JOHN HUSTON

INTERVIEWS

CONVERSATIONS WITH FILMMAKERS SERIES

PETER BRUNETTE, GENERAL EDITOR

Courtesy of Photofest

JOHN
HUSTON

INTERVIEWS

EDITED BY ROBERT EMMET LONG

UNIVERSITY PRESS OF MISSISSIPPI / JACKSON

www.upress.state.ms.us

Copyright © 2001 by University Press of Mississippi
All rights reserved
Manufactured in the United States of America

09   08   07   06   05   04   03   02   01   4   3   2   1

∞

Library of Congress Cataloging-in-Publication Data

Huston, John, 1906–
    John Huston : interviews / edited by Robert Emmet Long.
        p.   cm.—(Conversations with filmmakers series)
    Filmography: p.
    Includes index.
    ISBN 1-57806-327-2 (cloth : alk. paper)—ISBN 1-57806-328-0 (pbk. : alk. paper)
    I. Long, Robert Emmet.   II. Title.   III. Series.

  PN1998.3.H87 A5   2001
  791.43′0233′092—dc21   00-043516

British Library Cataloging-in-Publication Data available

CONTENTS

INTRODUCTION

IN 1950 IN *LIFE* magazine, poet and critic James Agee hailed John Huston as the most inventive director of his generation. There was nobody of his age at work in movies, he remarked, "who can excel Huston in talent, inventiveness, intransigence, achievement or promise." Yet Huston's career was then just beginning, and in the over forty-year extent of it he would be constantly productive, making films that displayed extraordinary versatility and that in their reach and ambitiousness exceeded even his signature early work. To be sure, not all of his pictures were successes, either artistically or commercially, but the list of his triumphs is extensive and enviable. To encounter Huston in this collection of interviews, given at different times in his career to various people, is to confront an American filmmaker of estimable rank and permanence.

One of the conspicuous features of the interviews is the way in which Huston's life assumes larger-than-life proportions. He had love affairs with glamorous women in addition to numerous marriages; knew all the most important and gifted people in Hollywood; traveled the globe; hunted big game in Africa and consorted with Ernest Hemingway; acquired a large country estate in Ireland, where he rode in full regalia on fox hunts; and late in life settled at Las Caletas, Mexico, near Puerto Vallarta, in a clearing between the jungle and the Pacific Ocean and accessible only by boat—a setting as unlike his life as an honorary member of the Galway gentry as could be imagined. His life was like one long series of adventures. After years of hard living he died at eighty-two, still in full possession of his creative powers and surrounded by an adoring family that included his now famous actress daughter Anjelica.

As this collection reveals, interviewers tend to ask Huston about his flavorful personal life as often as they do about his films themselves; and his responses to both kinds of questions provide a kind of self portrait that is spontaneous, incisive, and tinged with humor. One incident that is alluded to repeatedly is the fight that he and Errol Flynn were involved in one night in Hollywood. During a house party, Flynn spoke disrespectfully of Olivia de Havilland, a former flame of Huston's, and Huston asked the actor to step out into the garden, where they fought with bare knuckles for an hour. At the end of the hour two ambulances arrived to take them to different hospitals. The next morning, however, Flynn made a comradely gesture, calling Huston to ask how he was doing. In later years Huston cast Flynn as the male lead in *Roots of Heaven,* and when not shooting the picture they went hunting together and were on companionable terms. If the incident of the fight in the garden had not actually happened, it ought to have for it bears out Huston's reputation as one of the so-called "wild men" of Hollywood—a man partial to drink, a high-stakes gambler, and a genius of cinema.

Interviewers also frequently ask about his famous father, Walter Huston, the distinguished American stage and screen actor, and about his own early years and youthful wanderings. In fact, Huston wandered even as a child since his father, who was then playing the vaudeville circuit, and his mother, a journalist who wrote under her own name of Rhea Gore, divorced when he was three, and he was thereafter passed back and forth between them. At the age of ten, he staged a minor miracle. Sent to a sanitorium in Phoenix, Arizona, after he was found to have Bright's disease, a liver condition, and a seriously enlarged heart, he was expected to grow up as an invalid. But he confounded everyone by stealing out every night at midnight to swim in a nearby river, and within a year he walked away from the sanitorium in recovered health.

There was, in fact, a superabundance of life in him. He lived with his mother, who had remarried, in Los Angeles; but at fifteen he left high school to pursue a life of adventure as a boxer. Appearing in tank towns along the California coast, he won twenty-three out of twenty-six bouts as an amateur lightweight, and in one town remembers fighting twice in one night under different names. His other interests included horseback riding, French literature, opera, and painting. When he was not boxing, he pursued his interest in painting as a student at the Art Students League in Los Angeles. A many-faceted youth, he was considered a "romantic fantasist" by his mother; and he later remarked, "Nothing I ever did pleased my mother." He did, however, inherit her penchant for horses and gambling.

Before long Huston's wanderlust took him to New York City, where his father was becoming famous playing the lead in Eugene O'Neill's *Desire Under the Elms.* Watching Walter Huston prepare his performances became his first introduction to the stage; before long he was acting himself at the Provincetown Playhouse in Greenwich Village, and even tried his powers as an opera singer. At twenty, on an impulse, he went south to enlist in the Mexican cavalry, and as an honorary member indulged his love of horseback riding. On returning to New York he met and married the first of his five wives, and began writing fiction and a play, *Frankie and Johnnie,* which was produced in the Village. Before long he followed his father to Hollywood, which was then going through its awkward but exciting transition to talkies. There he was engaged as a screenwriter at Universal Studios and worked, with others, on his first films, two of which—*A House Divided* and *Law and Order*—were to star his father.

But Huston left Universal before long to write for the Gaumont-British studio in London, and after a short time left Gaumont to go to Paris and paint. His life as an indigent painter in Paris who slept on park benches ended a year later when he traveled to New York to write and act in the theater. By 1936, when he was thirty and in Hollywood again, he became a screenwriter for Warner Brothers and was given his first screen credits as scenarist for William Wyler's *Jezebel,* starring Bette Davis. Almost immediately he scored impressive successes, winning Academy Award nominations for his next screenplays, one of which was for Howard Hawks's celebrated *Sergeant York.* These successes launched him as a director. It was unusual to move up from screenwriter to director at that time; only Preston Sturges and Garson Kanin had become directors in this way before him, but with his much talked about Oscar nominations Huston had a strong hand and played it expertly. The first film he directed was *The Maltese Falcon,* a solid gold screen classic and a spectacularly auspicious beginning to his long career as a director.

One feature of the interviews in the collection that is particularly striking is the dual role of writer and director that Huston assumed; he was a literary director particularly well known for his adaptations of novels and plays. Huston was faithful to the material he adapted, but he was apt to choose works that were very challenging and reflected his own wide-ranging tastes. His sources have included Melville (*Moby Dick*), Stephen Crane (*The Red Badge of Courage*), Kipling (*The Man Who Would Be King*), James Joyce (*The Dead*), Flannery O'Connor (*Wise Blood*), Malcolm Lowry (*Under the Volcano*), Tennessee Williams (*The Night of the Iguana*), Carson McCullers (*Reflections in a Golden Eye*), Dashiell Hammett (*The Maltese Falcon*), and Mario Puzzo (*Prizzi's Honor*). He has even adapted the Bible. In interviews Huston talks about his work as a director who is also a writer. "I saw no great dividing line," he remarks, "between writing and directing. . . . The directing of a film to me, is simply an extension of the process of writing. It's the process of rendering the thing you have written. You're still writing when you're directing . . . a gesture, the way you make somebody raise his eyes or shake his head is also writing for films."[1]

It was typical of Huston that he worked closely with his writers on each of his pictures, frequently preparing scenes himself for his screenwriter to revise, and then having the writer submit a scene to him to revise. Huston's being highly literate had much to do with his concept of making films. A painter who sketched out exactly what a scene would look like before shooting it, he had a strong visual sense, as his movies reveal. But he was wary of overindulgence with the camera, which he felt should not call attention to itself. It was the *idea* holding the scene together that mattered most and that should be the controlling force in the making of a movie. In interviews he often speaks, like a good writer, in praise of form. He admires, he tells Rosemary Lord, "the form that pictures have: a beginning, a middle, and an end—because it seems to me that that form is significant. I'm classic-minded in this regard. A picture is supposed to reduce life into significant philosophic terms, if you like, so that it's a demonstration of one aspect of life."

The interviews reveal, moreover, how much he had been affected by certain writers, especially James Joyce. His long-term attachment to Joyce began early, when he was twenty-one and honeymooning with his first wife, who read *Ulysses* aloud to him in the original banned edition in a blue paper cover. Another important figure for him was Hemingway, whom he acknowledges to Peter Greenberg as an influence that "hit me right where I was trying to write. . . . I had one or two other literary influences, the biggest being James Joyce. And along came Hemingway, who was circuitously a

---

1. Gideon Bachmann, "How I Make Films: An Interview with John Huston," *Film Quarterly*, v. 19, n. 1 (Fall 1965), 3–13. Interview not included in this collection.

product of Joyce's too. . . . I was very influenced by his writing and his thinking. His values, his reassessment of the things that made life go were probably more important than his writing. Stories didn't come easily with him. Incidents did. And he had a wonderful way of being able to bring an incident to life." In time Hemingway and Huston became friends, an association deepened by certain resemblances one can see in their work—in the male-dominated worlds they create, with their masculine drives and fears, and in their sense of the individual's essential isolation. These are worlds in which men are tested and are likely to be defeated: Hemingway's title *Winner Take Nothing* could as well apply to Huston's boxers and drifters. Women are frequently on the margins of the action, as girlfriends or lovers, subordinate figures who are not explored as fully as the men.

The interviews also reveal the peculiar way that Huston found material to adapt into films. "I never start off," he observes, "by saying 'I'm going to make a specific film,' but from some idea twenty-five or thirty years ago, or when I was a child, and have played around with it in my thoughts, for a long time. . . . Suddenly, surprisingly, I discover that I am actually making it. . . . *The Man Who Would Be King* . . . was based on my reading of the story at age twelve or fifteen, and my impressions of it have remained with me. Most of my pictures begin with this kind of inbred idea, something that lives in me from long ago. . . . I believe in letting them have complete freedom, and imposing myself only when necessary. . . . I let my films make themselves."[2]

Huston was a maverick in the studio system in Hollywood under which he worked, and at times he worked outside the system, producing his pictures as well as directing them; in certain cases he also wrote the film and acted in it as well. His involvement in the studio system sometimes resulted in the frustration of seeing his work mangled before its release by the studio bosses. We learn in the interviews that *Freud* originally ran to two hours and forty minutes before being trimmed by half an hour, without regard for logic or continuity, by studio heads. The studio altered *The Barbarian and the Geisha* so that it was unrecognizable, even in its plot. *The Red Badge of Courage* was edited so barbarously by the studio, reducing its 135 minutes to barely sixty-nine, that the picture was deprived of the force it had possessed initially.

But equally of interest in this collection is the way in which the pieces reveal Huston's relationship to the craft of acting and to actors. Perhaps the

---

2. Bachmann, Ibid.

most startling observation of Huston's in this respect is his often quoted comment to Gene Phillips that "in working with actors, I try to direct as little as possible." The great consideration, he says, is that the casting of the film should be right, and in particular he favors using an actor whose own personality, or a part of it at least, overlaps with the personality of the character he is portraying. He prefers such an actor over even a very talented performer who, through his technical skills, can cast an illusion of being the character he plays. "I don't, as a rule," he says, "give an actor a script and have him try to change his personality into something that's suitable for the role. I prefer to let him discover whatever part of himself is that role and present it to me." Nor does he tell his actors what to do to begin a scene, but rather has them show him how they would do it. Generally they perform the scene in the way he had had in mind, and he then concentrates on the best way to photograph it. "As a result," he comments, "you get something that isn't mechanical—that isn't done for the camera."

The interaction of Huston with his actors is more a matter of intuition than of logic, is open and spontaneous rather than being consciously formulated. "The one thing I always try to experiment with," he tells an interviewer, "is accepting suggestions from people who work with me. I don't like to dictate, I like to receive stimuli from all: not only the cameraman and the actors, but the grips and the script girl, or the animal trainers in the case of *The Bible*. I try to create an atmosphere on the set where everyone feels he can participate."[3]

At times he speculates on what makes a superior actor, and on the mystery of the camera, which can give a larger-than-life size to one performer although not to another even though he may be very talented. "The very best actors, the ones that fill me with admiration," he remarks to David Robinson, "are those that furnish *surprises*. You don't know—I doubt that they do either—where it comes from. They reach down in some remote cavern and come up with something that reveals a principle, something mysterious and new." Huston speaks of Marlon Brando as the actor he has worked with who most fulfills this ideal; who conjures up moments from deep within himself that are like revelations and that reinforce the texture of the film. Of Marilyn Monroe, whom he directed in *The Asphalt Jungle* in her first significant acting role and in *The Misfits*, the last picture she completed, he observes that she

---

3. Bachmann, Ibid.

wasn't an actress in the strict technical sense yet had "the ability to go down within herself and pull up an emotion and put it on the screen."

One of the unique pleasures of Huston's interviews, in fact, consists of his perceptions of the actors who appeared in his films. He was a trained observer, and his comments are persuasive: candid and acute. Ronald Reagan, whom Huston never forgave for imposing the loyalty oath on members of the Screen Actors Guild, is characterized as an egotistical bore as well as a bad actor. But by and large his comments on actors are extremely generous. Marlon Brando, Robert Mitchum, and Humphrey Bogart are all praised by Huston in the strongest terms. The interviews also provide first-hand, insider accounts of what happened off-camera during the making of Huston movies, particularly *The Misfits* and *Freud,* when Marilyn Monroe and Montgomery Clift had reached a point of final breakdown.

Huston speaks, too, of pictures by others he had liked and of his favorite directors, who include John Ford, George Stevens, and his early mentor and friend William Wyler. He admires *Godfather II* and *Taxi Driver,* the Australian films *Gallipoli* and *Breaker Morant,* and a number of French pictures, like Henri-Georges Clouzot's tense, masterful *Wages of Fear.* He has a great liking for Alain Resnais's *Hiroshima, Mon Amour* and Vittorio De Sica's *Bicycle Thief*—but perhaps most of all for Robert Altman's *McCabe and Mrs. Miller,* John Schlesinger's *Midnight Cowboy,* and Arthur Penn's *Bonnie and Clyde.* Perhaps his most revealing comment on the filmmaking of others is on *Bonnie and Clyde.* "It is," Huston declares, "an extraordinary work, steeped in the unknown and in adventure . . . all those murders, robberies, assassinations . . . but they were succeeding in creating their own world. They were creating their own life! . . . What Warren Beatty conveys in the film is phenomenal, this mixture of psychopathic neurosis, of exaggerated attitude and of genius, all that skillfully combined. . . . *Bonnie and Clyde* is pure adventure."[4] His comments on *Bonnie and Clyde* are reminiscent of what he says elsewhere about letting his movies "make themselves," of setting the imagination free so that the picture becomes, as it were, pure adventure.

One of the questions most often asked of Huston by interviewers is about his remarkable versatility—the question of what it is that binds together the themes and concerns of the many different pictures he made. What is the

---

4. Rui Nogueira and Bertrand Tavernier, "Entretien avec John Huston," *Positif,* n. 116, May 1970, 1–22. Interview not included in this collection.

figure in the carpet? To this he invariably replies that he does not know himself. *The Treasure of the Sierra Madre* and *The Asphalt Jungle* are two of his exemplary pictures, both dealing with the undoing of men under pressure, yet other Huston movies are not like them at all. All that they have in common, perhaps, is Huston's strong craftsmanship and his willingness to go on another adventure, even if it should be as large as *Moby Dick*. Huston seems to have conceived of his life as an open-ended adventure: his pictures are an analogue of it.

That at least is one conclusion that can be drawn from these interviews, which reveal Huston in his work and in his temperament. They inevitably contain some repetitiousness, but this does not detract significantly from the portrait of John Huston that emerges from them. Literate, stimulating, completely frank and direct, surprising in their critically detached assessment of the shortcomings of his own work, and touched with the humor of a born storyteller, the interviews can be more than enjoyed. They can be savored.

CHRONOLOGY

1906 Born August 5, 1906, in Nevada, Missouri, to actor Walter Huston and Rhea (Gore) Huston, a roving journalist.

1909 Parents separate and are divorced four years later. As a child, Huston is shuttled back and forth between his father, playing the vaudeville circuit, and his mother, living at a series of different hotels.

1916 Doctors diagnose Huston at ten as having an enlarged heart and kidney disease, and he is placed in a sanitorium in Phoenix, Arizona, with the prospect of being an invalid for life. He rebels, however, taking midnight swims and somehow throwing off illnesses. Spends early years in California.

1921 At fifteen, drops out of Lincoln High School in Los Angeles to become a champion lightweight boxer in bouts along California coast. Also pursues his interest in painting, and studies at Art Students League in L.A.

1924–27 Lives in New York with father, then achieving fame in O'Neill's *Desire Under the Elms,* and acts at Provincetown Playhouse in Greenwich Village. In 1926, at twenty, marries Dorothy Harvey (divorce 1933) and, fascinated by horses, joins the Mexican cavalry.

1928–33 Returns to New York; writes short stories and has play, *Frankie and Johnnie,* produced in the Village. Travels to Hollywood, where father has migrated with arrival of talkies. Collaborates on four scripts, two starring his father, but leaves writing job at Universal for one with Gaumont-British in London. Then quits this, too, and goes to Paris to paint and lead indigent life.

1934–35   Returns to New York as writer-actor.

1936–37   Settles down, at thirty, to career as screenwriter for Warner Brothers. Marries second wife, Leslie Black. Given first screen credit as scenarist for William Wyler's *Jezebel*.

1938–40   Writes screenplays for *The Amazing Dr. Clitterhouse* (1938), *Juarez* (1939), and *Dr. Ehrlich's Magic Bullet* (1940), the last of which wins Oscar nomination.

1941   Script for Howard Hawks's *Sergeant York* also wins Oscar nomination. Writes *High Sierra*, in which Humphrey Bogart as gunman on the run makes breakthrough as a star. Persuades Warner Brothers to let him direct his first film, *The Maltese Falcon*. It becomes a screen classic.

1942–43   Makes two melodramas, *In This Our Life*, Bette Davis vehicle, and *Across the Pacific*, a war-time espionage story. Enters Army as lieutenant in Signal Corps, with assignment to make documentary film in the Aleutian Islands. *Report from the Aleutians* wins high praise; Huston promoted to captain.

1944   Sent to Italy to make *The Battle of San Pietro*, outstanding combat documentary controversial among Army officials because of its candor. Is nevertheless promoted to major and awarded the Legion of Merit.

1945   Makes documentary film *Let There Be Light*, about the rehabilitation of shell-shocked and psychologically disabled soldiers who have been through combat. Film barred from release by War Department as being too disturbing, but finally shown, to acclaim, in 1980. Discharged from Army and returns to Hollywood; divorces second wife, and has much-talked-about romance with Olivia de Havilland.

1946   Marries actress Evelyn Keyes; is uncredited co-scenarist of *The Kill-*

ers, adaptation of Hemingway story starring Burt Lancaster, and of another picture, *Three Strangers.* Directs Jean-Paul Sartre's *Huis Clos (No Exit)* on Broadway and returns to Hollywood.

1948   Makes *The Treasure of the Sierra Madre.* Earns Oscars as both writer and director; father Walter Huston also wins Oscar as best supporting actor. Makes *Key Largo.*

1949   With Sam Spiegel founds Horizon Films, and is co-producer and director of *We Were Strangers.*

1950   Films *The Asphalt Jungle,* about a jewel heist that goes awry; Marilyn Monroe makes her first serious acting appearance in the picture. Huston receives Oscar nominations for both best screenplay and best direction, as well as Screen Directors Guild Award. Divorces Evelyn Keyes and a day later marries Enrica Soma.

1951   Release of *The Red Badge of Courage* and *The African Queen,* for which Humphrey Bogart wins Oscar as best actor.

1952   Produces and directs *Moulin Rouge,* fictionalized life of painter Toulouse-Lautrec. Angered by House Committee on UnAmerican Activities scourging of entertainment industry, leaves America for Ireland, buying a large country house in Galway and eventually becoming Irish citizen.

1953   Co-produces and directs black comedy *Beat the Devil*; picture fails at box office but goes on to become cult favorite.

1956   Makes film adaptation of Herman Melville's *Moby Dick.* Ten years in the planning and three in the shooting, film has tepid reaction.

1957   Films *Heaven Knows, Mr. Allison,* about a marine and a nun stranded on a Japanese-held island during World War II.

1958   Makes *The Barbarian and the Geisha.* Picture badly mangled by studio prior to release. Makes *The Roots of Heaven,* set in Africa. This picture, too, regarded as fiasco.

1960   Release of *The Unforgiven.*

1961   Makes *The Misfits,* written by playwright Arthur Miller for his then wife, Marilyn Monroe; also stars Montgomery Clift and Clark Gable. Gable dies shortly after film is shot, Monroe never completes another picture.

1962   Films *Freud,* haunting psychological study featuring Montgomery Clift.

1963   Makes spoof murder mystery, *The List of Adrian Messenger.*

1964   Release of *The Night of the Iguana,* adapted from Tennessee Williams's play.

1966   Makes Dino De Laurentiis-produced epic, *The Bible;* upon release is savaged by reviewers.

1967   Directs and acts in *Casino Royale,* pastiche of James Bond films with David Niven as an aging secret agent. Also makes *Reflections in a Golden Eye,* adapted from Carson McCullers's novel of personal and sexual frustration at an Army camp in the South.

1969   Makes *Sinful Davey,* a picaresque adventure in early nineteenth-century Scotland, and *A Walk with Love and Death,* the tale of young love set against the turmoil of fourteenth-century France, starring daughter Anjelica Huston and Assaf Dayan. During shooting of *A Walk,* wife Enrica killed in automobile accident.

1972   Films *Fat City,* about a washed-up prize fighter in a seedy California town; draws rave reviews for picture and its star, Stacy Keach. Also makes light-hearted Western, *The Life and Times of Judge Roy Bean.* Marries fifth wife, Celeste Shane.

1973   Directs *The Mackintosh Man,* a spy film.

1975   Release of *The Man Who Would Be King,* from Kipling tale, which scores at box office and with critics, and earns Huston Oscar nomination for best screenplay. After finish of shooting Huston undergoes heart surgery and produces no feature films for four years.

1978   Marriage to Celeste Shane ends in divorce; Huston sells Galway estate and moves to Puerto Vallarta, Mexico.

1979   Makes *Wise Blood,* from Flannery O'Connor's novel of sin and salvation in the American South, which receives markedly favorable reviews.

1982   Brings Broadway hit musical *Annie* to the screen.

1984   Makes *Under the Volcano,* from Malcolm Lowry's novel about a British diplomat in late 1930s Mexico who drinks himself literally to death.

1988   Films *Prizzi's Honor,* black comedy of Mafia family mores starring Jack Nicholson, Kathleen Turner, and Anjelica Huston, who wins Oscar as best supporting actress.

1987   While suffering from terminal emphysema and a heart condition, makes last film, *The Dead,* from James Joyce's short story in *Dubliners.* Cast includes Anjelica Huston, with screenplay by Huston's son Tony. Picture ends career on note of triumph. Dies of pneumonia in Newport, Rhode Island, August 28, 1987.

FILMOGRAPHY

1941
THE MALTESE FALCON
Warner Brothers
Producer: Hal Wallis
Director: **John Huston**
Screenplay: **John Huston,** from the novel by Dashiell Hammett
Cinematography: Arthur Edeson
Art Direction: Robert Haas
Editing: Thomas Richards
Music: Adolph Deutsch
Cast: Humphrey Bogart (Sam Spade), Mary Astor (Brigid O'Shaughnessy),
Sydney Greenstreet (Kasper Gutman), Gladys George (Iva Archer), Peter
Lorre (Joel Cairo), Barton MacLane (Lieutenant Dundy), Ward Bond (Det.
Polhaus), Jerome Cowan (Miles Archer), Lee Patrick (Effie Perine), Elisha
Cook, Jr. (Wilmer Cook), Murray Alper (Frank Richman), John Hamilton
(Bryan), James Burke (Luke), Walter Huston (Captain Jacobi)
35 mm, B&W
100 minutes

1942
IN THIS OUR LIFE
Warner Brothers
Producer: Hal Wallis
Director: **John Huston**

Screenplay: Howard Koch (and **John Huston**, uncredited), from the novel by Ellen Glasgow
Cinematography: Ernest Haller
Art Direction: Robert Haas
Editing: William Holmes
Music: Max Steiner
Cast: Bette Davis (Stanley Timberlake), Olivia de Havilland (Roy Timberlake), George Brent (Craig Fleming), Dennis Morgan (Peter Kingsmill), Charles Coburn (William Fitzroy), Frank Craven (Asa Timberlake), Billie Burke (Lavinia Timberlake), Hattie McDaniel (Minerva Clay), Ernest Anderson (Passy Clay), Walter Huston (bartender)
35 mm, B&W
97 minutes

1942
ACROSS THE PACIFIC
Warner Brothers
Producer: Jerry Wald, Jack Saper
Director: **John Huston** (finished by Vincent Sherman)
Screenplay: Richard Macaulay, from the *Saturday Evening Post* serial "Aloha Means Goodbye," by Robert Carson
Cinematography: Arthur Edeson
Art Direction: Robert Haas
Editing: Frank Magee (montage sequences by Don Seigel)
Music: Adolph Deutsch
Cast: Humphrey Bogart (Rich Leland), Mary Astor (Alberta Marlow), Sydney Greenstreet (Dr. Lorenz), Charles Halton (A. V. Smith), Victor Sen Yung (Joe Totsuiko), Roland Got (Sugi), Lee Tung Foo (Sam Wing)
35 mm, B&W
97 minutes

1943
REPORT FROM THE ALEUTIANS (documentary)
Producer: Army Pictorial Service, Signal Corps, U.S. War Department
Director: **(Capt.) John Huston**
Screenplay: **John Huston**
Narrator: Walter Huston and **John Huston**

Cinematography: Jules Buck, Rey Scott, Freeman Collins, Herman Crabtree, Buzz Ellsworth
Music: Dimitri Tiomkin
25 mm, color
45 minutes

1945
THE BATTLE OF SAN PIETRO (documentary)
Producer: Army Pictorial Service Corps, U.S. War Department
Director: **(Maj.) John Huston**
Screenplay: **John Huston**
Narrator: **John Huston**
Cinematography: **John Huston,** Jules Buck, and other Signal Corps members
Music: Dimitri Tiomkin
35 mm, B&W
32 minutes

1946
LET THERE BE LIGHT (documentary)
Producer: Army Pictorial Service, Signal Corps, U.S. War Department
Director: **John Huston**
Screenplay: Charles Kaufman, **John Huston**
Narrator: **John Huston**
Cinematography: Stanley Cortez, **John Huston,** John Doran, Lloyd Fromm, Joseph Jackman, George Smith
Editing: George Fowler, Jr.
Music: Dimitri Tiomkin
35 mm, B&W
59 minutes

1948
THE TREASURE OF THE SIERRA MADRE
Warner Brothers
Producer: Henry Blake
Director: **John Huston**
Screenplay: **John Huston,** from the novel by B. Traven
Cinematography: Ted McCord

Art Direction: John Hughes
Editing: Owen Marks
Music: Leo Forbstein
Cast: Humphrey Bogart (Fred C. Dobbs), Walter Huston (Howard), Tim Holt (Curtin), Bruce Bennett (Cody), Barton MacLane (Pat McCormick), Alfonso Bedoya (Gold Hat), Arthur Soto Rangel (Presidente), Manuel Donde (El Jefe), José Torvay (Pablo), Margarito Luna (Panch), Robert "Bobby" Blake (Mexican lottery boy), Jacqueline Dalya ("Chiquita" Lopez), **John Huston** (American in the white suit)
35 mm, B&W
124 minutes

1948
KEY LARGO
Warner Brothers
Producer: Jerry Wald
Director: **John Huston**
Screenplay: **John Huston** and Richard Brooks, from the play by Maxwell Anderson
Cinematography: Karl Freund
Art Direction: Leo Kuter
Editing: Rudi Fuhr
Music: Max Steiner
Cast: Humphrey Bogart (Frank McCloud), Lauren Bacall (Nora Temple), Lionel Barrymore (James Temple), Edward G. Robinson (Johnny Rocco), Claire Trevor (Gaye Dawn), Thomas Gomez (Curly), Harry Lewis ("Toots" Bass), John Rodney (Clyde Sawyer), Marc Lawrence (Ziggy), Monty Blue (Ben Wade), Dan Seymour ("Angel" Garcia), Jay Silverheels (Johnny Osceola), Rodric Redwing (Tom Osceola)
35 mm, B&W
101 minutes

1949
WE WERE STRANGERS
Producer: S. P. Eagle (pseudonym for Sam Spiegel); a Horizon Production released by Columbia Pictures
Director: **John Huston**

Screenplay: **John Huston,** Peter Viertel, from a segment in *Rough Sketch,* by Robert Sylvester
Cinematography: Russell Metty
Art Direction: Gary Odell
Editing: Al Clark
Music: George Antheil
Cast: John Garfield (Tony Fenner), Jennifer Jones (China Valdes), Pedro Armendariz (Armando Ariete), Gilbert Roland (Guillermo), Wally Cassel (Miguel), Ramon Navarro (leader of the revolutionaries), David Bond (Ramon), **John Huston** (no credit)
35 mm, B&W
106 minutes

1950
THE ASPHALT JUNGLE
Metro-Goldwyn-Mayer
Producer: Arthur Hornblow, Jr.
Director: **John Huston**
Screenplay: **John Huston** and Ben Maddow, from the novel by W. R. Burnett
Cinematography: Harold Rosson
Art Direction: Cedric Gibbons
Editing: George Boemler
Music: Miklos Rozsa
Cast: Sterling Hayden (Dix Handley), Louis Calhern (Alonzo D. Emmerich), Jean Hagen (Doll Conovan), Sam Jaffe ("Doc" Erwin Riedenschneider), James Whitmore (Gus Minissi), Marc Lawrence (Cobby), John McIntire (Hardy), Anthony Caruso (Louis Ciavelli), Teresa Celli (Maria Ciavelli), Marilyn Monroe (Angela Phinlay), Barry Kelly (Dietrich), William Davis (Timmons), Dorothy Tree (May Emmerich), Brad Dexter (Bob Brannen), John Maxwell (Swanson)
35 mm, B&W
112 minutes

1951
THE RED BADGE OF COURAGE
Metro-Goldwyn-Mayer
Producer: Gottfried Reinhardt

Director: **John Huston**
Screenplay: **John Huston,** from the novel by Stephen Crane
Cinematography: Harold Rosson
Art Direction: Cedric Gibbons
Editing: Ben Lewis, supervised by Marguerite Booth
Music: Bronislau Kaper
Cast: Audie Murphy (Henry Fleming, "The Youth"), Bill Mauldin (Tom Wilson, "The Loud Soldier"), John Dierkes (Jim Mauldin, "The Tall Soldier"), Royal Dano ("The Tattered Soldier"), Arthur Hunnicutt (Bill Porter), Tim Durant (the general), Douglas Dick (the lieutenant), Robert Easton Burke (Thompson), Andy Devine ("The Fat Soldier"), Smith Bellow (the captain), Dixon Porter (a veteran). Added voice-over commentary by James Whitmore
35 mm, B&W
69 minutes

1951
THE AFRICAN QUEEN
Producer: Horizon-Romulus in association with S. P. Eagle (pseudonym for Sam Spiegel) for United Artists release
Director: **John Huston**
Screenplay: **John Huston** and James Agee, from the novel by C. S. Forester; additional dialogue by Peter Viertel
Cinematography: Jack Cardiff
Art Direction: Wilfred Shingleton
Editing: Ralph Kemplen
Music: Allan Gray
Cast: Humphrey Bogart (Charlie Alnutt), Katharine Hepburn (Rose Sayer), Robert Morely (Samuel Sayer), Peter Bull (captain of the *Luisa*)
35 mm, B&W
105 minutes

1952
MOULIN ROUGE
Producer: **John Huston;** a Romulus Production for United Artists release
Director: **John Huston**
Screenplay: Anthony Veiller, **John Huston,** from the book by Pierre La Mure

Cinematography: Oswald Morris
Art Direction: Paul Sheriff, Maracal Vertés
Editing: Ralph Kemplen
Music: Georges Auric
Cast: José Ferrer (Toulouse-Lautrec), Colette Marchand (Marie Charlet), Suzanne Flon (Myriamme Hayen), Zsa Zsa Gabor (Jane Avril), Katherine Kath (La Goulue), Glaude Nollier (Countess Toulouse-Lautrec), Muriel Smith (Aicha), Goerge Lannes (Patov), Rupert John (Chocolat), Tutti Lemkov (Aicha's partner), Eric Pohlmann (bar owner), Walter Crisham (Valentin le Desosse), Mary Clare (Mme Loubet), Lee Montague (Maurice Joyant), Christopher Lee (Paul Gaugin)
35 mm, color
123 minutes

1954
BEAT THE DEVIL
Producer: **John Huston** (with Humphrey Bogart); a Romulus-Santana Production for United Artists release
Director: **John Huston**
Screenplay: **John Huston**, Truman Capote, from the novel by James Helvick; Anthony Veiller, Peter Viertel (uncredited)
Cinematography: Oswald Morris
Art Direction: Wilfred Singleton
Editing: Ralph Kemplen
Music: Franco Mannino
Cast: Humphrey Bogart (Billy Dannreuther), Gina Lollobrigida (Maria Dannreuther), Jennifer Jones (Gwendolyn Chelm), Robert Morley (Peterson), Peter Lorre (O'Hara), Edward Underdown (Harry Chelm), Ivor Barnard (Major Ross), Marco Tulli (Ravello)
35 mm, B&W
89 minutes

1956
MOBY DICK
Producer: **John Huston**, Vaughan Dean; a Moulin Picture released by Warner Brothers
Director: **John Huston**

Screenplay: **John Huston,** Ray Bradbury, from the novel by Herman Melville
Cinematography: Oswald Morris
Art Direction: Ralph Brinton
Editing: Russell Lloyd
Music: Philip Stanton
Cast: Gregory Peck (Ahab), Richard Basehart (Ishmael), Orson Welles (Father Mapple), Leo Genn (Starbuck), Harry Andrews (Stubb), Bernard Miles (Manxman), Mervyn Johns (Peleg), Noel Purcell (Carpenter), Friedrich Ledebur (Queequeg), James Robertson Justice (Captain Boomer), Edric Conner (Daggoo), Seamus Kelly (Flask), Royal Dano (Elijah), Francis de Wolff (Captain Gardiner), Philip Stainton (Bildad), Tornelty (Peter Coffin), Tamba Alleney (Pip), Ted Howard (blacksmith), Tom Clegg (Tashtego)
35 mm, color
116 minutes

HEAVEN KNOWS, MR. ALLISON
Producer: Buddy Adler, Eugene Frenke for Twentieth Century–Fox Film Corp.
Director: **John Huston**
Screenplay: Oswald Morris
Cinematography: Oswald Morris
Art Direction: Stephen Grimes
Editing: Russell Lloyd
Music: George Auric
Cast: Robert Mitchum (Marine Corporal Allison), Deborah Kerr (Sister Angela)
35 mm, color
107 minutes

1958
THE BARBARIAN AND THE GEISHA
Producer: Eugene Frenke for Twentieth Century–Fox Film Corp.
Director: **John Huston**
Screenplay: Charles Grayson, story by Ellis St. Joseph
Cinematography: Charles G. Clarke
Art Direction: Lyle Wheeler, Jack Martin Smith, and Walter M. Scott
Editing: Stuart Gilmore

Music: Hugo Friedhofer
Cast: John Wayne (Townsend Harris), Eiko Ando (Okichi), Sam Jaffe (Henry
Heusken), So Yamamamura (Tamura), Norman Thomson (captain), James
Robbins (Lieutenant Fisher), Morika (prime minister), Kodaya Ichikawa (Dai-
myo), Hiroshi Yamato (the shogun), Tokujiro Ichikawa (Harusha), Fuji Kasai
(Lord Hotta), Takeshi Kumagai (chamberlain)
35 mm, color
105 minutes

1958
THE ROOTS OF HEAVEN
Producer: Darryl F. Zanuck for Twentieth Century–Fox Film Corp.
Director: **John Huston**
Screenplay: Romain Gary, Patrick Leigh-Fermor, from the novel by Romain
Gary
Cinematography: Oswald Morris
Art Direction: Stephen Grimes
Editing: Russell Lloyd
Music: Malcolm Arnold
Cast: Errol Flynn (Forsythe), Trevor Howard (Morel), Juliette Greco (Minna),
Eddie Albert (Abe Fields), Orson Welles (Cy Sedgewick), Paul Lukas (Saint
Denis), Herbert Lom (Orsini), Gregoire Aslan (Habib), Friedrich Ledebur
(Peter Qvist), Edric Connor (Waitari), André Luquet (governor), Olivier Hus-
senot (the Baron), Pierre Duban (Major Aholscher), Marc Doelnitz (De Vries),
Dan Jackson (Madjumba), Maurice Cannon (Haas), Jacques Marin (Cerisot),
Bachir Touré (Yussef)
35 mm, color
131 minutes

1960
THE UNFORGIVEN
Producer: James Hill for Continental Hecht/Hill/Lancaster; released by
United Artists
Director: **John Huston**
Screenplay: Ben Maddow, from the novel by Alan Le May
Cinematography: Franz Planer
Art Direction: Stephen Grimes

Editing: Hugh Russell Lloyd
Music: Dimitri Tiomkin
Cast: Burt Lancaster (Ben Zachary), Audrey Hepburn (Rachel Zachary), Lillian Gish (Mattilda Zachary), John Saxon (Johnny Portugal), Charles Bickford (Zeb Rawlins), Albert Salmi (Charlie Rawlins), Audie Murphy (Cash Zachary), Joseph Wiseman (Abe Kelsey), Doug McClure (Andy Zachary), Kipp Hamilton (Georgia Rawlins), Carlos Rivas (Lost Bird)
35 mm, color
125 minutes

1961
THE MISFITS
Producer: Frank E. Taylor for Seven Arts Productions; distributed by United Artists
Director: **John Huston**
Screenplay: Arthur Miller, from his novella published in *Esquire* in 1957
Cinematography: Russell Metty
Art Direction: William Newberry, Stephen Grimes
Editing: George Tomasini
Music: Alex North
Cast: Marilyn Monroe (Roslyn Taber), Clark Gable (Gay Langland), Montgomery Clift (Perce Howland), Eli Wallach (Guido Dellini), Thelma Ritter (Isabelle Steers), James Barton (old man in bar), Kevin McCarthy (Roslyn's husband), Dennis Shaw (boy in bar), Philip Mitchell (Charles Steers), Walter Ramage (aged groom), Peggy Barton (young bride), Estelle Winwood (woman collecting money), Marietta Tree (Susan), Bobby Lasalle (bartender)
35 mm, B&W
124 minutes

1962
FREUD (THE SECRET PASSION)
Producer: Wolfgang Reinhardt; a John Huston Production for Universal International Pictures
Director: **John Huston**
Screenplay: Wolfgang Reinhardt, Charles Kaufman
Cinematography: Douglas Slocombe
Art Direction: Stephen Grimes

Editing: Ralph Kemplen
Music: Jerry Goldsmith, with electronic music sequence by Henk Badings
Cast: Montgomery Clift (Sigmund Freud), Susannah York (Cecily Koertner),
Larry Parks (Dr. Joseph Breuer), Susan Kohner (Martha Freud), Eileen Herlie
(Frau Ida Koertner), Fernand Ledoux (Professor Charcot), David McCallum
(Carl von Schlosser), Rosalie Crutchley (Frau Freud), David Kossoff (Jacob
Freud), Joseph Furst (Herr Jacob Koertner), Eric Portman (Dr. Theodore
Meynert), Alexander Mango (Babinsky), Leonard Sachs (Brouhardier), Allan
Cuthbertson (Wilkie), Moira Redmond (Nora Wimmer)
35 mm, B&W
120 minutes

1963
THE LIST OF ADRIAN MESSENGER
Producer: Edward Lewis, Edward Muhl (in charge of production) for Joel Pro-
ductions–United Pictures; distributed by Universal Pictures
Director: **John Huston**
Screenplay: Anthony Veiller, from the novel by Phillip MacDonald
Cinematography: Joseph McDonald, Ted Scaife
Art Direction: Alexander Golitzen, Stephen Grimes, George Webb
Editing: Terry Moore, Hugh S. Fowler
Music: Jerry Goldsmith
Cast: Kirk Douglas (George Bruttenholm), George C. Scott (Anthony Ge-
thryn), Clive Brook (Marquis of Gleneyre), Dana Wynter (Lady Jocelyn Brut-
tenholm), Gladys Cooper (Mrs. Karoudjian), Herbert Marshall (Sir Wilfred
Lucas), Jacques Roux (Raoul LeBorg), Walter Huston (Derek Bruttenholm),
Bernard Archard (Inspector Pike), Roland D. Long (Carstairs), **John Huston**
(Lord Acton), Tony Curtis (organ grinder), Burt Lancaster (protesting
woman), Frank Sinatra (gypsy with a horse), Robert Mitchum (Jim Slattery)
35 mm, B&W
98 minutes

1964
THE NIGHT OF THE IGUANA
Producer: Ray Stark; a **John Huston**–Ray Stark Production for Seven Arts;
released through Metro-Goldwyn-Mayer
Director: **John Huston**

Screenplay: **John Huston**, Anthony Veiller, from the play by Tennessee Williams
Cinematography: Gabriel Figueroa
Art Direction: Stephen Grimes
Editing: Ralph Kemplen
Music: Benjamin Frankel
Cast: Richard Burton (Rev. T. Lawrence Shannon), Ava Gardner (Maxine Faulk), Deborah Kerr (Hannah Jelkes), Sue Lyon (Charlotte Goodall), James Ward (Hank Prosner), Grayson Hall (Judith Fellowes), Cyril Delevanti (Nonno), Mary Boylan (Miss Peebles), Gladys Hill (Miss Dexter), Billie Matticks (Miss Throxton), Emilio Fernandes (barkeeper), Adelmar Duran (Pepe), Roberto Leyra (Pedro), C. G. Kim (Chang), Eloise Hardt, Thelda Victor, Betty Proctor, Dorothy Vance, Liz Rubey, Bernice Starr, Barbara Joyce (teachers)
35 mm, B&W
118 minutes

1966
THE BIBLE . . . IN THE BEGINNING
Producer: Dino De Laurentiis for De Laurentiis Cinematografica; distributed by Twentieth Century–Fox Film Corp., Seven Arts Pictures
Director: **John Huston**
Screenplay: Christopher Fry
Cinematography: Giuseppe Rotunno
Art Direction: Stephen Grimes
Editing: Alberto Galliti
Music: Toshiro Mayuzumi
Cast: Michael Parks (Adam), Ulla Bergryd (Eve), Richard Harris (Cain), Franco Nero (Abel), Stephen Boyd (Nimrod), **John Huston** (Noah), George C. Scott (Abraham), Ava Gardner (Sarah), Peter O'Toole (the angel messenger), Gabriele Ferzetti (Lot), Eleonara Rossi Drago (Lot's wife), Pupella Maggio (Noah's wife), Grazia Maria Spina and Adriana Ambesi (Lot's daughters), Zoe Sallis (Hagar)
35 mm, color
174 minutes

1967
CASINO ROYALE
Producer: Charles K. Feldman, Jerry Bresler for Famous Artists Productions; a Columbia Pictures release

Director: **John Huston**, Ken Hughes, Val Guest, Robert Parrish, Joseph McGrath
Screenplay: Wolf Mankowitz, John Law, Michael Sayers, suggested by the novel by Ian Fleming; additional writing by Billy Wilder, Ben Hecht, **John Huston**, Val Guest, Joseph Heller, Terry Southern
Cinematography: Jack Hildyard; additional photography by John Wilcox, Nicholas Roeg
Art Direction: John Howell, Ivor Beddoes, Lionel Couch
Editing: Bill Lenny
Music: Burt Bacharach
Cast: Peter Sellers (Evelyn Tremble, 007), Ursula Andress (Vesper Lynd), David Niven (Sir James Bond), Orson Welles (Le Chiffre), Joanna Pettit (Mata Bond), Daliah Lavi (the detainer), Woody Allen (Jimmy Bond/Dr. Nash), Deborah Kerr (Agent Mimi/Lady Fiona), William Holden (Ransome), Charles Boyer (Le Grand), **John Huston** (McTarry/M), Kurt Kasnar (Smernov), George Raft (himself), Jean-Paul Belmondo (French legionnaire), Terence Cooper (Cooper), Barbara Bouchet (Moneypenny), Angela Scoular (Buttercup), Gabriella Licudi (Eliza), Tracy Crisp (Heather), Elaine Taylor (Peg), Jacqueline Bisset (Miss Goodthighs)
35 mm, color
130 minutes

1967
REFLECTIONS IN A GOLDEN EYE
Producer: Ray Stark for the **John Huston**–Ray Stark Productions; a Warner Brothers–Seven Arts International Release
Director: **John Huston**
Screenplay: Chapman Mortimer, Gladys Hill, based on the novel by Carson McCullers
Cinematography: Aldo Tonti
Art Direction: Bruno Avesani
Editing: Russell Lloyd
Music: Toshiro Mayuzumi
Cast: Elizabeth Taylor (Leonora Pemberton), Marlon Brando (Maj. Weldon Pemberton), Brian Keith (Lt. Col. Morris Langdon), Julie Harris (Alison Langdon), Robert Forster (Private Williams), Zorro David (Anacleto), Gordon Mitchell (stables sergeant), Irvin Dugan (Captain Weincheck), Fay Sparks

(Susie), Douglas Stark (Dr. Burgess), Al Mullock (old soldier), Ted Beniades (Sergeant)
35 mm, color
108 minutes

1969
SINFUL DAVEY
Producer: William N. Grof, Walter Mirisch (executive producer), for the **John Huston**–Walter Mirisch Production; distributed by United Artists
Director: **John Huston**
Screenplay: James R. Webb, based on the book *The Life of David Haggart,* by David Haggart
Cinematography: Freddie Young, Edward "Ted" Scaife
Art Direction: Carmen Dillon
Editing: Russell Lloyd
Music: Ken Thorne
Cast: John Hurt (Davey Haggart), Pamela Franklin (Annie), Nigel Davenport (Constable Richardson), Ronald Fraser (McNab), Robert Morley (Duke of Argyll), Fidelma Murphy (Jean Carlisle), Maxine Audley (Duchess of Argyll), Fionnuala Flanagan (Penelope), Donal McCann (Sir James Graham), Allan Cuthbertson (Captain Douglas), Eddie Byrne (Yorkshire Bill), Niall MacGinnis (Boots Simpson), Noel Purcell (Jock), Judith Furse (Mary), Francis De Wolff (Andrew), Paul Farell (bailiff of Stirling), Geoffrey Golden (Warden McEwan), Leo Collins (Dr. Gresham), Mickster Reid (Billy the Goat), Derek Young (Bobby Rae), John Franklin (George Bagrie), Eileen Murphy (Mary Kidd)
35 mm, color
95 minutes

1969
A WALK WITH LOVE AND DEATH
Producer: Carter De Haven III for a **John Huston**–Carter De Haven III Production; Twentieth Century–Fox Film Corp.
Director: **John Huston**
Screenplay: Dale Wasserman; adapted by Hans Koningsberger from his novel
Cinematography: Ted Scaife
Art Direction: Wolf Witzemann
Editing: Russell Lloyd

Music: Georges Delerue
Cast: Anjelica Huston (Lady Claudia), Assaf Dayan (Heron of Foix), Anthony Corlan (Robert), John Hallam (Sir Meles), Robert Lang (pilgrim leader), Guy Deghy (priest), Michael Gough (mad monk), George Murcell (captain), Eileen Murphy (gypsy), Anthony Nicholls (father superior), Joseph O'Connor (St. Jean), **John Huston** (Robert the Elder), John Franklin (Whoremaster), Francis Heim (knight lieutenant)
35 mm, color
90 minutes

1970
THE KREMLIN LETTER
Producer: Carter De Haven III, Sam Wiesenthal (executive producer); a **John Huston**–Carter De Haven III Production; Twentieth Century–Fox Film Corp.
Director: **John Huston**
Screenplay: **John Huston**, Gladys Hall, from the novel by Noel Behn
Cinematography: Ted Scaife
Art Direction: Elven Webb
Editing: Russell Lloyd
Music: Robert Drasnin, composed by Toshiro Mayuzumi
Cast: Bibi Andersson (Erika), Richard Boone (Ward), Nigel Green (Janis, alias "the Whore"), Dean Jagger (Highwayman), Lila Kedrova (Sophie), Michael MacLiammoir (Sweet Alice), Patrick O'Neal (Rone), Barbara Parkins (B.A.), Ronald Radd (Potkin), George Sanders (Warlock), Raf Vallone (Puppet Maker), Max Von Sydow (Kosnov), Orson Welles (Bresnavitch), Sandor Eles (Grodin), Niall MacGinnis (Erector Set); Anthony Chinn (Kitai), Guy Degny (professor), **John Huston** (Admiral), Fulvia Ketoff (Sonia), Vonetta McGee (Negress), Marc Lawrence (priest), Cyril Shaps (police doctor), Christopher Sanford (Rudolph), Anna-Maria Pravda (Mrs. Kazar), George Pravda (Kazar), Ludmilla Dutarova (Mrs. Potkin), Dimitri Tamarov (Ilya), Pehr-Olof Siren (receptionist), Daniel Smid (waiter)
35 mm, color
90 minutes

1972
FAT CITY
Producer: Ray Stark; a **John Huston**–Rastar Production; Columbia Pictures release

Director: **John Huston**
Screenplay: Leonard Gardner, from his novel
Cinematography: Conrad Hall
Editing: Marguerite Booth
Music: Marvin Hamlisch (supervision)
Cast: Stacy Keach (Billy Tully), Jeff Bridges (Ernie Munger), Candy Clark (Faye), Susan Tyrell (Oma), Nicholas Colosanto (Ruben), Art Aragon (Babe), Curtis Cokes (Earl), Sixto Rodriquez (Lucero), Billy Walker (Wes), Wayne Mahan (Buford), Ruben Navarro (Fuentes)
35 mm, color
100 minutes

1972
THE LIFE AND TIMES OF JUDGE ROY BEAN
Producer: John Foreman for National General
Director: **John Huston**
Screenplay: John Milius
Cinematography: Richard Moore
Art Direction: Tambi Larsen
Editing: Hugh S. Fowler
Music: Maurice Jarre
Cast: Paul Newman (Judge Roy Bean), Ava Gardner (Lillie Langtry), Victoria Principal (Marie Elena), Anthony Perkins (Reverend La Salle), Tab Hunter (Sam Dodd), **John Huston** (Grizzly Adams), Stacy Keach (Bad Bob), Roddy McDowell (Frank Gass), Jacqueline Bisset (Rose Bean), Ned Beatty (Tector Crites), Jim Buck (Bart Jackson), Matt Clark (Nick the Grub), Steve Kanaly (Whorehouse Lucky Jim), Bill McKinney (Fermil Parlee)
35 mm, color
120 minutes

1973
THE MACKINTOSH MAN
Producer: John Foreman, William Hill (associate) for Warner Brothers
Director: **John Huston**
Screenplay: Walter Hill, from *The Freedom Trap,* by Desmond Bagley
Cinematography: Oswald Morris
Art Direction: Alan Tomkins

Editing: Russell Lloyd
Music: Maurice Jarre
Cast: Paul Newman (Reardon), Dominique Sanda (Mrs. Smith), James Mason (Sir George Wheeler), Harry Andrews (Mackintosh), Ian Bannen (Slade), Michael Hordern (Brown), Nigel Patrick (Soames/Trevelan), Peter Vaughan (Brunskill), Roland Culver (judge), Percy Herbert (Taafe), Robert Lang (Jack Summers), Jenny Runacre (Gerba), John Bindon (Buster), Hugh Manning (prosecutor), Wolfe Morris (Malta police commissioner), Noel Purcell (O'Donovan), Donald Webster (Trevis), Keith Bell (Palmer), Niall MacGinnis (Warder)
35 mm, color
105 minutes

1975
THE MAN WHO WOULD BE KING
Producer: John Foreman, James Arnett (associate) for Associated Artists; released by Columbia Pictures
Director: **John Huston**
Screenplay: Gladys Hill, **John Huston**, from the story by Rudyard Kipling
Cinematography: Oswald Morris
Art Direction: Tony Inglis
Editing: Russell Lloyd
Music: Maurice Jarre
Cast: Sean Connery (Daniel Dravot), Michael Caine (Peachy Carnehan), Christopher Plummer (Rudyard Kipling), Saeed Jaffrey (Billy Fish), Karrovin Ben Bouih (Kafu-Selim), Jack May (district commissioner), Doghmi Larbi (Ootah), Shakira Caine (Roxanne), Mohammed Shamsi (Babu), Paul Antrim (Mulvaney), Albert Moses (Ghulam)
35 mm, color
127 minutes

1976
INDEPENDENCE
Producers: Joyce Ritter, Lloyd Ritter for National Park Service and Twentieth Century–Fox
Director: **John Huston**
Screenplay: Joyce Ritter, Lloyd Ritter, Thomas McGrath

Cinematography: Owen Roizman
Cast: Ken Howard (Thomas Jefferson), Patrick O'Neal (George Washington), William Atherton (Benjamin Rush), Eli Wallach (Benjamin Franklin), Anne Jackson (Abigail Adams), Pat Hingle (John Adams), Paul Sparer (John Hancock)

1979
WISE BLOOD
Producer: Michael Fitzgerald, Kathy Fitzgerald for Ithaca-Anthea; released through New Line Cinema
Director: **John Huston**
Screenplay: Benedict Fitzgerald, from the novel by Flannery O'Connor
Cinematography: Gerry Fisher
Editing: Roberto Silvi
Music: Alex North (composition and adaptation)
Cast: Brad Dourif (Hazel Motes), Ned Beatty (Hoover Shoates), Harry Dean Stanton (Asa Hawks), Amy Wright (Sabbath Lily), Mary Nell Santacroce (landlady), **John Huston** (Hazel's grandfather), Daniel Shor (Enoch Emery), William Hickey (preacher)
35 mm, color
108 minutes

1980
PHOBIA
Producer: Larry Spiegel for Spiegel-Bergman Films
Director: **John Huston**
Screenplay: Ronald Shusett, Gary Sherman, Lew Lehman, James Sangster, Peter Bellwood
Cinematography: Reginald Morris
Editing: Stan Cole
Music: Andre Gagnon
Cast: Paul Michael Glaser (Dr. Peter Ross), John Colicos (Inspector Barnes), Susan Hogan (Jenny St. Clair), Alexandra Stewart (Barbara Grey), Robert O'Ree (Bubba King), David Bolt (Henry Owen), David Eisner (Johnny Venuti), Lisa Langlois (Laura Adams), Kenneth Walsh (Sergeant Wheeler), Neil Vipond (Dr. Clegg), Patricia Collins (Dr. Alice Toland)
35 mm, color
107 minutes

1981
VICTORY
Producer: Freddie Fields for Lorimar; a Paramount release
Director: **John Huston**
Screenplay: Evan Jones, Yabo Yablonsky, from a story by Yablonsky, Djordje
Milicevic, Jeff Macquire
Cinematography: Gerry Fisher
Art Direction: J. Dennis Washington
Editing: Roberto Silvi
Music: Bill Conti
Cast: Sylvester Stallone (Robert Hatach), Michael Caine (John Colby), Pélé
(Luis Fernandez), Max Von Sydow (Maj. Karl Von Steiner), Anton Diffring
(chief commentator), Tom Pegott-Smith (Rose), Daniel Massey (Colonel Wal-
dron), Gary Waldron (Coach Mueller), Carole Laure (Renee), Julian Curry
(Shurlock), Bobby Moore (Terry Brady)
35 mm, color
110 minutes

1982
ANNIE
Producer: Ray Stark for Rastar; a Columbia Pictures release
Director: **John Huston**
Screenplay: Carol Sobieski, from the stage play by Thomas Meehan, based on
the comic strip created by Harold Gray
Cinematography: Richard Moore
Editing: Margaret Booth (supervising), Michael A. Stevenson
Music: Ralph Burns; songs by Charles Strouse, Martin Charnin
Cast: Aileen Quinn (Annie), Carol Burnett (Miss Hannigan), Albert Finney
("Daddy" Warbucks), Ann Reinking (Grace Farrell), Bernadette Peters (Lily),
Tim Curry (Rooster), Geoffrey Holder (Punjab), Edward Hermann (FDR),
Sandy (himself)
35 mm, color
128 minutes

1984
UNDER THE VOLCANO
Producer: Moritz Borman and Wieland Schulz-Kiel in association with
Ithaca-Conacine; a Universal release

Director: **John Huston**
Screenplay: Guy Gallo, based on the novel by Malcolm Lowry
Cinematography: Gabriel Figueroa
Editing: Roberto Silvi
Music: Alex North
Cast: Albert Finney (Geoffrey Firmin), Jacqueline Bisset (Yvonne Firmin), Anthony Andrews (Hugh Firmin), Katy Jurado (Señora Gregoria), James Villiers (Brit), Ignacio Lopez-Tarzo (Dr. Vigil), Dawson Bray (Quincey), Jim McCarthy (Gringo), Rene Ruiz (Dwarf), Emilio Fernandez (Diosdado), Carlos Requelme (Bustamente)
35 mm, color
109 minutes

1985
PRIZZI'S HONOR
Producer: John Foreman; an ABC Motion Pictures Presentation; released by Twentieth Century–Fox Film Corp.
Director: **John Huston**
Screenplay: Richard Condon, Janet Roach, based on the novel by Richard Condon
Cinematography: Andre Barthowiak
Editing: Rudi and Kaja Fehr
Music: Alex North
Cast: Jack Nicholson (Charlie Partanna), Kathleen Turner (Irene Walker), Robert Loggia (Eduardo Prizzi), John Randolph (Angelo "Pop" Partanna), William Hickey (Don Carrado Prizzi), Lee Richardson (Dominic Prizzi), Anjelica Huston (Maerose Prizzi), Michael Lombard (Filargi "Finlay"), Lawrence Tierney (Lieutenant Hanley), Joseph Ruskin (Marxie Heller)
35 mm, color
129 minutes

1987
THE DEAD
Producer: Wieland Schulz-Keil and Chris Sievernich for Liffey Films; released by Vestron Pictures
Director: **John Huston**

Screenplay: Tony Huston, based on the short story from *Dubliners,* by James Joyce
Cinematography: Fred Murphy
Editing: Roberto Silvi
Music: Alex North
Cast: Donal McCann (Gabriel Conroy), Anjelica Huston (Gretta Conroy), Helena Carroll (Aunt Kate), Cathleen Delaney (Aunt Julia), Frank Patterson (Bartell D'Arcy), Rachael Dowling (Lily), Katherine O'Toole (Miss Furlong), Bairbre Dowling (Miss Higgins), Maria Hayden (Miss O'Callaghan), Cormac O'Herlihy (Mr. Kerrigan), Colm Meaney (Mr. Bergin), Ingrid Craigie (Mary Jane), Dan O'Herlihy (Mr. Brown), Marie Kean (Mrs. Malins), Donal Donnelly (Freddy Malins), Sean McClory (Mr. Grace), Maria McDermottroe (Molly Ivors), Lydia Anderson (Miss Daly)
35 mm, color
83 minutes

Films Written Wholly or in Part by John Huston But Directed by Others

A House Divided (1931), Universal, directed by William Wyler
Murders in the Rue Morgue (1932), Universal, directed by Edward L. Cahn
Jezebel (1938), Warner Brothers, directed by William Wyler
The Amazing Dr. Clitterhouse (1938), Warner Brothers, directed by Anatole Litvak
Juarez (1939), Warner Brothers, directed by William Dieterle
Dr. Ehrlich's Magic Bullet (1940), Warner Brothers, directed by William Dieterle
High Sierra (1941), Warner Brothers, directed by Raoul Walsh
Sergeant York (1941), Warner Brothers, directed by Howard Hawks
The Killers (1946), Universal, directed by Robert Siodmak (Huston uncredited)
The Stranger (1946), RKO, directed by Orson Welles (Huston and Welles uncredited)
Three Strangers (1946), Warner Brothers, directed by Jean Negulesco

Films in which John Huston Appeared as Actor or Narrator

Report from the Aleutians (1943), directed by John Huston
The Battle of San Pietro (1945), directed by John Huston
We Were Strangers (1949), directed by John Huston

Freud (The Secret Passion (1962), directed by John Huston

The List of Adrian Messenger (1962), directed by John Huston

The Cardinal (1963), directed by Otto Preminger

The Bible . . . In the Beginning (1966), directed by John Huston

The Life and Times of John Huston (1966), directed by Roger Graef

Casino Royale (1967), directed by John Huston, et al.

Candy (1968), directed by Christian Marquand

De Sade (1969), directed by Cy Enfield

A Walk with Love and Death (1969), directed by John Huston

The Kremlin Letter (1970), directed by John Huston

The Other Side of the Wind (never completed production) (1970), directed by
    Orson Welles

Myra Breckenridge (1970), directed by Michael Sarne

The Bridge in the Jungle (1971), directed by Pancho Kohner

The Deserter (1971), directed by Burt Kennedy

Man in the Wilderness (1971), directed by Richard Sarafin

The Life and Times of Judge Roy Bean (1972), directed by John Huston

Battle for the Planet of the Apes (1974), directed by J. Lee Thompson

Chinatown (1974), directed by Roman Polanski

Breakout (1975), directed by Tom Gries

The Wind and the Lion (1975), directed by John Milius

Sherlock Holmes in New York (1976), directed by Boris Sagal

Tentacles (1977), directed by Oliver Hellman (Ouido Assonitis)

The Rhineman Exchange (1977), directed by Burt Kennedy

Hollywood on Trial (documentary) (1977), directed by David Helpern, Jr.

The Hobbitt (animated) (1977), directed by Arthur Rankin, Jr.

The Word (1978), directed by Richard Lang

The Bermuda Triangle (1978), directed by Rene Cardona, Jr.

Angela (1978), directed by Boris Sagal

Jaguar Lives! (1979), directed by Ernest Pintoff

Winter Kills (1979), directed by William Richert

The Battle of Mareth/The Greatest Battle (1979), directed by Hank Milestone

Head On (1979), directed by Michael Grant

John Huston's Dublin (documentary) (1980), directed by John McGreevy

Agee (documentary), (1980), directed by Ross Spears

The Visitor (1980), directed by Michael J. Paradise

John Huston: A War Remembered (1981), directed by Jim Washburn

Cannery Row (1982), directed by David S. Ward

Lights! Camera! Annie! (documentary) (1982), directed by Andrew J. Kuehn

The Directors Guild Series: John Huston (documentary) (1982), directed by William Crain

Lovesick (1983), directed by Marshall Brickman

A Minor Miracle/Young Giants (1983), directed by Terry Tanen

Momo (1986), directed by Johannes Schaaf

JOHN HUSTON

INTERVIEWS

Interview with Huston

KAREL REISZ/1952

THE DRIVE AND RUTHLESSNESS of his films and the gory pub-
licity stories (there's a particularly nasty one about a fight with Errol Flynn—
but they are probably all apocryphal) had led one to expect a formidable
man, tough, probably difficult. The first encounter dispelled these fears at
once. A tall, impressive figure, immaculately dressed in a lounge suit, quietly
in command of his film—and, one imagines, anything he touches—John
Huston turned out to be accessible and rewarding to interview. On the sound
stage of Isleworth Studios, during the shooting of *The African Queen,* he was
calmly in control, though a little remote from his unit.

Huston is completely frank and direct about the merits and faults of his
past films, assessing them with surprising critical detachment. He is a little
different about discussing technique—"all the trouble one takes over composition and lighting may be pleasing to oneself and one's friends but it's usually lost on the audience"—and says that the visual style of his films usually
crystallises of its own accord after the first few days shooting: he makes no
conscious, formulated plan but lets the writing and performances determine
the pictorial style. In *The Maltese Falcon*—of which he speaks with a particular affection—he was chiefly concerned with capturing the taut, personal
tensions of Hammett's novel and therefore used the long, uninterrupted
group shots staged in depth which characterise the film. But though he likes
to work out the compositions of his images with great care, he is uncertain

From *Sight and Sound,* January/March 1952, 130–32. © 1952 by *Sight and Sound.* Reprinted by
permission.

whether the effort is finally worth while. "I've seen Wyler's *The Heiress* three times and got great 'aesthetic' pleasure from just watching the images, one by one. But how much does the average audience get of this? Not much, I suspect." To the obvious reply, that there is a difference between merely "aesthetic" compositions and ones that are dramatically telling, he responds, frankly from experience: "In theory—yes. In practice—only sometimes. There are shots where the way you put them on the screen makes your point; in others, the actors are really doing all the work and it doesn't really matter how you shoot them." In those cases, the "pretty" images are, to him, a matter of personally satisfying a professional pride rather than an essential of storytelling.

Of the technical experiments he has made, he speaks only in concrete terms—theoretical considerations seem to interest him little. *Key Largo* was very much a tracking shot picture: the action was confined within a small space and the continual camera movements gave a sense of the confined, claustrophobic atmosphere. *The Asphalt Jungle* was quick, sharp, ruthlessly cut for tempo. All this, however, he is only prepared to discuss briefly, without much real interest. He appears to be a director whose conception of a film is in the first place literary and the visual style largely a matter for intelligent improvisation on the floor.

For a director with so marked a consistency of approach to his material, it was surprising to hear Huston discuss his method of working with actors. He says flatly—and refuses to qualify the statement—that he does not direct actors. "The trick is in the writing and casting. If you cast the right people, using only good actors, and adjust the script to suit the actors you've chosen, then it's best to leave them to work out their own gestures and movements. Your job is to explain to them the effect you want, and your skill lies in being able to do that exactly and vividly. Then, if they're good actors, it's best not to interfere in *how* they get your effect across—you'll only throw their natural performance out of gear if you try." What if they don't succeed in putting his point across? "They usually do." Well then, how about X—I mentioned a minor actor whose performance in one of Huston's films seemed to me inconsistent with the rest of the playing. "Oh, X—he's a very bad actor. Only has two expressions: handsome, and tough." And that seemed to end the discussion as far as he was concerned; there was no suggestion that Huston's responsibility as a director had not ended with his thus assessing the actor in question. But he is quick to point out that this method of treating actors happens to suit him and is not necessarily the right one for other directors.

This technique of handling the cast, though perhaps surprising for a director whose films have always been notable for their fine performances, becomes more understandable when one has seen Huston at work and read one of his scripts. Clearly, his sympathetic, quietly authoritative manner allows him to get loyal and accurate responses to all his demands from his actors and technicians. Where another director may stage-manage his actor's every movement as he works out the progress of his sequence, Huston knows what he wants before he goes on the floor and can then allow his actors some latitude within his conception. He is also obviously the sort of person for whom actors will do anything and perhaps the freedom he allows them is in many cases more illusory than real.

Huston works on the scripts of all his films, writing them in great detail, in a lively, lightly sophisticated literary style. His shooting script for The African Queen (adapted from C. S. Forester's novel by John Collier, James Agee, and Huston) contains only comparatively elementary camera directions and provides only a rough guide to the formal *decoupage:* what guide there is, he explains, is largely to allow the front office to work out a schedule and is not binding to himself in any way. In the description of characters' behaviour, intonations of speech and so on, the script is minutely detailed, designed to give his actors and his unit the fullest possible insight into the effects he intends to make.

Huston's scripts are surprisingly faithful to their originals. Once he has chosen a novel for adaptation, he treats it with the greatest respect. *The Maltese Falcon* and *The Asphalt Jungle* ("Burnett seems almost to write for me," he says) are among the most faithful adaptations ever filmed. In *The African Queen,* apart from condensing the climax and dramatising the ending by an ingenious plot twist, he has largely retained C. S. Forester's continuity and dialogue.

We Were Strangers, Huston's most considerable film seen in this country so far, is unique in that his expansion of the source material is more drastic and original; one had felt, seeing it, that more of Huston was behind it than behind his larger, more commercial films. I mentioned with surprise that the maker of *We Were Strangers*—a film which, by inference, makes out a case for political violence—should also have been attracted to make a film of Stephen Crane's *The Red Badge of Courage.* The ideologies of the two films, if not actually contradictory, seem distinctly alien. Huston did not really recognise this. *We Were Strangers,* he says, was scripted very quickly and the central character of Fenner was not as fully motivated as he would have wished. The point the film makes—that violence under certain circumstances may become a duty and be morally justified—emerges too rigidly. Fenner never rationalises the problem to himself, nowhere expresses doubts about the rightness of his action, and this makes the film's final gesture too simple. This apart, Huston feels that the inconsistency between the two works should not necessarily preclude a director from tackling both subjects. In working with other people's material, the director is primarily an interpretive artist and as such may respond to different materials provided he feels the characterisations of both to be genuine.

Huston's high position among American directors rests, so far, on his ability to apply immense drive and a penetrating analytical skill to popular material. Unlike Zinnemann, whose material is generally of a more serious nature than the average commercial film, and unlike Milestone, who leads a double life between worthy and meretricious subjects (and accords each appropriate treatment), Huston has tended to work with above-average thrillers (*The Maltese Falcon, The Asphalt Jungle*) which he has directed straight, or with action adventure stories (*The Treasure of Sierra Madre, We Were Strangers*) in which he could bring the moral issues to the forefront. But the cold, almost cynical detachment which has served him so well in the thrillers, has also limited the validity of the two more ambitious films, particularly *We Were Strangers.*

Whether this detachment—of which Huston's respectful treatment of others' material and his partially negative approach to acting are symptoms—is an indelible part of his temperament as a director, or whether he has simply refused (or failed) to engage his complete creative personality in his films so far, it is difficult to say. *The Red Badge of Courage*—which, strangely, he regards as a completely objective novel—might, but for the circumstances of its production, have provided the answer. Huston's uncompromising treatment had, according to trade reports, produced a film lacking box-office appeal, and M.G.M. have re-edited it into an action picture. The resulting film contains several powerfully realised episodes but is scrappy and inconsistent, and it would be unreasonable to draw any conclusions on Huston's future work from it.

The African Queen may well prove to be a turning point. Essentially a slight, good-natured fairy-tale about a prim, dowdy lady missionary who falls in love with a boat-captain, the script has a gentle, affectionately humorous quality which is new in Huston's work. It may be that with the freedom of working for his own company and with material whose overtones are in some ways more sophisticated and adult than anything he has so far tackled, Huston will now produce the unreservedly complete film which his admirers have been awaiting.

Paris in the 90s

AL HINE/1953

ONE OF THE TOURIST attractions of Paris last summer, in addition to the Arc de Triomphe, the Eiffel Tower and other stand-bys, was a motion picture called *Moulin Rouge. Moulin Rouge* wasn't being shown on any Parisian screens; it was still in production. The reason for its popularity, for the crowds of native Parisians and foreign visitors who crowded the streets where it was on location, was more than anything else the personalities involved in its filming.

Its director was John Huston, whose *African Queen* was still winning box-office and critical honors and who had been one of the central figures in Lillian Ross's controversial book *Picture,* about the making of *The Red Badge of Courage.* Its star was José Ferrer, a sort of perpetual-motion machine with built-in talent, who had been copping stage and cinema honors as actor, director, and producer. Also involved were such glamorous figures as Zsa Zsa Gabor and ballerina Colette Marchand. The internationally famed fashion artist Marcel Vertes was designing the costumes; Eliot Elisofon, an outstanding still-color photographer, was said to be tinkering with the Technicolor camera work. With all this, the story of *Moulin Rouge* was a sort of biography of Henri de Toulouse-Lautrec, the warped, degraded and dwarfish artist of the late 1800s who had made the Paris of the cancan, of the rowdy café and the garish brothel, of champagne, brandy, absinthe come to life in his posters and canvases.

So, when I learned that John Huston was flying in with the first print of

From *Holiday,* April 1953, 26–27. Reprinted by permission of *Travel Holiday* magazine.

Moulin Rouge the following day, I jumped at the chance to talk to Huston and to see the picture.

Mr. Huston and a United Artists representative were eating a late lunch in the hotel room to a background accompaniment of telephone rings. Mr. Huston was tall and lank and tousled in a print dressing gown. He was attentively attacking a small steak. His face was rugged, deeply lined and youthful, dominated by live and interested eyes.

"I think it's a good picture," he said happily.

The man from United Artists explained wryly that this was as high praise as Huston would give himself. "When he brought back *African Queen,* he said he thought it wasn't too bad. *African Queen!*"

We talked around the picture. What had it been like to make? Fun. What about the color, which I had heard was something special?

"Wait till you see it," Huston said. "We drove Technicolor crazy. We had Eliot Elisofon and Vertes and Ossie Morris, the cameraman, all working on some way to get into color the feeling of Toulouse-Lautrec, and to get color that looked real, not just splashy and bright.

"They worked it out with filters and with lighting and with other filters—not just on the camera, these were big gelatin filters in front of the lights—and took stills till we got what we wanted.

"Then the battle began with Technicolor. They couldn't understand what we were trying to do. All their thinking is to make everything equally bright and sharp and clear. Like a beer ad, where you can see every bubble in the foam. And here we were with color that was hazy in some places, that was light or dark according to mood, that sometimes showed the central figures clear and then let the background go into vagueness. They told us we were crazy. They wrote letters to us and to the money, trying to get pressure on us, or to stop us from doing this evil thing.

"We went ahead and did it, and now they want to know how to do everything that way. It's a joke now and we kid about how much I should sell them back their letters for."

What about the problems of shooting the picture in Paris?

"You mean *les citoyens?* It was a problem, but it was fun too. *Les citoyens* are individualistic. It isn't that they are trying to hold you up financially; it's more that they insist upon being recognized as individuals. There was one woman who ruined scene after scene in one sequence. Every time we were ready to shoot, just as soon as the sound equipment went on, she began banging a piece of metal against a fire escape. There didn't seem to be any solution, until we found a fortuneteller. We got the fortuneteller to tell the banger that, if she didn't stop banging, she'd have unbelievably bad luck. So she stopped."

What about Ferrer to work with?

"Wonderful. Never saw such an amazing guy, so many talents. I knew he spoke French fluently, and Spanish. Then one day Silvana Mangano visited the set; he spoke Italian fluently too. Anything he tries, he does well and he tries everything. I don't think he'd ridden a horse since he was a kid, but he heard I was going to Ireland to do some riding and he came along and soon he was taking jumps as if he'd been riding all his life.

"In the picture he's perfect. One thing you'll notice is that in playing this dwarf, this grotesque, he never for one minute gives the character any self-pity. It's a proud and whole character, which is what Lautrec should be."

Any interesting side lights on the picture in production?

"Maybe one. You know, most important people you wouldn't walk around the block to meet. Especially if you like their work; it's going to be too disillusioning. At any rate, that's the way I've always felt. But there's one exception. Picasso. I'd like to meet Picasso.

"Well, it wasn't until we'd finished shooting that I found Picasso had been on the set every day we'd been on location. He'd had someone who tipped him off every day where we'd be shooting the next day and he'd rent a room in a house or a hotel there and peek out and watch what was going on.

"Why? I don't know. He was just interested. Maybe he thought seeing what the movies were doing with Lautrec would be some kind of clue to his own future fate. I don't know. It was tantalizing as hell to find out what had been going on though."

How closely had he followed the Pierre la Mure novel for which the movie had been taken?

"Pretty closely. The novel really gave me the final impetus to make the movie. For a long time I'd wanted to do something with Lautrec in a movie. I felt he could be used to present the Paris of his times, to let the movie-goer see what Lautrec had seen—within the limits of moral censorship, of course. The book gave his life the kind of a frame we could use."

I saw *Moulin Rouge* the following night. It was as good, as new and exciting, and as beautiful as Huston had predicted. After almost twenty years of Technicolor which has mostly been as abusive to the eye as to the aesthetic sense, this was a long-delayed triumph. There is great art in the direction and the photography of *Moulin Rouge,* but there is never artiness. Once and for all (I hope) Huston and Ossie Morris, Vertes, Elisofon, and art director Paul Sheriff have shown that color is not something to hit customers over the head with, that its effects may be subtle and casual as well as blaring and stridently chromatic.

The outdoor country scenes have the quality of Corot, and the Paris scenes, interior and exterior, are beautifully Paris and accurately Lautrec. From the opening cancan to the ghostly dancers in the death scene, there is a vibrancy and honesty in the color that has not been seen on the screen before.

As to the story of the movie itself, there is here, too, color and excitement all the way, although it is much more the color and excitement of Toulouse-Lautrec's Paris than of his own life. The artist's story is well told and played to awesome perfection by José Ferrer, but it is the vignettes of a Paris long dead that come most sharply to life for the viewer.

There is a marvelous sequence in which Lautrec's drawings are projected on the screen, one after another in a sort of magic-lantern progression, which proves decisively that great art can be great excitement and entertainment. But other sequences, more subtly perhaps, have the same quality. I have never seen a movie where I had so much the feeling that any given frame of film could be isolated and stand on its own beauty and design. Yet this quality in no way makes *Moulin Rouge* slow or static. Exciting is still the key word.

José Ferrer has to be seen to be believed for the vitality and empathy he brings to his portrayal of Lautrec. Colette Marchand's Marie Charlet is a tramp who makes even the Millie of *Of Human Bondage* look like a leader in the local Young People's Sunday Evening Assembly—a great and thrilling actress. Zsa Zsa Gabor emerges, unbelievably, as a creditable actress. Suzanne Flon, as the decent love of Lautrec's later years, takes her own honors. But the full feeling, the excitement, the Lautrec-Parisian mood, belongs to the cancan girls, to Katherine Kath as La Goulue, to Muriel Smith as Aicha, to Rupert John as Chocolat, to all the dancers, drinkers, brawlers who populate this Paris, this moving poster of the splendid Nineties, in a swirl of life and music and color.

An Encounter with John Huston (Excerpts from a Conversation)

EDOUARD LAUROT/1956

HUSTON: Speaking about the philosophic content of *Moby Dick*—I am re-minded of Jean-Paul Sartre's *The Devil and God Almighty,* which I read recently. He also deals in ultimates—that ultimate evil may in turn become ultimate good, for example. I feel that I'm saying what you are more familiar with, but it seems to me that one of the themes of the play is precisely the fact that there is an unpredictable interplay between Good and Evil and that therefore, no Manichaean distinction between them can be made—though in this country there is a tendency to oversimplify moral and political issues.

LAUROT: There is no doubt about that. One of the main reasons for my having written the English version of *The Devil and God Almighty* was, precisely, my realization of how significant its ideas are for the modern world, and how important an American production of it would be. There haven't been any plays on Broadway in the past few years that could compare with the scope of its thought and the power of its dramatic impact.

HUSTON: I entirely agree with you. Aside from its purely theatrical qualities, it can be read as a sort of dramatic essay of ideas. I would risk saying that it's his best play. Don't you think so?

LAUROT: Yes, insofar as Sartre's expression through theatre goes, this play may be taken as his most advanced one. No other contemporary dramatist seems to have approached the dilemma of the modern intellectual with such boldness and perspicacity. *Waiting for Godot,* a play currently so popular with

From *Film Culture,* vol. 2, no. 8, 1956, 1–4. © 1956 by *Film Culture Magazine.* Reprinted by permission.

the *Saturday Review* type of intelligentsia, is at best a poetic prolegomenon to the problems affronted in *The Devil and God Almighty* by Goetz, the protagonist. For Goetz, of course, represents a type of the modern intellectual—at least the European intellectual—torn by an anguished conflict between his divided ethical, therefore political, allegiances. He describes a full circle of possibilities afforded by the modern world in his existential search for an ethic. But the play has a more universal meaning in that it presents both man's craving for the Absolute and his rebellion against it.

HUSTON: This is what I really meant when I said that the ultimates are oversimplified here.

LAUROT: I'm very glad to hear this from you for, as you most certainly know, Existentialism, as a philosophy—as well as its personal and political implications—has been regrettably misinterpreted here—even in academic circles. And then—there are those popular conceptions that consider it either as an eccentric pose or as a gloomy philosophy of foredoom preaching moral anarchy and, therefore, an abstention from all responsibility. The whole of Sartre's creation and activity, as well as the fact that he has announced as his new project a work on ethics, should be known to at least the intelligentsia of this country. That's why at present I am making plans for a stage production of *The Devil and God Almighty.*

HUSTON: I'd very much like to see this play produced in New York. As a director, I'm also interested in it and have entertained thoughts of putting it on film. Sartre would be very strong medicine for Hollywood. They engage moral issues constantly, but on a superficial level. Here in New York, I believe he could meet with response; although when I staged *Huis Clos,* its depths escaped audiences and critics. Many thought it was a play about Lesbians. . . .

LAUROT: I have a feeling that if *The Devil and God Almighty* were to be filmed under your direction, it might not suffer from a reduction in significance. You seem to be one of the very few directors who attempt to retain the substance of an original they adapt—insofar as this is possible.

HUSTON: You're very kind to think so. Sometimes, of course, one doesn't have to follow the original literally to remain faithful to the spirit. For instance—take *Moby Dick.* So far I've encountered only one person that did not approve of what I had done with it—he is a rabid reverer of every line in Melville's book—and, while I respect his opinion very much, I do believe that my interpretation penetrates to the deepest parts of Melville. It emphasizes them and does not try to avoid any of them. What do you think about *Moby Dick*'s message?

LAUROT: I think the book's content extends beyond the concept of message. In the first place, it is a book on the human condition, with all the complexities and contradictions that it implies; and it could not be reduced, as it has been by many, to the presentation of a struggle between "good" and "evil" forces. There is a poetic overtone in it, a song of man and the element transcending the dramatically presented conflict. And, for the same reason, the book's power transcends the symbolism of images and situations. Even if we see Melville's world as a world humanized by an ethic, this ethic surpasses the Christian *Weltanschauung*. . . . Remember Father Mapple's words? "Mortal or immortal, here I die. . . . I have striven to be Thine, more than to be this world's, or mine own. Yet this is nothing; I leave eternity to Thee. . . ." Ahab, on the other hand, is haunted by the Absolute, and that is why he, literally—hunts It. In this, he is comparable to Orestes in *The Flies:* they both want to liberate man from the Supreme Being. And beyond that . . . every work of art is a departure from the given world that is Nature, but it is an organized, explained world. The greatest works of art, however, go beyond the presentation of an intelligible world and create one that is recognizable and yet as complex and subject to as many interpretations as the phenomenal world in which we live. . . .

HUSTON: Yes, certainly. That is why I also think that Melville goes much further than just the presentation of opposing, warring concepts. He seems to have written the book with several parts of his nature. It isn't just one man and one point of view—it is a half a dozen men and different points of view. It is the writer, the moralist, the philosopher, the scientist, the cetologist, the dramatist. I don't attempt consciously to correlate all his facets in my film, but let them exist in their original richness and spontaneity. For example, I think that he wrote the Father Mapple speech in a completely different spirit from that in which he approached the philosophical vein that runs through the book and underlies the events. He wrote the sermon as a religious man, deeply passionate in his belief. And this is somewhat mysterious and puzzling, for the sermon is in conflict with his philosophical concepts. It is, in fact, as you pointed out, a denial of it. It also occurred to me that the story of Noah is the story of Ahab in reverse, but even that cannot be taken as ultimately true. Melville was carried away by the magnitude of his thought. Theologically, the book is a blasphemy. Ahab is at war with

God, there is no question about this. He sees the mask of the whale as the mask that the deity wears. He sees the deity as a malignant, rational being that is out to torment the race of men and all other creatures. And Ahab is the world's dark champion who grapples with this omnipresent and enslaving force.

LAUROT: Without this dimension, *Moby Dick* would have been reduced to such an orthodox presentation of Good and Evil as is literally incarnated in the characters of Billy Budd and Claggart.

HUSTON: *Billy Budd* is indeed that, a very simple book, though a later one. *Moby Dick* says God is evil, or at least, Ahab says God is evil. The pragmatic-minded Starbuck interprets the blasphemy on a bourgeois level. He thinks that the mission of the whaler men is to furnish oil for the lamps of the world. But Ahab's blasphemy is even greater than Starbuck dreams.

LAUROT: You seem to be taken with the ideas in *Moby Dick* aside from its narrative aspect. I understand you began writing the script many years ago—is it the same script?

HUSTON: Yes and no. I wrote some parts of the scenario some years ago; then, I had my father in mind for the part of Ahab. I'd planned the script for years. Bradbury and I worked on the version that was used in the film. But the reflection of years has gone into it, so in some respects, I feel it to be close to my original conception.

LAUROT: Being such a compelling and original world, *Moby Dick* would demand a corresponding originality and forcefulness from the director, also. . . .

HUSTON: That was my main preoccupation. I wanted to find fresh ways to deal with the substance of Melville's book. On the most obvious level—that of color—I tried to discover the tones that would tell *Moby Dick* as a picture—this particular picture and no other. So we devised a new color photography process and found a palette to paint Melville's story. We shot *Moby Dick* in Technicolor. From the color film we made two sets of negatives—one in color, one in black and white. The two negatives were printed together on the final print, achieving a completely new tonality. The dancing purples, for instance, are absent.

LAUROT: The rather amorphous, narrative construction of the book must have presented difficulties in dramatization.

HUSTON: Yes, we had to dramatize some of the narration, and aside from that, create dramatic situations. But always—without exception—they come from the book, although sometimes, from just an important line in the text. For example, Starbuck discovered through Ahab that the purpose of the voyage, so far as the master of the ship is concerned, is to kill Moby Dick. In the book, Ahab has a chart. In the film, the chart has been made into a scene. The original scene where he declared himself and what he conceived the white whale to be took place on the quarter deck where he spoke to the mariners and where they drank to the death of Moby Dick. In the picture, as they drink to the death of Moby Dick, the crew sees him for the first time, and he studies them. Then, after that, they have their first lowering, or engagement with the whales, and the barrels are stored in the hold. Starbuck goes to report to Ahab so many barrels, and then Ahab shows him his charts. He believes he has discovered the movements of the whales around the world—"I know them as I know the veins of my arm." Starbuck sees this as a way of filling the hold in record time and Ahab says, "so we shall, once we have accomplished the bigger business." Starbuck ought to know what that business is. Then into that comes his accusation of blasphemy and the first revelation on Ahab's part—"Talk not to me of blasphemy, I'd strike the sun if it insulted me." That is what I meant about dramatizing the narrative. I hope the picture will be successful because production costs are in the millions and unfortunately, you can't get funds for anything that is in the least way a departure from the established pattern. When I went to Hollywood, there were only a few who had broken away from it—Flaherty, Murnau. *Trader Horn* was the one great adventurous undertaking. This represented the sum total of shooting done anywhere other than in Hollywood. My going to Mexico to shoot *The Treasure of the Sierra Madre* was a big step for the studio to take. Now, the situation is completely changed—companies are shooting all over the world. So, the industry's decentralization and the growth of East Coast production, for instance, is encouraging. But it will be utterly meaningless if it does not bring about a complete breakaway from standard Hollywood patterns.

LAUROT: You seem to speak with intimate knowledge about the "patterns. . . ."

HUSTON: On, the worst frost I ever had was with *The Red Badge of Courage*. It was "rearranged," as you know. During the preview, large sections of the audience just left in the middle of one of the best scenes, the one in which the tall soldier dies and then the boy and the tattered soldier leave him. They tried to salvage what looked to them like a hopeless mess. *The Red Badge of*

Courage was made during the Korean War and this might have had something to do with it. It was too much for audiences, they wanted no part of it. All their feelings were magnified by the Korean War. It had something to do with bad timing. Now, if somebody else comes along and wants to do something like *The Red Badge,* many would be opposed.

LAUROT: Before, when we talked about dramatisation, I recalled that some people wondered if you had attempted to shoot *Moby Dick* in accordance with the "style" that is commonly attributed to you—which, of course, might present certain limitations. . . .

HUSTON: It is a curious thing that so many people ascribe to me a distinct style. Believe me, I am not conscious of any such thing. Whenever I undertake to direct a film, I do so out of the deep feeling that it inspires in me. It is precisely this feeling that dictates the way in which I direct a picture. It is a matter of spontaneous sensitivity. I direct actors as little as possible, and do not strive to impose a monotonous unity of style upon the whole. There may be some general principles that are abiding, but the rules are there only to be broken, not to be adhered to. The direction of a scene depends upon its quality as a scene. For example, we are having a certain kind of conversation right now. It is a spatial relationship that is directed by the thoughts. In photographing this scene, in composing, lighting and editing, this sort of encounter would be rendered according to the varying distances between the participants.

LAUROT: It's this freedom, then, from a preconception of style that keeps you from subordinating given situations, and that accounts for the spontaneous feeling of life. . . .

HUSTON: Oh yes. This frees me to retain the particular style of the film— not my own "personal, permanent style—and within the film, to create spontaneous variations of the style that make for unity and fortify the whole conception. I do not think any filmmaker should—though many do— consciously strive to maintain a permanent style in all his films. This could be possible only if he made the same picture over and over again. Some styles, for example, Westerns, have become a noble convention; they tell the same kind of story in the same way and there is no reason to change this approach. From time to time, people say to me, "We'd like to see you make a Western." If I ever made a Western, I'd make the same kind of Western. I don't want to put my brand on the Western; it has its adequate style already.

LAUROT: Then would you agree with me that neo-realism is primarily an attitude toward life, rather than a style?

HUSTON: Certainly; I have the greatest admiration for the neo-realist directors. De Sica's *Bicycle Thief* is an ever-renewed experience for me. He knows how to make people in his films behave naturally and yet he gives them the intensity of his vision.

LAUROT: It's all the more to be regretted, don't you think, that the American filmmakers who have attempted an imitation of neo-realism have conceived it as a style rather than as a way of seeing the world which, in turn, would command an artistic interpretation.

HUSTON: That is true. Neo-realism has influenced many American filmmakers, but their films, for example, on juvenile delinquency are juvenile, thematically superficial and self-conscious. They fail to understand that what matters is not a new method, but the return to the sources of life, of people, of society that the European neo-realists have affected. It all comes back to a matter of heart and vision, not only talent. So long as these elements are neglected, we shall not have films here made with the intensity and compassion of the neo-realists.

Huston: "I Direct as Little as Possible"

KIMMIS HENRICK/1968

JOHN HUSTON IS MAKING a film about a boy and girl working out answers against a background that could be now. It isn't. It's the Middle Ages.

This is *A Walk with Love and Death,* taken from a novella by Hans Koningsberger. Its theme, as Mr. Huston says, is always new. Youth has to find its way through the Establishment—in any period, any place.

Mr. Huston loves this sort of thing. He has been directing films since 1941, but "veteran" doesn't seem like the apt word for anything he says or does. "Explorer," maybe, or "adventurer." Youth crowds in on him.

His producer for this picture and the next to follow is a young man, Carter De Haven. His stars for *A Walk with Love and Death* are two beautiful young people. The boy is Assaf Dayan, son of Israel's Defense Minister, who has already made pictures in Italy and Israel and is barely in his twenties. The girl is Mr. Huston's daughter, who has never made a film before.

"The problem about Anjelica," says her pleased parent, smiling, "has been to keep her off the screen until now. I never wanted her to be a child actress. But she has been proposed by associates of mine for important roles ever since she was a little girl."

Mr. Huston's present film has been forming in his thought for years. He visited Austria for the first time 20 years ago and was royally entertained in feudal castles from one end of the country to the other. He knew one day he must make Austria the setting for a film. When he read *A Walk with Love and Death,* he had his story.

This one, to be released by 20th Century–Fox, makes the twenty-eighth film Mr. Huston has directed. His first was *The Maltese Falcon,* which starred Humphrey Bogart and established both men as preeminent figures in the world of cinema. Today Mr. Huston says, "I direct as little as possible," meaning that he likes to let actors develop their own characterizations, and apparently that's always been his way of working.

He remembers, though, that there was one film in which Mr. Bogart kept feeling uncertain. It was in *The African Queen,* in which he played opposite Katharine Hepburn, and they both were marvelous. Mr. Bogart would say to Mr. Huston, "Keep me in it." That, Mr. Huston says, really sums up the director's job.

John Huston was born in Nevada, Mo., both his parents were, as he puts it, "itinerent" actors, so he was always on the go. He says he can probably still recite most of the stops on the Santa Fe and Northern Pacific. He went to high school in Los Angeles, but most of that time, he says, he wasn't studying. He was boxing.

Evidently it was when his father, Walter Huston, starred in the Broadway production of Eugene O'Neill's *Desire Under the Elms* that John Huston first really felt drawn to drama. But he wanted something else for himself. He got an honorary commission in the Mexican Cavalry. He wrote short stories which H. L. Mencken published in the *American Mercury.* He wrote a play for marionettes published by Alfred Knopf. He took a Left Bank studio in Paris and painted.

Then Mr. Huston got a job in Hollywood as a writer of special dialogue for a film called *A House Divided,* which starred his father. This led to a screenwriting job at Warner Bros. John Huston took it with the brash proviso that he'd be allowed to direct something. This intrigued Jack Warner. Eventually he gave him *The Maltese Falcon* to work on, and his name was made.

He left Hollywood for Ireland in 1952 and ten years later became a citizen of the Irish Republic. He is now at work on a project to give Ireland a national film industry. After his next picture, *The Kremlin Letter,* which he will start filming early next year, Mr. Huston intends to do a great one out of modern Irish history.

"I hope to do it," is the way he says it. "It will be *Easter Rising.*"

A Talk with John Huston

DAN FORD/1972

WHEN I VISITED JOHN Huston he was staying in a canyon house that looked across a dry stream bed where thin shadows danced over rocks hot and dry in the sun. He was dressed in a billowing saffron robe and sat with his bony shoulders hunched over, elbows on his knees, long thin fingers trailing down. A little over six feet, Huston has the moves of a much larger man. He is loose-hipped and is both gangling and graceful, like a basketball giant. He speaks with a rich mellifluous voice that handles eight syllable words, florid metaphors and four-letter blasts with equal alacrity. This voice makes him one of the most sought after narrators in the business, perhaps second only to Orson Welles. Like Welles, his voice conveys tremendous literacy and dignity. But the most striking thing about Huston is the leathery face that this voice comes out of. God must look something like John Huston. It's a thin, deeply grooved face framed by wispy grey hair and a beard. The eyes are an opaque reddish brown. They are watchful, yet curiously empty of all feeling. Despite the heartiness of his manner I suspected that the eyes were like a curtain to a closely guarded soul and that John Huston was perhaps a deeply introverted and very private man.

John Marcellus Huston was born in Nevada, Missouri. The town, if family legend is to be believed, was won by his grandfather in a poker game. His father, Walter Huston, was on a hiatus from the boards and was gainfully employed as a local power engineer. One night the town caught fire and the

From *Action*, vol. 7, no. 5. September/October 1972, 21–25. © 1972 copyright by Dan Ford. Reprinted by permission.

firefighters kept telling engineer Walter to give them more water pressure. Being an amiable man he obliged them and overstrained the water system. The Huston family thought it prudent to leave what was left of Nevada, Missouri that same night. A few years later, Huston's parents separated, and Walter returned to the stage. John shuffled between the horse-loving, gambling life of his mother and the three-shows-a-day and catch-the-sleeper-to-Cleveland life of his father.

At twelve John was pronounced deathly ill, and fears for his survival were expressed. Appropriately he was put in a sanitarium where he could live his remaining years in comfort. But he was too irrepressible for such nonsense. Late at night when all the medical sages were asleep, he would sneak out and slide down a nearby rocky, moss covered waterfall and frolic in the icy water. Young John was soon judged healthy and returned home. At first he wanted to be a painter and studied at an art school in Los Angeles. He took nine flings at prize fighting and claims to have become amateur lightweight champion of California.

"I had talent for it as a kid," he recalls, "When I put on the gloves, I felt easy and I hit straight off the bat. But I was so damned skinny that I'd feel a beating for several days afterwards. I had in mind to become middleweight champion of the world."

He wandered down to Mexico and served in the Mexican Cavalry. He wrote for a while, publishing a play, *Frankie and Johnnie,* and sold a number of short stories about horses and fighters to H. L. Mencken of the *American Mercury.*

Huston's writing landed him a job at Universal where he scripted William Wyler's *A House Divided* and the Edgar Allan Poe classic, *Murders in the Rue Morgue.* But he was still restless and bolted Hollywood to study art in Paris, be a bum in London, a newspaper man in New York, and an actor in Chicago.

Huston's varied early life taught him lessons he has never forgotten. His recent film, *Fat City,* captures the lives of the Stockton fieldhands and boxing hopefuls with a Steinbeckian flair. It sees that city as a bum sees it, the flophouses, park benches, littered streets and sweaty gyms. The men work in fields under a hot white sky. The boxing is fast and painful. There is knowledge of and empathy for Huston's characters.

In 1938 Huston was at Warner Brothers as a writer, married and settled; he began his career in earnest, collaborating on Wyler's *Jezebel* (1938); *The Amazing Dr. Clitterhouse* (1938); *Jaurez,* (1939); *Dr. Ehrlich's Magic Bullet,* (1940); Howard Hawks's *Sergeant York,* (1941); and Raoul Walsh's *High Sierra* (1941). Huston's contract with Warners expired while he was working on *High Sierra,* and he brashly announced that he was leaving unless they let him direct. Warners agreed, not because they foresaw he would emerge as a great director; rather, they wanted to keep him as a writer.

He made his directorial debut with what Warners had planned to be a B picture, Dashiell Hammett's *Maltese Falcon.* It had been filmed twice before with Ricardo Cortez and Warren William in the role of detective Sam Spade but had never been a success. Huston was determined to be true to Hammett's gritty style and terse dialogue.

Falcon was a miracle of casting. Bogart made the perfect Sam Spade. He was brutal, cunning, unsentimental, yet somehow admirable. For the heavy, Casper Gutman, Huston cast Sydney Greenstreet, a 285-pound veteran stage comic who had never been in a motion picture. Mary Astor, Peter Lorre, and Elisha Cook rounded out the cast.

The Maltese Falcon under Huston's taut direction achieved a drive from first frame to last. Harsh lighting set off gritty sets, low camera angles enhanced Greenstreet's menacing bulk. Huston's roving deep-focus camera set up perfectly what would eventually become a John Huston directorial trademark: group tension, contrasting personalities thrown together by circumstance, abrading against one another, sparks flying off. Huston's script adhered to one of the classic rules of tragedy: unity of time, place, and action. *The Maltese Falcon* was completed in eight weeks and cost less than $300,000. Warners released it as a B but were quick to cash in on its enormous popularity. It was hailed as a classic and James Agee called it "the best private eye melodrama ever made." It was nominated for an Academy Award as best picture of 1941.

Huston's better films are noted for their superb camera work. Never flashy, his is a more subtle camera. It is used to establish mood and reveal character without relying on dialogue. Huston has an artist's delicate eye for space relationships and distances. In *Treasure of the Sierra Madre,* which many consider Huston's best film, Ted McCord's camera is immobile, medium-distance. It stands off sardonic and passive until the final orgy of violence.

"I just wanted them to look like they were stewing in their own juice," says Huston.

Moulin Rouge is a landmark for the color film. Oswald Morris's muted and filtered photography is hazy in spots, sharp in others with the tonal range of

an oil painting. It establishes the mood perfectly for this biography of Toulouse-Lautrec. In *Key Largo* Huston's camera is a moving close-up, one which
at once keeps the action moving and conveys the fungoid claustrophobia of
a small Florida hotel during a hurricane.

In *Treasure* the camera is used to contrast the gold-hunting trio in a memorable scene where they discover the body of intruding Texas, Bruce Bennett.
Bogart, the disintegrating tough guy, looks on the corpse as though he's
about to put his foot on it and have his picture taken. Tim Holt, a decent
young man, brings his hands together, a hint of prayer. Walter Huston, the
wise old sage who has spent a lifetime looking for gold, surgically goes
through the dead man's pockets like a worker in a morgue.

In *Key Largo* Edward G. Robinson is introduced sitting naked in a bathtub,
chewing a cigar. "I wanted the look of a crustacean with its shell off," says
Huston. Robinson is immediately established as obscene and dangerous, like
an animal caught out in the open.

In *The African Queen* one of the earliest scenes establishes the conflict and
comic dimension. Bogart, the low-life, alcoholic river rat, visits prissy missionary Katharine Hepburn and her brother, Robert Morley. As Morley be-
moans the fact that fate has left him far behind the other "old boys,"
Bogart's stomach growls like a man used to food and drink more substantial
than tea and crumpets.

Much of Huston's best work is based on having contrasting characters
together by circumstance. He is a master at regulating the interplay between
characters. It would almost seem that he functions best as an artist when the
story limits him from the outset, when he is forced to rely on interplay and
confrontation. Not only is this true of early Huston classics like *Treasure of
the Sierra Madre, Key Largo,* and *African Queen,* but also in more recent works.
In *Night of the Iguana* a sodden, defrocked Richard Burton is beset by a prim
spinster, Deborah Kerr, dissolute innkeeper, Ava Gardner, and temptuous
nymphet, Sue Lyon, in a sleazy Mexican hotel. In *Heaven Knows, Mr. Allison,*
Deborah Kerr, a nun, and Robert Mitchum, a tough Marine, hide together in
a cave. Because they are both such attractive people there is an overriding
sexual tension, but Huston never surrenders to cheap sensationalism, and a
delicate platonic love develops between them.

At sixty-six, Huston is trim and fit. He has remained uncompromisingly
athletic. He is a superlative horseman and rides as often as he can. He is a
good drinker and holds it well.

"I get a little cockeyed before dinner but always go to bed sober," he says.

An impulsive man of action, his courage knows no bounds. During the Second World War he continually exposed himself to danger making documentaries; his *Battle of San Pietro* is among the best ever made. He publicly called the McCarthy hearings an obscenity, consistently has bucked the powers of the moment in Hollywood, has gamely tackled Melville, Hemingway, Tennessee Williams, and Freud. Huston has no politics, but he is an anti-authoritarian cop-hater who is quick to jump to the defense of the underdog. He is incredibly well read and can talk endlessly about Portuguese wines, African elephants, or Italian wives.

Huston describes his recent forays into acting as a lark. His real interest now, as always, is directing. Recently he has completed two entirely different pictures: *Fat City,* based on Leonard Gardner's terse boxing novel, and *The Life and Times of Judge Roy Bean,* a wide open western based loosely on the west Texas hanging judge. He discussed his work on the latter location.

FORD: *You certainly had a varied early background. By the time you were thirty-two, you had been a bum, a boxer, a soldier, a writer, actor, artist, and editor.*

HUSTON: Well, I don't think it's quite as good as Keats. Thirty-two seems to me a pretty ripe old age. I didn't know it at the time, but it was all preparatory to becoming a director. Like any artist he must know and experience life, and I think most of the better ones have a varied background and a variety of interests.

FORD: *When did you first want to direct?*

HUSTON: At first I wanted to become a painter, but meeting O'Neill in New York, when my father was doing *Desire Under the Elms,* first drew me to the theater. I think I learned more about films from O'Neill than anyone—what a scene consisted of and so forth. By the time I came to Hollywood as a writer I was conscious that I wanted to direct. Working with such greats as Wyler and Howard Hawks only served to reinforce it. It was not easy to jump from writer to director in those days. There was just one other man who had made the jump, and I wasn't able to do it until much later, of course. I worked for a while at Universal, but I was no great shakes there, what I wrote didn't really go down.

FORD: *How did the volatile, independent John Huston get along with the old studio system?*

HUSTON: Well, there are certain advantages to having a kind of police state. It gave you something to buck. We were writers in revolt, fighting to write well. With rare exception they believed only in the cliché and making pictures to formula. Of course, the fact that you were on salary gave you a luxury that is unknown today. Writing is a form of madness anyway. One time I was with Hemingway on his boat and he was talking about the joys of writing, when the words took wing and so forth. I listened to this and thought, "Yeah, sure, Hemingway." About a month later we were together again and were talking about dancing. Papa was saying how he loathed dancing, getting up and walking around a crowded floor with some broad. He said, "Jesus, I hate it so much, I'd rather write." I was relieved to hear that.

FORD: *Did writers and directors collaborate much then?*
HUSTON: No, not much. The director was given a finished script. There was a period in pre-production in which the writer, director, and producer worked together, but when the picture went on the floor, that was the end of the writer. I remember after I had written *Sergeant York,* Hawks called me on the set about something. This was extraordinary, and I was delighted to be able to spend some time on the set. Warner Brothers just before the war was the peak of the studio system, by the way. They started the gangster thing, which had tremendous relevancy at the time. More than anyone else they had their hand on the pulse of the times. A very creative atmosphere.

FORD: *I don't know how original this is, but I've always viewed Bogart as the personification of the Hemingway hero, and you were certainly an important figure in Bogart's career.*
HUSTON: There was no conscious effort on my part to translate Hemingway into film or anything of that sort. I'm sure I was influenced by him and by Joyce and some of the other voices of my generation. If there is any connection it was just a thing of the time, something people were moved by. Unfortunately I never made a Hemingway picture. I worked on the screenplay for Hellinger's *The Killers,* and was to direct *A Farewell to Arms* for Selznick but that never came to be.

I was fortunate to work on a number of Burnett and Hammett stories, and I always thought they were vastly underrated writers. The heroes are of the same genre, and they helped reinforce some of the definitions that Hemingway made.

FORD: *Like what?*

HUSTON: Well, simple pleasures like eating, drinking, and loving. We used to eat because we were hungry and drink just for the effect. Papa and some of the others reminded us that these things had value in and of themselves in a period when we had forgotten about them. Of course, there was the codal thing, a man's pride in his behavior, not on parade as it were, but important to himself. As far as Bogart being the Hemingway hero, you're right—not only because he is tough and unsentimental. Papa was in reality a romantic. Papa fell in love. You were moved not by what he said, but rather by what he left out. Sometimes you got that from Bogart. I'm thinking of *Casablanca* primarily. Not a case of lacking sentiment, but *why* he lacks sentiment.

FORD: *Has that concept influenced your work?*

HUSTON: Oh, perhaps, but in a visual sense rather than a literary one. It's what the painter calls space. One of the things I did as a young man was to study art. I'm something of a collector of pre-Columbian and Etruscan art. It's simple and direct like some of the better modern art. But before Cezanne, painting was concerned too much with flesh tones, lacy trees, sugary clouds, an artificial and corrupt sentimentality. Cezanne got back to the basics, he rediscovered the angle, used color not so much for effect, but to describe form. His was a unique vision, piercing through all that was artificial. He also used space. On the canvas where he didn't paint, the void had meaning. He was one of the great revolutionists who returned painting to some of its purest and most original form and beauty.

I've always been a great admirer of Robert Flaherty. Not only was he the first great documentary filmmaker, but his vision was that mankind at its source was pure and uncorrupt. Civilization was the spoiler. And his work was like his vision in that it had the purity of the primitive artist. Perhaps civilization corrupts the filmmaker too. I've always felt I learned a lot about film by studying art. It's very important, for example, to use your lighting to capture the mood of the scene.

FORD: *You're known for a very passive work style. Some construe it as indifference and some actors find it difficult to work with you.*

HUSTON: Well, I believe the most important part of picture making is the casting—matching the actor to the proper character and making sure the actor understands the character. In a given scene, I have an idea what should happen, but I try not to tell the actors. I think they should follow their own hunches. I just tell them to do it their own way and sometimes they improve on it, add something by accident. When they do, I print the accident. Sometimes this works exceptionally well. Take Alfonso Bedoya, Gold Hat in *Treasure*. A delightful man, the heart opens right up to him. He looked great for the part, but he didn't know how to act. My not telling him exactly how things were to be done only confused and frustrated him. There was an uncertainty there that added a dimension of volatility and unpredictability and made him even more terrifying.

Acting is part intuitive and part technical. The English train their actors to be superb technicians. Americans tend to rely on charisma. Most critics that attacked *Moby Dick* attacked Greg Peck. I swear by him. I thought he was very good in a very demanding role. I was afraid of a melodramatic approach to Ahab, someone fierce and pyrotechnic. That would have been too easy. There were a number of Englishmen at that time who had a great gift in that direction, but I wanted more than that.

The better American actors like, of course, Brando, Paul Newman, Mitchum, young Stacy Keach, and so many others have a way of expressing their internal conflicts in nonverbal ways. Englishmen tend to rely too much on the written word. I saw the magnitude in Ahab rather than the madness. Ahab was not insane, his was a terrible sanity. His arrogance was the naked fist raised against the deity. Melville saw the Almighty as a malignant being and the whale as the symbol of God. There is a line—I'm paraphrasing it badly—"What is the judge? Himself to be himself who is dragged before the bar. If God almighty is to be judged what punishment would he deserve?" Greg had the nobility and dignity so necessary for Ahab as I believe Melville to have conceived him. It was important for a charismatic American to have played him, not merely because he is a uniquely American character, but the role required that sort of soulful depth.

In terms of being passive I can only say that I believe filmmaking to be a collaborative medium. Rather than being a tyrant, I believe in getting ideas from as many sources as possible. Let me tell you about Tennessee Williams on *Night of the Iguana*, which he so generously lent himself to. Tony Veiller and I had a pretty good scene written where Burton is alone in his room in a fever and in a drunk, and all these things are going on inside of him. The girl, Sue Lyon, comes in and tries to seduce him and he is doing everything in his power to keep away from the girl. Well, we gave the scene to Tennessee to see what he thought of it. The only change he wrote was the thing that made the scene. When the girl opens the door suddenly, a glass falls onto the floor leaving broken bits of glass scattered about the room. When the scene is played both of them are barefoot. Burton walks on it and doesn't even feel his feet being shredded. The girl sees this and joins him walking barefoot across the glass. It was the difference between an extraordinary scene and a pedestrian one. It's also an example of Tennessee's extraordinary powers of dramatization. It certainly was a welcome idea.

FORD: *Isn't it difficult to find consistent themes that summarize your work?*
HUSTON: I agree. I don't see any line through my work and I'm not conscious of those things. After *Treasure* the European critics said my message was that the end didn't matter, it was the means, the undertaking rather than the achievement. Well, that sounds pretty good.

FORD: *Perhaps they were influenced by the fact that you brought No Exit to Broadway?*
HUSTON: That's possible, although I didn't get to know Sartre until *Freud*. He did a treatment and, my God, it was 450 pages long! I don't think I have ever known anyone with the capacity for concentrated work to compare with Sartre.

FORD: *Why Sartre to write on Freud?*
HUSTON: He had this power of logical thinking to sift through all this material, and we agreed that there was the presence of the devil, the smell of sulphur in Freud. I liked the picture but it was too long, two and a half hours, I think, and that's an awful long time to sit with no relief or no action to speak of. It was conceived as a super detective story but when it was cut for the sake of brevity, the symmetrical line of logic was broken. And that sort of picture must have the logic of an equation to stand up.

FORD: *Much has been made of your life style in Ireland. How did you come to emigrate?*
HUSTON: There was never any conscious withdrawal on my part. I first went to Europe to do *African Queen* and went to Ireland for the hunting. One thing led to another and I seemed to be working mostly in Europe so I took a house in Galway; eventually I bought it and after twelve years living there I became a citizen. I just fell into the lifestyle. There is a healthy moral climate there, and it's a great place to raise my children.

The Innocent Bystander

DAVID ROBINSON/1972

THEY WERE SHOOTING JOHN Huston's *The Mackintosh Man.*
The scene was a fight in the exercise yard of a prison, started up to cover a
jail break by Paul Newman. The yard was an oppressive vista in the huge set
that had been built at Pinewood, something of a masterpiece of the studio
plasterers' craft. The jail buildings were thirty feet high; the outer walls some
seventeen; and they looked as solid and mature as Pentonville. Everything
was a merciless grey. The prisoners' uniforms were grey also, and their shoes
had been carefully greyed with simulated mud. Even the leaden October sky
above and beyond the vista of the yard seemed blue and brilliant by comparison.

The bleakness was pervading. The assistant director, who seemed totally
in charge of the scene, was rehearsing maybe a hundred extras and stuntmen
through a loud-hailer: "Miserable now. Miserable . . . No smiling during the
fight. . . ." Ossie Morris, the lighting cameraman, anxious-looking at the best
of times, was balefully eyeing a break in the clouds where the sun threatened
to come through and spoil his lighting. John Foreman, the producer, sat by,
a man evidently oppressed.

Huston, however, was undoubtedly having fun. He looked like a stage
Irishman, though it was hard to say whether a flamboyant poacher or a dis-
reputable landowner. He was wearing a crumpled ginger suit and russet
shoes, a coarse grey overcoat with a cape and brown velvet collar, and a kind

From *Sight and Sound,* Winter 1972/73, 20–21. © 1972 by *Sight and Sound.* Reprinted by permission.

of tweedy deerstalker. He smoked a cigar. Sometimes in full face the deer-stalker made him look like a First World War *poilu*. Talking with the crew he changed again, and was more like a genial priest-confessor, too gentle even to pretend to these infants that their naughtiness was sin.

He roamed about contentedly, and every time the assistant said "Turn over" he gazed with the rapt curiosity of someone just come in off the street. Sometimes he would murmur "Cut" himself, but so quietly that no one heard him but the assistant. He explained that the assistant was handling the sequence by himself. "He told me his ideas for his scene, which involves a lot of people. I let him stage it entirely; then I come in. He worked all day yesterday and part of the day before. I play the role of innocent bystander. Until the last moment; then I make corrections. But the staging of this is largely due to him. I make not very significant suggestions."

Beside the camera stood a large board, with a very precise camera plan for the scene, and a detailed story-board of drawings for every set-up. Did this indicate that his role as innocent bystander was earned by very detailed advance planning and preparation? "Not at all. This was done by the people who staged the scene and then sent to me for approval. Just for this one scene. For my first picture I did that, made my own drawings from set-up to set-up. But that was because I didn't want to appear too uncertain on the set for my first picture. And about half the time, without directing them, why, the actors fell into those positions by themselves. And about a quarter of the time they had something better."

For the last couple of takes, and for the succeeding shot where smoke bombs were thrown in to heighten the confusion, Huston leapt on to the camera platform (he was using two Panavision cameras for the scene, one fixed and one mobile). Then he resumed his role as looker-on; and talked meanwhile about his old films. "I am particularly set on *Reflections in a Golden Eye,* and it's only now beginning to become appreciated. More and more people like yourself mention *Reflections in a Golden Eye* as one of my better films. And I quite agree. This is not a new experience. A number of pictures which I've made were not particularly popular at the time and later achieved considerable popularity. Designated as classics, whatever that means. *Red Badge of Courage.* It had no success whatever, critical or otherwise. Yes, it was received very well critically in England, but not in the United States. And I think *Reflections* will take its place eventually. *We Were Strangers* I haven't seen for a long time. I don't think I've seen it since I made it. I remember it. Of course I always think when I work on a picture that it's the best thing I ever did. *We Were Strangers* was based on a true incident. A lot of it was shot in Cuba. I liked Jennifer Jones in it, and John Garfield. It was a good cast; and there were good moments in it. Whether it was overall a good film I'm not sure; but I remember some excellent moments."

He recalled films he did not like with the same sort of objectivity. "There are some so bad that it would pain me a little bit to think about them. I wasn't responsible for a couple of them being as bad as they are. And for one I was entirely responsible. I regret that failure as much as any sin I've committed in my time. That was *The Roots of Heaven,* which could have been a very fine film. And largely owning to me was not a good film at all. The ones which were very bad films were in fact at one time good films, and nothing has been made of what happened to them as it was in the case of *Red Badge of Courage.* But they were ruined by their producers—in both cases I was away working on other films. One picture that is ghastly to look at today—and even when I first saw it I wanted to take my name off right away—was *The Barbarian and the Geisha* (an awful title, by the way); and another picture that was *very* good, and spoiled beyond recognition, was *Sinful Davy.* I recommend you staying away from all three of those.

"*The Bible* . . . It was an interesting one, very interesting. Unfortunately called *The Bible.* The title might have been a little more modest. Aside from the great *falsehood,* in so far as it was only half the Book of Genesis. . . ."

For his latest picture, *The Life and Times of Judge Roy Bean,* he was full of enthusiasm: "It was a joy to make. Altogether. I had a wonderful time. We had a marvelous time on the desert near Tucson. I lived in a trailer and the whole thing was done on this one location. It's a big picture. I don't mean just physically. It has a big spirit. The wind blows through it. Adown the corridors of time."

The great veteran Hollywood editor, Margaret Booth, was credited as supervising editor on the film before that, *Fat City,* although twenty years earlier she had appeared as one of the baddies in Lillian Ross's book *Picture,* about the making of *Red Badge of Courage.*" No, not at all. She was not a villain. I'll tell you a little bit about that. There was a complete rejection for *Red Badge of Courage* on the part of the audience. It was the worst preview I've ever attended: they left the theatre in droves. I've speculated on why that was. Maybe the country was in the same state of mind as it is now over the Vietnam war; it was the Korean war then. And I remember myself turning fast through the pages of *Life* magazine. And this film—though it was set back in Civil War times—was . . . the photographs were made with an idea of the reality of war, of combat. . . .

"So there was an attempt—I think it was a mistaken attempt—to save something. There was one scene, if you know the book, where the Tall Soldier, the Tattered Soldier, dies; and it was probably the best scene in the picture; and it was the scene that most people walked out of. So that was cut, and a few other things were cut. Maggie was acting on instructions, and the instructions were not all that severe. It was an attempt . . . it was one of the few times when cuts were made to a picture of mine that I could understand; and even by sympathetic about. I don't think anyone could have protested too much. It was under the pressure of public reaction. And it's very interesting, two or three months ago I had a request from MGM: did I by any chance have an original print, because they would like to put it out again as it was originally made. . . ." The script of *The Mackintosh Man* was still not finished, two weeks into shooting. It is by Walter Hill, and based on a novel by Desmond Bagley, *The Freedom Trap*. Everyone was reticent about the qualities of the original book. "Every now and then a good novel is at least as good, sometimes better, as a film. Now and then an awful thing occurs, as witness such a picture as that one I mentioned, that I did such a bad job on. That was a very interesting novel. But novels that are something less than first class have often been made into excellent films."

For a shot which was to show in detail the start of the fight, Huston stepped behind the camera himself. He lowered his great height to the viewfinder, removed his cigar to relish a lengthy smoker's cough, and gazed for a long time through the instrument, before giving Oswald Morris instructions for the meticulous placing of the extras in the frame. The crew were slightly foxed by his placing of two figures in the foreground, talking together but back to back. "Shall I put another figure here?" asked the assistant. "Won't it look funny if they're talking and facing away from each other?" "No," said Huston gently. "No. This man can look back over his shoulder."

"It's not often I look through the camera. I know what lens they're using, and I know what it's going to look like. . . . I direct actors about as little as possible. The better an actor, the less I have to direct. I want to get as much out of the actor himself as I can. Because wonderful accidents occur. I guide an actor rather than direct; expand a performance or reduce it. So far as the mechanical element goes—why, that's just being a traffic cop.

"I choose an actor as a rule for his . . . no, not as a rule, but *always* . . . for his *kinship* to the role. I cast personalities rather than actors. Then if they're superior actors, why that's so much velvet. But the trick is also in the casting, your assistant director, and all the people round you. I look for them to be very, very good. And try to reduce my own role to its minimum function. . . .

"But actors. I've had a long acquaintance with actors because my father was one. Each one is different of course, and their reactions are not so given and sure as with a good animal, for instance. People always say that more time has been spent working with animals and children. I think quite the opposite is true. With any understanding, you know pretty well what an animal is going to do and by the same token what a child is going to do. Actors are a step or two removed from that simplicity and innocence."

(Huston had just previously broken off his innocent bystanding to audition a beautiful, hopeless animal who had been brought to read for the part of a guard dog. Huston had sat on a pile of boards and watched with intense interest and patience and kindliness as the dog had muffed all his chances, grinning, sniffing and leaping about in foolish gaiety when he was supposed to be attacking with intent to kill.)

"Each man that you work with is different. Some actors like to talk about what they're going to do, and I've discovered over the years it's not really to get information, or your opinion, but just to talk their way into it. Others do almost no talking. On *Reflections in a Golden Eye,* I don't suppose I addressed myself to Brando more than half a dozen times during the making of the picture. Just stood back and watched this *phenomenon.*

"Now Paul Newman is full of innovation. He has wonderful immediate ideas. Very often supplements mine, or has something better than my notions. Some action, perhaps. The very best actors, the ones that fill me with admiration, are those that furnish *surprises.* You don't know—I doubt that they do either—where it comes from. They reach down into some remote cavern and come up with something that reveals a principle, something mysterious and new.

"I don't distinguish between actors and anyone else. Just because they're professional, it doesn't make them actors. Some of the best performances in *Fat City,* come from non-actors. The trainer in that film is a director. Art Aragon was only a fighter, never acted in his life. The black boy, an extraordinary talent, a seventeen-year-old high school kid with whom they were having trouble in school. My God—this is a young black Brando! And the black man that as he hoes talks of wine and roses never acted. We gave him his lines and let him read—and they were his own.

"There are fine black actors in the States now. Until this last experience, I had not been back there for a long time. And what surprised and delighted me most was the emergence of the black man. They are making greater progress than the whites of my acquaintance! I had seen a lot of them for the part of the girl's man friend; and they were all good. All very good, but a certain quality was not there. I was at the fights one night, at the Cow Palace in San Francisco. And man came in with the right face; and he was quickly in the center of a little group. They told me it was Curtis Cokes, the welter-weight champion. I went over and spoke to him, and said, were you ever interested at all to be an actor for five minutes? When I went away he said, "Who's that? What's that guy want?" Thought I was some kind of a drifter. Then he came back to San Francisco in a week or so for a fight; and I gave him a script. He lost the fight; and read the script that night to me. And he was just perfect. There's something in that face, a melancholy and a worldliness and a cadence in his voice. . . ."

The scene had moved on to a shot with Paul Newman, who was to move away from the crowd, under cover of the smoke bombs, to wait for his rescuers under the prison wall. (There had been an idea for a motorcycle assault on the seventeen-foot walls; but the stunt-riders were having second thoughts.) Huston watched, as happily curious about it all as ever; then went over and murmured a couple of words to Paul Newman. He watched the next take appreciatively. "Just now—this is when you're really in touch with an actor—I saw the way that was done, and I said, 'Paul, try to be the invisible man when you come over.' That's all. That's all you have to tell him. He is really extraordinary."

After a couple more takes he said, "O.K. That will do." But the cameraman wanted another. He shook on the track, and did it again. Huston watched with the same abstracted interest. Then just at the end called out, "Paul, Paul! Look this way." Newman was thrown, puzzled; then looked interrogation at the director. "That's it. That's just the way I wanted you to do it," said Huston, and shook with merry laughter.

Talking with John Huston

GENE D. PHILLIPS/1973

R ECENTLY, WHILE HE WAS making his latest film, *The
Mackintosh Man,* in London, John Huston took time out to discuss
his career with Gene D. Phillips, author of *Graham Greene: The Films
of His Fiction* and *The Movie Makers: Artists in an Industry.* Herewith
is the transcript of his remarks, rearranged by topic.

Sam Goldwyn brought me to Hollywood in the early thirties on the
strength of some short stories that I had published in *The American Mercury,*
but I was a dismal failure trying to write scripts for him. Then I went to
Universal, which was going downhill at the time. So I left Hollywood and
went to Europe where I worked for Gaumont-British briefly. Finally I returned to Hollywood and became part of the writers stable at Warner Brothers, where I collaborated on *Jezebel* for my good friend William Wyler and
went on to work on *Sergeant York, High Sierra, Juarez, Dr. Ehrlich's Magic Bullet,*
and other films.

In those days the Hollywood set-up was much different than it is now.
There was an executive producer who had a number of individual producers
working under him. A producer would be given a property to film and he
would select from among the contract writers, directors, and actors that the
studio employed those people who could handle the material that was to be
made into a film. Screenwriters at the time were much more concerned with

From *Film Comment,* vol. 9, no. 3, May/June 1973, 15–19. © 1973 by *Film Comment.* Reprinted
by permission.

the perfection of their work than they are now. They were on salary; when they finished an assignment they would either be moved on to another film or let go if their work wasn't satisfactory. Hence a writer fought for the leisure to be able to polish and improve his material before it went before the cameras. The writer handed in twenty pages or so of the script at a time, not the finished product. If he got behind schedule he would be urged on. Writers and directors often had no control over their material once they had finished it.

The writer never came on the set unless he was asked for in extraordinary circumstances. By the same token, when the director finished shooting a picture, the footage was turned over to the editor. This kind of set-up in the studio gave the creative writer and director something to fight against. Those who say that there is too much freedom today in the filmmaking business may have a point.

Once I had become established as a screenwriter at Warners I got a clause put into my contract that if I stayed on there they would give me the chance to direct. I saw no great dividing line between writing and directing, although few writers had become directors at the time—Preston Sturges and Gar Kanin were, I believe, my only predecessors. After Allen Rivkin and I finished the screenplay of *The Maltese Falcon* [1941], I asked to direct it. Dashiell Hammett's book had been filmed twice before, but the previous screen adapters didn't have the faith in the story that we did. Our script simply reduced the book to a screenplay, without any fancy additions of our own.

Before I started shooting I made drawings, set-up by set-up, of the action. I discovered that about half the time the actors automatically fell into the blocking that I had worked out in my drawings, and the rest of the time I would either bring them into line with my original conception of the blocking or let them work out something for themselves. I was extremely lucky to have such a fine group of actors to work with. I had known Humphrey Bogart, who played detective Sam Spade, for a long time. I had written *High Sierra* for him earlier. George Raft had been approached to play Spade, but he didn't want to work with a director who was a newcomer.

Warner Brothers was indulgent with me, and I was allowed to work with the editor to some extent after shooting was finished, and with the composer. Ever since I have made it a point to involve myself in the making of a film from the pre-production work right through to the end of the post-production work. Even when I have made a picture from a screenplay written by another writer, I have worked on it with him.

During the war I made three documentaries for the Army. I was attached to the Air Corps and made *Report from the Aleutians* in the Aleutian Islands in 1942. Then I went to Italy where I did *The Battle of San Pietro* [1944], a combat picture made to explain why we hadn't swept over Italy after we came up from Salerno and took Rome. When I put the film together it was described as anti-war by the brass at the Pentagon. The picture was shelved until General George C. Marshall saw it, because it was thought that the film would discourage men who were going to go into combat. He felt, however, that it should be used as a training film to show men what was in store for them in combat. There were some cuts, but I believe they were justified. For example, some of the soldiers with whom I had dialogued during the making of the film had been subsequently killed in action. I had used their voices over later shots of their dead bodies covered with blankets, and it was thought that this would have upset their families should they see the film.

The other documentary which I made has never been released by the Pentagon for screening. It was called *Let There Be Light* [1945] and was about combat neuroses, about men who had been torn up emotionally by their experiences in battle. For some reason to see a psyche torn asunder is more frightening than to see people who have physical wounds. Some of the brass said that there was a question of invasion of the privacy of the men shown as patients in the film. The men themselves, however, after they recovered, said that they as a group were all in favor of the film being shown. What I had done in making the film was to follow a group of seventy-five patients from their admission into the hospital until their release. To me it was an extraordinary experience—almost a religious experience—to see men who couldn't speak, or remember anything at the beginning of their treatment, emerge at the end, not completely cured, it is true, but restored to the shape that they were in when they entered the Army.

While making *Let There Be Light* I had the benefit of a quick course in psychiatry by constantly asking Army psychiatrists questions about various aspects of what they were doing. The figure of Freud began to emerge, and that was the beginning of my later film about Freud. My original orders in making *Let There Be Light* was to reassure industrialists that they should hire veterans, even those who had been hospitalized, since they were as capable as the next man. Since the Pentagon didn't feel that the film accomplished this goal, however, the film was shelved, and has never been shown theatrically to this day.

When I returned to the United States after the war, I directed Sartre's *No Exit* on the New York stage, but the critics didn't know what it was all about. They thought it was a French love triangle instead of a rather strongly philosophic work. So I went back to Hollywood, where I co-scripted with Richard Brooks and directed *Key Largo*, and won Oscars for writing and directing *The Treasure of the Sierra Madre*, which grew out of my time in Mexico years before as a horseman in the Mexican cavalry. My father, Walter Huston, won an Oscar as the gritty old prospector in the film.

There is an objectivity on the set that does away with any of the regular relationships that one might have with these same people off the set. The director is always the father figure on the set, so I suppose that, while the film was being made, I was my father's father figure. For my part, when I appear as an actor under another director, as I have, for example, for Preminger in *The Cardinal*, I am the most obedient of actors. My intention is to set a good example for the other actors in the film, looking toward the time when I might have to direct them. I have no standard approach to actors. I try to guide each actor through his part without letting him know that, as director, I am really acting all of the parts myself.

Furthermore, I look upon the camera as still another actor on the set. The relationship between the actors is important but the relationship between the actors and the camera is also important. The camera can be as eloquent as the finest actor if you know how to use it. You have to be the right distance from an actor when he says a line, for example. Very rarely has my best camera work been remarked on by either an audience or the critics because good camera work should be unobtrusive. One set-up should naturally lead to the next without anyone noticing—it's like a ballet. A good scene tells you how it should be shot. I begin by letting the actors sort themselves out; and often, as I found in directing my very first film, they do the scene fairly well without any suggestions from me at all, falling into some of the set-ups quite naturally. A bad scene is the most difficult to shoot, since there is no way that you can shoot it to make it look any better than it is.

One of my favorite films, at least as I shot it, is *The Red Badge of Courage*. Lillian Ross in her book about the making of the film, *Picture*, is extremely accurate about what went on during production. She was a fine journalist, and I say this even though I myself come in for some body blows in the course of the book. So, you see, I am speaking with a certain detachment. I think that she was a little harder on the studio than perhaps was fair. There was a power struggle going on at MGM at the time: one group wanted to make the film an the other group didn't. Whoever won that battle would be in charge of the studio. Louis B. Mayer's power was waning. I told him that if he was against my making the picture that I wouldn't pursue it. He replied, "You believe in the project, don't you? You continue to defend it, even though I am against it. I would be deeply disappointed in you if you didn't fight for it."

I fought for it and the picture was made, and then I had to witness a disaster at the preview. The best scene in the film was the one in which the Tall Soldier dies a kind of mystical death. "Don't touch me," he says, and then he falls dead. His death is witnessed by the hero (Audie Murphy) and by the Tattered Soldier, who begins to wonder around in circles; then he too falls dead. This is particularly shocking because the viewer was not aware that the Tattered Soldier was even wounded until he drops dead. One third of the audience walked out at this point. The scene was too emotionally taxing, and so it was cut, as were some others, bringing the film down to one hour and forty minutes. I hear that the film has since been cut to sixty-nine minutes. Of course I couldn't bring myself to look at the present version, but I have been given to understand that MGM is thinking of re-releasing the original version.

My next film, *The African Queen,* in contrast with *The Red Badge of Courage,* was a joy to make. We shot it in Africa with two delightful people, Katharine Hepburn as the spinster-missionary, and Humphrey Bogart as the river-boat bum. Kate Hepburn was enchanted with the whole thing; Bogey would rather have been back in his house in Beverly Hills. I suggested to Kate that she play her role as a lady something like Eleanor Roosevelt. She did and it was fine.

I went abroad to make *The African Queen* and continued traveling to make other films, so finally I bought a house in Ireland and settled there. But I have never thought of myself as an expatriate. I became an Irish citizen because I believe in being a citizen of the country where I live. If I move back to the United States I will become a citizen there again.

Another of my favorite films is *Moby Dick,* although neither the public nor the critics have agreed with me. For me the point of *Moby Dick* as Melville wrote it is that Ahab hated God, and in essence felt that he was bringing the Judge himself before the bar of judgment and condemning Him. This theme of blasphemy was missed by most people who saw the picture, and who think of Ahab simply as a madman. Hence Gregory Peck's performance as Ahab didn't coincide with their preconceived notions of the story.

I have often been asked if I have had final cut on my films since becoming an established director. My answer is always the same: no director ever has final cut because ultimately the picture always belongs to someone else who may tamper with it after you think the film is finished and have delivered it for distribution. After I finished *The Barbarian and the Geisha,* I went on to Africa to make *The Roots of Heaven.* After I left, the studio altered the film considerably, and when I saw it a year later I wanted to take my name off it. Even the plot was unrecognizable.

Freud was another of my films that was cut after it was finished. As I mentioned earlier, the importance of Freud to the psychiatric scene loomed larger and larger while I was making *Let There Be Light.* I began reading Freud in the intervening years, and it took some time before the idea for a film about his life developed in my mind. I got Jean-Paul Sartre to do the screenplay, but he wrote a four hundred fifty-page script. Then he revised the first version into another script more than twice the length of the first! We cut this down to the bone, but the final shooting script nevertheless contained the strongest of his ideas and is still very much his script.

The picture was difficult to make. Montgomery Clift was quite ill during shooting; halfway through he could hardly see because he had developed cataracts on his eyes as a result of damage sustained in an automobile accident, and this made the film a real ordeal for him. When the picture was completed it ran two hours and forty minutes, for this was the length needed to explain Freud's discovery of infantile sexuality to a movie audience. But the audience had no opportunity to relax during the whole running time of the film. It was too much to ask filmgoers to give such close attention to a film for that length of time. All of the subsequent cuts made in the picture— about twenty-five minutes of screen time—were at the film's expense, however, since vital steps in the continuity and progression of the story were eliminated.

In dealing with psychosexual matters so frankly, *Freud* was ahead of its time, as was *Reflections in a Golden Eye,* one of the first American films to broach the subject of homosexuality. I seem to have a knack for making films that are either a few years ahead of or behind the times—and one is as bad as the other. Such films of mine are better liked today than when they were released.

I had no directorial problems with Elizabeth Taylor and Marlon Brando during shooting. I don't cast an actor for his technique but for his personality, and because of my vision of what he will do with his personality in a given part. My faith in the actors in *Reflections in a Golden Eye,* I think, was justified. Taylor and Brando, Brian Keith and Julie Harris all had different acting styles, but people are different too. They turned in an extraordinary group of performances that amounted to ensemble playing. I had originally intended Montgomery Clift to play Brando's role of Captain Penderton, but he died before the film was made. In that role Marlon Brando gave me one of the best performances that I have ever had from an actor.

The color process in which the film was originally shot was the result of considerable experimentation, and was perfectly suited to this study of a group of neurotic people. This color process basically had a golden amber quality to it; other colors, toned, impinged on the screen, as it were, from behind this golden hue. This served to separate the audience somewhat from the characters, who were in various ways withdrawn from reality, and to make their story a bit more remote and erotic. One of the executives at Warner Brothers objected to this concept of color for the film. (I think he had seen a beer ad at age eleven and that was the extent of his aesthetic growth.) I got the concession that the film would be released initially in this special color process in key cities, but the response wasn't good. Prints in Technicolor had also been processed at the same time the original prints were made, and it is the Technicolor prints that have been in circulation ever since.

Among my more recent films, the success of *Fat City* was a pleasant surprise. I didn't expect a commercial success; I believed very much in the film but would have been happy if it was well received by a selective audience. I had a great interest in the characters in the film, since I was a boxer briefly when I was seventeen. Personally I admire the down-and-outers depicted in the film, people who have the heroism to go on taking it on the chin in life as well as in the ring.

Stacy Keach, who played the worn-down pug in *Fat City,* is also in *The Life and Times of Judge Roy Bean,* are Ava Gardner, Anthony Perkins, and myself.

Paul Newman plays the title role, which was played back in 1940 by Walter Brennan in William Wyler's film *The Westerner*. *Judge Roy Bean* couldn't be more different from *Fat City*. Whereas *Fat City* took place in one concentrated area, a big city slum, *Judge Roy Bean* is all over the map. It is romantic, sad, and funny—a high, wide, and, I hope, handsome film. We departed from the historical facts and made Bean more of a scalawag than he really was; but the film is, after all, more of a romance than a historical document.

Paul Newman is also the star of my latest film, *The Mackintosh Man*, which, like *The Kremlin Letter*, is a spy thriller with some amusing moments. Critics have never been able to discover a unifying theme in my films. For that matter, neither have I. Of course, as a director I do interpret reality. Just pointing a camera at a certain reality means an interpretation of that reality. But I don't seek to interpret reality by placing my stamp on it. I try to be as faithful as I can to the material I have chosen to film. Everything technical and artistic in the picture is designed to depict that material for an audience. That, in the end, is what really matters.

John Huston

LOUISE SWEENEY/1973

W E A R E S I T T I N G I N a brick mews house in the middle of London, and director John Huston is giving a thirty-second course in filmmaking.

"To me the perfect film is as though it were unwinding behind your eyes, and your eyes were projecting it themselves, so that you were seeing what you wished to see. It's like thought. It's the closest to thought process of any art."

Mr. Huston illustrates the point in his own unique way. "Look at that lamp," he says, pointing to a brass floor lamp halfway across the dark green room. "Now look at me. Look back at the lamp. Now look at me. Do you see what you did? [the second time]. You blinked. Those are cuts. After the first time you know that there's no reason to pan from me to the lamp, because you know what's in between. Your mind cuts [the scene]. You behold the lamp. And you behold me. So in cutting the scene you cut with the physiology."

We have been sitting in the gathering dusk, talking about why film has so much more impact than any other medium. The reason, he thinks, is physical. "In the theater," Mr. Huston says, "there's a different time factor because with your concentration on the screen things move much slower . . . the closer one's attention is held to something, the slower time goes. If you're sitting in the theater, you're aware of the stage, and the stage is lighted, and that reflected light comes out at you. You're not in a tunnel (as in a movie theater) where this oblong of light has your complete attention."

He is leaning forward in the oatmeal tweed chair as he talks, his long and lanky frame a study in right angles: sinewy arms elbowing out of a short-sleeved black knit shirt, tall legs in tan whipcord pants folded praying-mantis style high above the floor. There is the familiar roof of white hair, the outline of a narrow white beard around his jaw, the long, almost medieval-looking face with its surprisingly twentieth-century eyes. Very brown they are, and supercharged, under scraggly black eyebrows. When he moves, an image comes to mind. The overall impression of this man who loves riding as much as films is of the tallest horse in the stable, a gray champion still full of spirit who likes to sniff the wind and go galloping off if that wind is right.

Mr. Huston, who gave up his U. S. citizenship when he moved to Ireland twenty years ago, says, "I went over to Ireland originally because I am a horseman and it's the greatest country for that kind of riding . . . fox hunting over there is just wonderful. All the excitement of a battle and twenty-five percent of the risk." Although Mr. Huston has just sold his Irish Georgian mansion in Galway ("I was having to stay away and work just to support the house and its staff of fifteen"), he maintains a smaller home in Connemara.

And a place in Los Angeles, where the fox hunting is not as good. But he has this new wife (his fifth), an American named Celeste Shane, whom he married in August, 1972. When pressed with a question about her, he becomes absolutely skittish, gets up and canters around the room, saying only, "She's a horsewoman. Young. Thirty-five, I think that's how old she is. I also think she has read a book, I'm not absolutely certain about it, *Black Beauty* or something." That is followed by a burst of the great, deep laughter that is very characteristic of John Huston in conversation—he is an entertaining man, full of stories and anecdotes and one-liners and the laughter that springs from them.

Mr. Huston, who has made twenty-seven films, has just finished editing *The Mackintosh Man* in London, which is why we are sitting in this house he's borrowed from a friend. *The Mackintosh Man,* a thriller shot in London, Malta, and Ireland, has now opened in New York. The director puts it rather objectively on a list of his films that are superior technically to their story: "There are pyrotechnics and facility rather than ideas or content." The film stars Paul Newman and the enigmatic Dominique Sanda. "She does carry a very interesting mystery around with her, doesn't she?" says Mr. Huston. He speaks with great warmth of Paul Newman—"he's a joy to work with"—and explains that *Mackintosh* came about just because he and Newman and the crew had "such a wonderful time" making their last film, the exuberant western *The Life and Times of Judge Roy Bean*.

His latest picture is the twenty-eighth in a distinguished career which includes some great moviemaking, like *The Maltese Falcon, The Asphalt Jungle, The African Queen, The Red Badge of Courage, The Night of the Iguana,* and the picture many consider his masterpiece, *The Treasure of the Sierra Madre*.

His directing career, which spans thirty years, has had some checkered moments. But even his less successful films, like *The List of Adrian Messenger,* are full of the zest of the man himself, this writer-prizefighter-cavalry lieutenant-actor-painter-director. Norman Mailer has said, in writing about Huston's *The Misfits* in his biography *Marilyn* that "Huston is of course the only celebrated film artist to bear comparison to Hemingway. His life celebrates a style more important to him than film. His movies do not embody his life so much as they emerge out of a pocket of his mind." If that is so, his mind is deeply rooted in America in spite of his Irish life. John Huston's most extraordinary films, no matter where they were shot, are about central characters as American in spirit as hot dogs and Conestoga wagons. His very recent success, *Fat City,* about California boxers, is a case in point. And then of course there was the quartet of films he did (*African Queen, Maltese Falcon, Key Largo, Beat the Devil*) with Humphrey Bogart, that growling essence of Americana. "His sort of person fitted into my kind of picture," the director says.

Huston's voice is like what I'd imagine the pads of the lion's paw to be: deceptively soft, with lots of power behind it. "He has a theatrical way of inflecting his voice that can give a commonplace query a rich and melodramatic intensity," says Lillian Ross in her book *Picture*. Her fascinating step-by-step study of Huston's making of his Civil War classic *The Red Badge of Courage* is full of some probing insight into the director (then forty-three) and filmmaking. He calls the Ross book "beautiful journalism."

I remember his beaming a welcome at Lillian Ross a few years ago when he was shooting a scene for *The Kremlin Letter*. She was one of several people who dropped by on the sort of family set that John Huston runs, to watch a taxi-kidnap scene at the UN. Many of the crew were Huston regulars, familiar to each other from other pictures, and they worked like old friends. Between the quick, apparently effortless, takes, the director would shoot the breeze with Ms. Ross or other visitors: his darkly beautiful daughter Anjelica, who starred in his *A Walk with Love and Death,* or Mrs. Walter Huston, widow of the actor-father whose memory means so much to the director. For this interview I asked him:

"If you could put just one scene from any of your films in a time capsule and label it John Huston, director, what would it be?" "Well," he said, "it would have to be my old man dancing in *Treasure of the Sierre Madre.*" And there was a long, almost painful pause after that. This famous son of a famous father adopted an Indian-Mexican orphan named Pablo while he was shooting *Treasure* in Mexico. He has another son, Walter, as well as his daughter, Anjelica, by his previous marriage to Enrica Soma.

John Huston has been accused of having a weakness for losers, but there is none of the acrid smoke of defeat in his work. We talk about this paradox and about a scene that sums it up, in his boxing film *Fat City.* It is a final scene in which Stacy Keach, as a washed-up fighter, is sitting with young contender Jeff Bridges late at night in one of those diners that never closes. You see Keach realizing that tough as life is for him, it's tougher for the 100-year-old Chinese counterman serving them. There is a sense of compassion and a kind of all-night hope there. Says director Huston, "Their defeat is everlasting . . . and then they recover from this, they share this emotion for the moment and then they recover. And there's that valor to ignore it and proceed. It's the fighting heart. . . . I was left with love and admiration for these men."

We talk about the fact that in films today there are a lot of downers, a lot of pictures that give audiences a feeling of absolute wretchedness and hopelessness for the moments they are identifying with the film. I say that I've never found that in John Huston's films. He says, "Well, I've never found that in life. I've never felt utterly desolate for very long [a rumble of laughter] which is of course suicidal. I suppose that those who do feel it, that utter desolation, [think they] have only one recourse, whether they commit the act or not. But they can commit the act unconsciously, too, just the same. I think more people kill themselves than ever we know."

Part of John Huston's affirmation of life is the energy that pulses through his best work and the true grit he has shown in making films on some of the toughest locations going. Mel Gussow writes of a Huston picture, *Roots of Heaven,* in his Darryl F. Zanuck biography *Don't Say Yes Until I Finish Talking.*

He says, "Never has a movie been filmed under such adverse circumstances." Speaking of *Roots of Heaven,* Gussow vividly describes the searing heat of French Equatorial Africa, the resulting nightmares of physical and mental illness and lethal drinking bouts. Mr. Huston says of *Roots:* "That was tough. That was a rough one, all right. I like working on location. The location, just like an actor, gives something to the picture and helps to color it, you know, envelop it in an atmosphere." But he concedes, "We may have gone a bit overboard in *The Roots of Heaven.* The hard-living crew fell by the wayside. The temperatures never dropped. At midnight it was 100 and before that 120, even 130, day after day.

"I guess the next hardest location was *Moby Dick,* but that was at sea. We just happened to hit a summer and winter that were the roughest and stormiest in, I think, seventy years of English maritime history. And the good ship *Pequod* was bound for the bottom certainly on three separate occasions. We were dismasted, three times. Tugs had to rescue us. It was a wonderful thing there were no calamities, . . . we could have lost men."

To create the moody, sea-misted look of *Moby Dick* he used two sets of negatives, one color, one black and white, then superimposed and printed them together.

Huston is a painter himself who has a rich and subtle eye for color on the screen. But he sometimes surprisingly shoots in black and white, as he did in *Freud* and *The Misfits.* He says, "I think that color can get between you and the thought of a picture. Your eye can be so entertained that your mind stops. When the material is psychological [as it was in *Freud*], you rather want to know what's happening behind the eyes than the color of the eyes, so black and white can be more serviceable than color.

"Now if you do use color, I think it's got to be done with thought. Color must combine and become part of the idea." He mentions the fights he had with the studio over using a special muted amber color for his film of Carson McCullers's *Reflections in a Golden Eye.*

John Huston has made his extraordinary reputation as an Oscar-winning director. But much of his directing career has been braided with his other life as a screenwriter. "I think directing is an extension of writing. I can't say where the writing stops and the directing begins. Directing is a synthetic. You get a number of factors together and hope to combine them into a wedding, into a harmonious whole. . . ."

In the last decade Huston has begun a third film career as actor, too. Has his acting ever interfered with or colored his directing in any way? "Unless an actor needs help, why I try to interfere with him as little as possible, to get as much out of him and get him to develop his own personality, to reveal it to its fullest saturation, otherwise they'd be weaker shadows of myself." He is obviously not one of the despot-directors, this man who says, "I direct actually as little as possible. I like to get my people to do it for me. . . . Some of my best ideas have come from grips and electricians."

John Huston Talking to Rosemary Lord

ROSEMARY LORD/1974

THE BITPART PLAYER WHO wins Oscars: well that's one way of describing director-actor John Huston. Huston had just finished appearing in Roman Polanski's new film *Chinatown* in Hollywood when I arranged to talk to him.

We met in the corridor of the Paramount Productions Los Angeles office in Beverly Hills on a hot, Monday afternoon. I was lost, and so was John Huston—he stopped me and asked the way to the boardroom; I was looking for the same thing, so we went in together. As we made ourselves comfortable at the large boardroom table a Paramount secretary appeared with a tray of coffee and sticky pastries and also offered the services of an interpreter—which I assured her I didn't need!

In his seventies, John Huston has the enthusiasm of a man just starting his career—and in his soft American drawl he began to talk.

ON ACTING: I don't take myself seriously as an actor at all. It's always a lark as far as I'm concerned. It's when it's done by an interesting director, or in a place that interests me—or it's amusing to me and then they pay me large sums of money to do it. It's all just a prank—an antic. It wouldn't worry me if I never acted again.

ON *FAT CITY*: It was part of an atmosphere I knew as a young man—right here in Los Angeles: the so-called Sporting Scene. It has its sad aspect,

From *Transatlantic Review*, Autumn/Winter 1974, 140–45.

surely, but there's something that always moves me. Not only moves me—but also I have a great admiration for those people that throw themselves into the part rather than gambling with other people's money. A number of the fighters that were in the film were old friends of mine from the time I lived there. Well . . . when I was boxing I went to high school—Lincoln Heights it was called, and there were three future world champions at my school and I went there because of the boxing. The school was in a rather poor area of town, and my family were much better off than most of the other kids in the school; it took me nearly an hour to get there on the street-car. And we were then boxing amateur—then some became professionals. And as I say, three world champions came from that little group. And we'd box in little towns all up and down—and they'd pay us sometimes in watches or goods—we were amateurs then. And later we'd get perhaps fifty dollars. I remember there was one place here called Madison Square Gardens and it was on Central Avenue which was a black community. They used to make up posters for the fights—make up weights. The fighters would go round the night of the fight and pick out names—they'd say—"That's gonna be your name." If you had red hair, you'd be Red O'Reilly, something like that. I remember fighting there one night under two different names!

In the earlier days—particularly when my father got the Acadamy Award—there were many sentimental associations for me, and most of all with *The Treasure of the Sierra Madre*. Not only a memorable film, but Bogart being a friend of mine, it was also a very happy one. Well today there is a nostalgia about the old days and when it came to doing this picture *Fat City* it evoked all those memories and I felt very tender towards them. It's surprising how the world continues—maybe it's to bad, because for the most part it's a hard life, a tragic life almost and except for the very rare one—they're doomed I'm afraid. I still see many of my old friends from those boxing days. Often my friends from that time will ring up and say "D'you like to go to the fight tonight, John?"—and I go and I thoroughly enjoy myself.

ON THE CHANGE IN FILMS: The preamble to filmmaking—what goes on beforehand is certainly more difficult. Oh, today they have to get a package together. But when it comes to making the movie itself it's pretty much the same. I'm talking about the difference between now and the time we were working for a major company. Majors were always very sympathetic. If they respected a writer or director they did everything they could to aid and

abet . . . to further his creativity. There were many things to be said for working for a major studio—for one thing you had somebody to fight against!
The soul may appear to have gone out of movies in a way—but then again
they suddenly come up with something really quite remarkable.

ON THE LAND: I like Europe very much. I have a great fondness for it.
Well, my home is in Ireland—I've been living there for twenty years—in
County Galway, but I don't manage to spend much time there. It's in the
country, and I like country life much better than I like city life. You can get
away from everything there—and the people think I'm an eccentric because
I go away and I make pictures. My wife has a house here in Los Angeles and
I stay there whenever I'm here. But in Ireland—sometimes I'm there for six
months at a stretch—that's usually when I'm writing a script, but then the
year before last I was only there two weeks. I find it easier to write in any
place where you are away. If I can't be in Ireland then I go down to Mexico—
anywhere where I'm away from telephones. I'm a very weak character and I
yield to any temptations that might present themselves. But in Ireland there
aren't really any temptations. The only thing I do there is get on a horse, or
drink.

ON WALTER HUSTON: I admired my father very much—he had a great
effect on my attitude to life. Father didn't encourage me with words—but by
example. He was a great influence on me but I don't think he ever gave me
any advice—it was always through what he did, and I would imitate him.

ON CINEMA NOW & THEN: I can't talk of a distinction between the
Hollywood of yesterday and today—it's only what is a good film, a good
picture. I've seen amongst these pictures some which impressed me very
much—like *McCabe & Mrs. Miller, Midnight Cowboy,* and *Bonnie & Clyde*—
these are extraordinary films. And some of these wouldn't have been made—
couldn't have been made—so in that particular sense, why, I think there is a
kind of freedom that exists today that didn't exist before. We'd have ways of
getting round things and that wouldn't have been as pure, wouldn't have
been as direct. I still admire the form that pictures have: a beginning, a middle, and an end—because it seems to me that that form is significant. I'm
classic-minded in this regard. A picture is supposed to reduce life, reduce a
book or a play, down into significant philosophic terms, if you like, so that
it's a demonstration or one aspect of life; it should be an organization.

Today, though, everyone talks about realism in the cinema. It's not a bad thing—as long as realism isn't forced down my throat. I don't care to be forced to witness automobile accidents and I don't think that's realism necessarily. When violence is called for, when violence is implicit in the material, by all means—or when sexuality is called for. And I have no quarrel with pornography at all if it is well done. I say this without ever having had the advantages of seeing a pornographic film. But I know I would enjoy it if it were well done. I don't go to the cinema much. To see a bad film depresses me enormously. It discourages me from ever making another film myself. Oh God, it's awful.

ON RETIREMENT: I think of myself as a painter thinks of himself. You don't stop painting until you can't see the colors any more. Although in movies they can stop you—they can stop giving you money to make the pictures. There are some pretty good directors around, as a matter of fact, that can't get work anymore. Well that's unfortunate—so they better have something else they can do—like painting.

ON WRITING: I wrote the picture that I'm going to do next: *The Man Who Would Be King.*—we're going to make it in Turkey I think. D'you know the story—it's an old Kipling tale. In Victorian times, two adventurers out of the army have an idea that there is a part of the world that no one has ever been in—and it's only in the past five years that anyone has visited there. It's in the northwestern corner of Afghanistan, and is composed of warring tribes. So these two soldiers go up and they think they'll lead one tribe against another and then they'll subvert the king and become king themselves. And that's briefly the story—Sean Connery and Michael Caine are to star, and I think it has very interesting overtones.

But of course I started out as a writer. I was brought out to Hollywood by Sam Goldwyn, who didn't use me at all. And then I worked with Universal—but they were suspicious of my kind of writing. There was a kind of cannabalism that went on at the studios then—they made pictures that were like other pictures and they mistrusted anything they called "arty"—anything that was original, and they were to have conventional endings and so on. So I didn't go down very well and my services weren't sought after at all. So then I left and came to Europe for two years, then came back. I'd always been infatuated with movies, so I wrote a story—an original—Warners bought it—but it never got made. So then I was asked to help my old friend Willy Wyler out of script trouble on *Jezebel*—I did—then they asked me if there was something I'd like to do myself. And then a whole new thing opened up—and it was at Warners I first directed.

ON DIRECTING: Sometimes I watch my own movies—and I feel quite detached from them, they have their own independent life. They seem to have nothing to do with me. I just watch them with interest—like I would any other film. Although sometimes I watch a film and just wish I hadn't made it!

The greatest piece of advice I ever had—when I made my first film—a wonderful producer named Henry Blanke, who was responsible for *Zola, Pasteur* and many more—he was my champion, if you like, and saw to it that I directed. When I went to make my first film *The Maltese Falcon*, Henry said, "Just remember one thing John: all I ever need to tell you . . . each scene, as you make it, is the most important scene in the film. Whether it's somebody getting out of an automobile or whatever—it's the most important scene at that moment." And that's the best advice I could give to a new director.

I was one of the first writers to become a director. So this was highly experimental as far as the industry was concerned. Everyone was leaning over backwards to help me—they were very kind. The crew and the cameraman were very good to me, but I knew pretty well what I was doing—I'd gone to great pains: sketched out each set-up. I'd draw not just each scene, but each cut, as well. And about half the time the actors did things without me having to tell them and the camera fell into position without me saying anything. About a quarter of the time I had to bring them into it and about a quarter of the time something better happened than I had anticipated.

ON ACTORS: I could tell you things about most of them: I remember Orson Welles, for instance, when he was playing Father Mapple in *Moby Dick* and it was a long, long speech that went on for five minutes. Orson got up into the pulpit and started turning pages—he said, "John I'm so nervous: I don't think I've ever been so nervous in my life. Could I have a drink . . . could I have a brandy?" So we put a bottle of brandy in the pulpit and Orson had a drink. "Would you like to rehearse?" I asked. He said, "WELL, give me a minute." It was going to take three days to shoot this scene—and this had gone on for an hour or more—Orson looking at the script, having a drink—a whole congregation waiting. So finally I said, "Well let's have a rehearsal: once over lightly." Orson said, "Look go ahead and shoot this. Shoot the rehearsal," and POW . . . SNAP . . . SNAP . . . SNAP . . . right through. He did five pages right through, and then I moved the cameras in closer and he did it again right through: five pages. Marvelous—a superb performance. The finest thing in the film as far as I'm concerned. And we finished in three hours.

And there was Bogey: I took Bogey to many places in the world and some of them were hardships. Well Bogey didn't like that at all. Bogey gave the air of being an adventurer, but really he loved being at home. But he was wonderful to be with—he never complained—except when he was making fun of himself. He would never know his lines when he came to the set—and in rehearsals he would learn them—and they would have a spontaneity that was remarkable.

A great film favorite of mine—I only worked with him in one complete picture—is Bob Mitchum, who is a great actor. He's never even scratched the surface. He should have played Shakespeare. Wonderful actor—and he's always so retiring; so modest in his self-estimation. Only sometimes do you get a glimpse of the center—this is an extraordinary man. Everyway.

I'd put Katey Hepburn at the top of my list of actresses—and Marilyn Monroe of course. What they say about her now . . . well I guess almost all that they say is true—but it disturbs me a little, seeing all the birds lighting on the body and just exploiting it. It's tragic exploiting a tragic memory. Good hearted girl—a great heart she had. I think the Bogarts and the Monroes were new in their own generation—they weren't like anybody else, and people are never replaced. People that we don't know about will live in the lives and hearts of people to come. They won't be the same. And there they are: The Bogeys and Monroes—thanks to this medium they'll be there for a long time. It's a shame when anybody we love dies—and where do you look next? Well you can't find them, can you? You can never hope to find them on the screen or off the screen.

The secretary appeared to tell John Huston his car was waiting to take him to the next appointment so reluctantly we finished our conversation.

We walked out to the front of the Paramount building, and the Happy Bit-part Player climbed into his chauffeur-driven limousine and rode off into the hot, smoggy, sunshine of North Canon Drive, Beverly Hills, California, U.S.A.

John Huston Finds That the Slow Generation of *King* Has Made It a Richer Film

JOSEPH McBRIDE / 1975

THE MAN WHO WOULD Be King, John Huston's finally realized dream project of twenty years, is, he observes with understandable pride, "the sort of considered, organized, thought-out picture that is a rarity today." Though his concept of the story didn't change much over the years, he feels the final result is "richer" for the long germination. "It's become banal to say that a good novel works on several levels," he says, "but I think this picture has several levels—the legendary one, the element of history in it, the adventure story, and also the psychological aspect, the thing that Bolitho wrote about in *Twelve Against the Gods*—we've all believed that we were gods, at one time or another."

Though the over-$7,000,000 Allied Artists–Columbia Pictures cooperation is lavishly mounted ("it's all on the screen," the director notes), he says he had "no intention ever for it to be a spectacle—in fact I would often turn the spectacle inside out."

Huston says he wanted to stress the ideas in the Rudyard Kipling tale of two soldiers of fortune setting themselves up as rulers in Afghanistan during the last century. "To me, dialogue can be action; what goes on behind the eyes can be action. It doesn't require flashing sabers."

Originally planned in 1956 to star Clark Gable and Humphrey Bogart in the roles eventually filled by Sean Connery and Michael Caine, the film was formerly on the production slates of Universal-International (in 1959) and Seven Arts (in 1964), though Huston says it never went beyond the talking stages at either studio. He credits producer John Foreman with finally making the film a reality; an Emanuel L. Wolf presentation, it is being released domestically by AA (premiering tomorrow in New York City) and overseas by Columbia.

Bogart and Gable would not have been acceptable in the roles today because contemporary audiences expect British actors in British roles, Huston notes. But when Bogart died in 1956, Huston shelved the project "because I didn't like the thought of going on without him."

Then, during the making of *The Misfits,* Gable persuaded him to reactivate it—"and I'll be damned if he didn't die." Pleased with the final casting, Huston says, "Everybody wanted to do it. The first two to respond were Sean Connery and Michael Caine, and I said fine."

The final screenplay adaptation was done in less than three months by Huston and his frequent collaborator Gladys Hill. The director says some elements remain from previous drafts by Anthony Veiller and Aeneas MacKenzie: "there are shreds of everybody in there." Always intended to be shot entirely on location, the film was made in Morocco; earlier locations considered included India and Afghanistan.

One important difference between the final film and earlier conceptions was the minimal emphasis on the only female character of significance, played by Shakira Caine (Michael Caine's wife). "In one script, they were both in love with the girl and the quarrels were over her," Huston recalls. "I felt that was wrong. But in those days you had to have a romance in it."

In fleshing out the 12,000-word short story, Huston also relied on ideas and phrasing from other works by Kipling, of whom he is an afficionado. "Stored in my subconscious," he says, "I have reams of Kipling's verse."

What attracted him to the story, essentially, was its combination of "the absurd and the great at the same time." He tried to look at the imperialist theme in the context of its time, even though "there was an element of the intellectuals of Kipling's time, and I surely would have been amongst them, who were highly cynical and took a very dim view of colonization."

Huston's fondest memory of the filming was a comment made by Karroum Ben Bouih, a nonprofessional actor who played the native chieftain in the film. Over a hundred years old, he had never seen a film until Huston showed him the rushes; after a conversation with the other elderly tribesmen who appear in the film, Ben Bouih told Huston, "We will never die."

In terms of technique, Huston rejects the flashy approach, which he notes is usually the one most appreciated by critics: "I'm quite elaborate with the camera, but that goes unobserved, as it should. That way you get three shots for the price of one, and the audience's mind is free to follow what it wants to follow.

"*Time* magazine, at the end of its film reviews, used to write, 'Best shot,' and they would always have a shot a good director would never dream of using—such as somebody reflected in a doorknob."

Huston's next film is an adaptation of Ernest Hemingway's novel *Across the River and Into the Trees* for producer Roberto Haggiag. He expects to start it next winter on locations in Venice.

As for casting the lead, a fifty-year-old military officer, Huston says, "I try to delay [casting] until the last moment. When I'm all through writing, I think, 'who do I know who was like that person?' and then try to find an actor who resembles him."

For the officer in *Across the River*, Huston has been reminiscing about "a colonel in the 36th Infantry division who was quite like Gable, with big ears."

Though his opinion of the novel is that Hemingway "was trying something that didn't come off—it's an experiment, kind of an indulgence," he feels the film will be "oddly faithful to it, but introducing another element that is implicit in the book—his memories." The film will contain a continuous stream of memory shots ("every scene is interrupted"), though they won't be flashbacks in the conventional dramatic sense.

Some of Hemingway's work has become dated today, Huston feels, but he adds that "the important thing about Hemingway was his redefinition of values," something Huston thinks is crucial today. The film will deal with "what it means to be a soldier," but it will also express "a side of Hemingway that most people don't know—the compassionate and sensitive side."

The search for values was also Huston's motive for making *Independence,* a twenty-eight-minute short about the U.S. colonial period he directed last June for the National Parks Service and Twentieth Century–Fox (the film is being screened twice daily at a theater across from Independence Hall in Philadelphia). He feels that Fox's "behavior [was] absolutely reprehensible" in trying to shutter the film when it went over budget with one day remaining on the one-week schedule; Huston chipped in $5000 of his own money to keep it going, and the cast and crew also donated their time.

The director intends to continue his acting career, which he calls a "lark."

The first film in which he has played the lead role, Orson Welles's *The Other Side of the Wind,* is still in progress after five years' shooting; Welles says Huston's character, a legendary film director, is modeled on Hemingway.

"I'll have to find out where Orson is," Huston muses. "I'm going to call him up and say 'Why the hell don't you finish it?' "

Watching Huston

GIDEON BACHMANN/1976

W H E N   J O H N   H U S T O N   W A S   playing Noah in his *Bible,* shot in
Rome exactly ten years ago this January, I asked him what his next film was
going to be. He answered that ten years previously he had written a script
based on a Kipling story, "The Man Who Would Be King," reputedly the
favorite story of Hemingway, Proust, and Faulkner, and that he was finally
going to shoot it. Since it seemed to me that Kipling was a natural source of
material for Huston, I said I would like to watch him. Huston promised, and
kept his promise. But I had to wait another ten years to cash in on it.

Twenty years have passed since Humphrey Bogart and Clark Gable agreed
to play the two adventurers in Queen Victoria's India who undertake to trek
into remote Kafiristan to seek their fortune, find it, and are felled by their
own pride. On a visit to Huston's Ireland retreat John Foreman, producer of
Butch Cassidy and the Sundance Kid, discovered some drawings Huston had
made in preparation for that venture, dug deeper, and came up with the
script, production notes, exact breakdowns, and the diaries of Huston's trips
to India and Afghanistan in the search for sites. Now Michael Caine and Sean
Connery play the two ill-fated blokes who go through triumph and disaster,
meet these two impostors as men, but can't keep it up, thus offering what is
perhaps a more realistic view of the nature of man than Kipling's famous
romantic poem did.

It starts romantically enough with a pact the two men make not to in-

From *Film Comment,* vol. 12, no. 1, January/February 1976, 21–22. © 1976 by *Film Comment.*
Reprinted by permission.

Humphrey Bogart as Sam Spade, Peter Lorre as Joel Cairo, Mary Astor as Brigid O'Shaughnessy, and Sydney Greenstreet as Kasper Gutman, *The Maltese Falcon*, 1941

Humphrey Bogart as Fred C. Dobbs and Tim Holt as Curtin, *The Treasure of the Sierra Madre*, 1948

Humphrey Bogart as Frank McCloud and Edward G. Robinson as
Johnny Rocco, *Key Largo*, 1948

Sam Jaffe as "Doc"
Riedenschneider and
Sterling Hayden as
Dix Handley, *The
Asphalt Jungle*, 1950

Audie Murphy as Henry Fleming, *The Red Badge of Courage*, 1951

Katharine Hepburn as Rose Sayer and Humphrey Bogart as Charlie Alnutt, *The African Queen*, 1951

José Ferrer as Toulouse-Lautrec, *Moulin Rouge,* 1952

Gregory Peck as
Captain Ahab,
Moby Dick, 1956

Clark Gable as Gay Langland, James Barton as old man, Marilyn Monroe as Roslyn Taber, Dennis Shaw as boy, Thelma Ritter as Isabelle Steers, Eli Wallach as Guido Delini, and Montgomery Clift as Perce Howland, *The Misfits*, 1961

Ava Gardner as Maxine Faulk and Richard Burton as Rev. T. Lawrence Shannon, *The Night of the Iguana*, 1964

Sean Connery as Daniel Dravot and Michael Caine as Peachy Carnehan, *The Man Who Would Be King*, 1975

Jacqueline Bissett as Yvonne Firmin and Albert Finney as Geoffrey Firmin, *Under the Volcano*, 1984

Kathleen Turner as
Irene Walker and
Jack Nicholson as
Charlie Partanna,
Prizzi's Honor, 1985

Donal McCann as Gabriel Conroy and Angelica Huston as Gretta
Conroy, *The Dead,* 1987

dulge in the commoner varieties of pleasure, an obvious plant set up by the author for the second-act curtain of this morality play: once crowned, the flesh calls Connery, and succumbing, his image shatters, as does, eventually, his body, in a San Luis Rey–type drawbridge disaster. Caine, surviving, at the end is back in Christopher Plummer's Kipling office, having come full circle, geographically and psychologically. Useless—although the effort is rewarding—to pretend to more than one is. Not a bad message for today.

The size of the film bears no relation to its source: $8\frac{1}{2}$ (magic film figure) million dollars patiently await transport to the coffers of the Moroccan government, a score of stars' bank accounts, and the British and American film industry's experienced system of expenditures. Two mountaintops were planed to make way for opposing Kafiristani cities. Folklore abounds as I arrive. Twelve hundred extras have their scalps shaved daily, an unfortunate habit of the monks they portray. Yorkshire pudding and roast lamb lunches are supplied to the British crew from a kitchen van brought from Pinewood Studios in England, while the locals light fires among their forest of donkey legs to brew their interminable mint tea. In front of the cameras it's all British Rahj, behind them it's the organizational ability that may be its legacy.

For three days I watch the special effects team trying to cause a few mules to fall down a hillside. Mules don't usually fall down at all, being mules, and all the trapdoors dug into the footpath, hot potatoes under the tail suggested by Connery, yelling on the part of the twelve hundred tea-drinkers, and blind shots from Caine's antediluvian rifle can't make them do it. The cursing is quadrilingual: Arabic, French, English, and Cockney. Huston is taking it all sitting down; it gives us a chance to talk. When the mules finally topple, his concern is with their well-being. The film seems to take care of itself.

G.B.: *Somehow, I have always thought, you and Kipling were going to get together. Observing your own trajectory, and comparing it to his path through difficulties and his constant search for the spirit of man, I am surprised that you have waited this long.*

J.H.: I have been intending to get together with Mr. Kipling for about twenty years, but it took a long time for it to come about. I was, of course, a great Kipling reader when I was a kid, and I've got reems of Kipling verse stored away in my unconscious to be tapped on drunken occasions. In fact, I have been looking forward to making this picture for a long time.

G . B . :   *Why didn't you do it before?*

J . H . :   I had originally intended to make it with Bogart and Gable. Then Bogie died and I put the thought away. After several years Gable said, well, let's go along and do it with someone else. We were in the process of doing that, during the making of *The Misfits,* but at the end of that picture, why, Gable died. And again I put it away. It was resurrected a couple of years ago by John Foreman, who saw that I had done a lot of preparation. I had been to the frontier countries scouting the locations, with the intention of perhaps making the film in Afghanistan or India. Where we are is supposed to be the upper right-hand corner of Afghanistan, looking at the map, then known as Kafiristan, which was the most locked-in, remote, secret country, perhaps, in the world. Much more so than Tibet. Only very recently have those frontiers been crossed. They had remained as closed in my time as they had in Kipling's, until just two or three years ago.

G . B . :   *Do you identify in any way with Kipling's quest, with his attempt to define man's struggle against nature, for example, and his fight to maintain an individuality in the face of encroaching progress? I think that's what had attracted Robert Flaherty, your old friend, to try and film* The Jungle Book, *before Korda took the film away from him and turned Sabu into a Hollywood cutie.*

J . H . :   I think that's a universal quest. Kipling himself identified, not only with people, but with animals, and even things, living in a kind of pantheistic world when trees and rocks had identities. It's this universality in Kipling that I feel close to, although it goes much deeper than that, of course.

G . B . :   *More specifically, I was wondering whether you identified with Kipling's fear that so many of our universal values were disappearing, and whether with this film, and by going back to him as an author, you were hoping to stress man's need to heed to his origins instead of the future alone?*

J . H . :   I only hope that man's future entails going back to his origins. This, it seems to me, is the only hope for man. Otherwise he will be destroyed.

G . B . :   *Hope is a very abstract quality.*

J . H . :   I thoroughly agree. In fact I believe we must do more than that. Each man, every day, must attempt his own little voyage of discovery, follow his own quest, to try and rediscover those things. It is this examining into one's own spirit which is what this film is all about. But this is rather highfalutin talk, as far as the picture is concerned, and I may be guilty of a profundity in a moment. The two men in this picture are indeed one man, and it's a dialogue that one man has with himself. They are divided into two men, because it cannot be all that introspective, in film. When the story calls for them to be divided, it's a kind of a division of a single personality, and when they come together again, the individual is united. One half of "him," as one half of ourselves very often does, falls prey to that illness that attacks us when we get to high places, *folie de grandeur*. Imagining that we are more than we are. Gods, in fact. The other one is that half of ourselves that chides us and says that we are absurd.

G.B.:   *Your profession, in our society, gives you sway over an enormous number of fates and means. Does the temptation you mention never manifest itself in the life of a major film director?*

J.H.:   I am not aware of it in myself. Nor am I aware of it in any of the better directors that I know. None of them seem to have ever fallen that deeply in love with themselves. With their work perhaps, but not with themselves.

G.B.:   *The theme we are discussing runs through your work like a red thread. Doesn't your concern, in these human terms, sometimes make you feel rather alone?*

J.H.:   I think I share that concern with many who have ideas, and I think it's important for any creator, to be obsessed, briefly, with his idea, and as long as he's sufficiently fascinated by the idea he hasn't that much time to think about himself.

G.B.:   *Is it always easy to distinguish? Obsession might just be the bridge between idea and self.*

J.H.:   Perhaps; in fact, during those periods of obsession there is no clean division between oneself and the idea. And my two characters in the film represent these two facets. It becomes a question of how to convey all this in images, and I think that this film has got rather more symbolic images than any that I've ever done. Of course they are of a simple order. I use a Masonic emblem to symbolize a universal connection between men, and my protagonists' lives are saved in a remote mountain town because the unfriendly high priest recognizes in the emblem on Sean Connery's chest an old holy insignia he believes belonged to Alexander the Great. It's just a pictorial device

for translating an idea into images. The same goes for the arrow that Michael
Caine gets stuck in him during a battle, but which fails to kill him. Pretty
soon he is carrying a golden one around as a scepter. I am sure that at some
moment every man alive, no matter how lowly, has dreamed for a split second, at least, that he himself was a god. This goes for a painter as well as for
a film director or a dice player. When the spirit is in him he is inspired, but
he better not go away from that dice table imagining that he is a deity. Or a
painter, when he puts his brushes down. He better give up the idea.

G . B . : *Is that what happens to you in your own painting?*
J . H . : The temptations come to every painter who has, however briefly,
command of his medium. And to every dice player or filmmaker. Every discipline has its advantages and its disadvantages. In film one sometimes becomes surfeited with personalities. I like painting because when I leave the
set I like to retire and be by myself or perhaps with one other person. I can't
go on being in a group; too many voices. That doesn't mean that I'm not
sociable when I am not making a film, but a set presents such kinetics in the
course of a day that I prefer to go into retreat at night.

G . B . : *Did you move to Ireland because you felt that the kinetics of life there are
more kin to your nature?*
J . H . : There are so many things that I like to do that Ireland offers. I am a
horseman, and it's a great horse country. And I like to fish, and the fishing is
good. I like the sport of hunting—the riding to hounds, that is—and the
country itself has a serenity and a tranquility that assuages the spirit. I go
back to Ireland to lick the wounds that have been inflicted on me in the
outer world.

G . B . : *What is your feeling about the use of animals in film, where there is
always a danger of their being hurt?*
J . H . : Every precaution is taken. As a matter of fact, the mules came
through without a scratch, as you saw. They are so wise. The risk is so slight;
I would myself assume risks, or a man would, in the film, just as an animal.
I've never lost a man on a film that I've made, and I've never lost an animal.

An Interview with John Huston

DAVID BRANDES/1977

DAVID BRANDES: *Mr. Huston, you're a writer, you're a director, and you're an actor. And you're famous in all three areas. Which do you prefer?*

JOHN HUSTON: I don't make a distinction between writing and directing. But to write and to direct one's own material is certainly the best approach. The directing is kind of an extension of the writing. So far as the acting is concerned, that's just a sort of lark—a well-paid lark, I might add—to relieve the responsibilities of being a director.

DB: *Why would a creative person like yourself become a filmmaker rather than, say, a novel writer?*

JH: I was raised in the tradition of films—that is, like so many children of my generation, we looked to the screen for our heroes; we imitated and emulated William S. Hart; people like Hart and Chaplin were gods. The films were every bit as much alive as literature, and I was always fascinated by films. So I started out to become a writer but I wasn't aware I wanted to become a director until after I had written for films for several years. Then I decided I could do my own material better than someone else. So I really just drifted into directing.

DB: *Yet you seem to prefer to adapt material rather than write your own original material.*

From *Filmmakers Newsletter,* vol. 10, no. 9, July 1977, 20–24. Reprinted by permission.

JH: I become fascinated by certain things and look for a way to bring them into immediacy. For instance, *Moby Dick*. I loved the book as a great work of art over many years, and finally saw what I thought was a way to bring it to the screen. It was a problem, but I enjoyed working it out enormously. Or *The Maltese Falcon*. It's very much the book only expressed in pictorial, dramatic terms.

DB: *What about the writing itself? Is there anything about the screenplay form which makes it appeal to you?*
JH: The ideal screenplay has a kind of discipline. You must make your points with a certain clarity and decisiveness which makes the ideal screenplay closer to poetry than to the novel. I find the form itself attracts me.

DB: *Yet poetry is such a pure form whereas film seems to be much more of a composite, so much less pure.*
JH: I think of pictures as being quite pure when they are truly realized. And closer, perhaps, to the thought processes than any other form. The ideal picture is almost as though the reel were behind your own eyes and you were projecting your own thoughts. It's only when the picture falters that your thoughts stumble as a result of the picture's faltering. Something "wrong" appears on the screen and the dream is broken.

DB: *When you read a novel and say, "This is it—this work speaks to me," what do you do then?*
JH: First, I read a lot, but I never read looking for material. I only read for the joy of reading. And it's usually some years after I've read something that one day I say, "Well, I think that will make a film." It's not an immediate process; it's something that occurs over a period of time.

DB: *When you say, "That'll make a film," do you mean "make a film for me" or "that material will be a winner in the marketplace."*
JH: I mean *for me*.

DB: *How and when do you know something will make a film "for you"?*
JH: When it has an *idea* and when I can *see* that idea in my imagination. It must all come together in my mind before it comes together on the screen or on the set.

D B : *Can you give me an example of such an "idea"?*

J H : For instance, an essential conflict or contradiction. Let's say there are two men: you admire both and see each one's point of view equally well. In addition, each man understands the other's point of view. Yet one or both must be destroyed. There is a paradox in that, and consequently the making of an idea out of which a picture can come. The idea, for the sake of representation on the screen, might be developed as the monarchical principle versus the democratic, where both have valid cases to make.

D B : *When you're making an adaptation, do you see the shots in your head?*

J H : Yes. When I did *The Maltese Falcon* the writing of the screenplay took all of three weeks and I did the drawings for the set-ups of every shot in the picture. For the most part they were adhered to—I'd say 75 percent of the time the scenes were the same as the drawings I made for the positions of the actors and the camera.

D B : *Do you still work that way?*

J H : I don't make drawings anymore, but there's a logic to shooting a scene. After your first shot, everything else falls into place. And shooting on location as I do and not in the studio, the circumstances usually tell you what the first shot is going to be.

By the way, I'd like to make an observation here. Very seldom does an audience realize what you're doing with the camera. When the camera is performing at its best, the audience isn't aware of it. It's so close to the thought process that you're watching the scene, not the movement of the camera—no matter what kind of ballet it might be doing.

As a rule, I think of the camera as part of the scene. It's the camera as protagonist. You enter the scene through the camera's eyes. It has a physiological function. Like the physiology of the cut. Try this little trick yourself. Look at something directly in front of you. Then look at something to the direct right of you. You've made a complete right angle. But notice that in doing it you blink your eyes. In other words, because you're familiar with the whole area in between, you blank it out and go directly from point A to point B. That is a cut.

Only when that intervening space—the relationship *between* those two objects—is important do you pan. If it isn't important, you cut.

DB: *Then you cut with the camera.*

JH: Yes, I cut with the camera.

DB: *I've noticed an element of your style is the use of reaction shots to give the substance and meaning of a scene.*

JH: Yes, I like that explicitness. It carries its own satisfaction, too. But I don't think of it as *my* style. I'm not even aware of *a* style. In fact, I don't think most people are aware of *a* style; they are just doing it to the best of their abilities.

DB: *In other words, it seems to you that there is no other way of shooting it.*

JH: Exactly.

DB: *Would you describe in detail how you would go about shooting a scene.*

JH: First, there's the atmosphere of the scene. If I'm being interviewed, for instance, we might start with a close-up of the camera and then pull back from that. But it's over my shoulder so we haven't seen me yet. Since I'm the one being interviewed, there's a certain suspense in what I look like—and you play that for its suspense. Finally you come around to the right shot of me and the right size. Now that's very important. You come around and do a big head close-up, instantly, and that immediately divorces the camera. Then, having established our relative sizes, if I say something that's utterly fascinating, why the camera might even be moved to come closer to me; it will search that thought out by coming even closer.

Now having come to a close-up, as it were, then I should want to come around and see you and what your reaction was to what I was saying. But unless you as the questioner had some sort of plot in mind, say an intent to confuse me, there would be no particular reason to move in on you. You would remain the interlocutor.

DB: *Now how does this work on a large scale? Something like* The Man Who Would Be King, *for instance, where you had a huge production and dealt with thousands of people.*

JH: If you start thinking about it in terms of thousands, you'll get confused. You must always stay with a simple thought: what you are trying to say in the scene. I never think in terms of spectacle. It's always in terms of idea. How best to put over the idea. *Idea* in italics.

DB: *I sometimes get the feeling those early pictures—*Treasure of the Sierra Madre, Maltese Falcon, African Queen*—were more like a bunch of friends going out on location or on the set and just making a movie and having a good time. Was it like that?*

JH: That's like Venetian painting. It looks very easy. Those painters were wonderful with a brush—very suave and very swift. But an awful lot of preparation goes into that final look.

The films that were well-written and well-prepared beforehand had fewer of the kinds of problems that are really disturbing than the ones that weren't. The ones that got you down were those where you were working with material that wasn't very good—and you were trying to hide from the audience the fact that what they were seeing was not all that good.

But when you're working with material that is really good, then it just becomes a matter of how to get it and what lengths you have to go to to do so. You know it's there and you're well prepared, so the physical discomforts are unimportant—even though they may be very difficult. (I've worked at times in Africa when people were falling down from sunstroke and going crazy from loneliness and disease.)

DB: *Let's talk for a moment about working with actors. How do you work with actors?*

JH: I always do as little directing as possible. Always. Because I don't want to color characterizations with my own personality. I try to get as much out of the actor as possible and tell him as little as possible. I try to develop what is there—whether the actor is a professional or has never done anything. Some of the best performances I've ever had have been by people who've never been before a camera or on a stage. In that case it's largely a matter of the personality and how to bring that out—produce it and give the audience the joy of discovering them.

DB: *Do you at least tell them what the scene means?*

JH: They find out through playing the scene. I don't have those discussions before a scene that many directors do. Actors sometimes like to talk about a scene, and in that case I accomodate them. But it's only to gratify some emotional requirement in them rather than to tell them how to play the scene.

I give them the script in the first place because I think they are right for it in their personalities. What I want to see is what they do—what comes naturally to them. I don't, as a rule, give an actor a script and have him try to change his personality into something that's suitable for the role. I prefer to let him discover whatever part of himself is that role and present it to me.

DB: *What about the set-up itself? How do you make sure they'll actually walk in the right place?*

JH: I don't tell them what to do to begin the scene, I just say go ahead and show me. And with a rehearsal, as a rule, they fall right into the right positions. You don't have to tell them. Just let nature take its course. Sometimes of course you have to give some help, but generally speaking they present you with the scene and then you discover what is the best set-up to photograph the scene. As a result you get something that isn't mechanical—that isn't done for the camera. And because it's true, you can just naturally introduce the camera into the scene.

DB: *What happens if you've miscast a scene?*

JH: It's never happened to me. I've occasionally had to work with actors, but I've never fired an actor. Never had to.

DB: *Do you rehearse a lot?*

JH: When there are long dialogue scenes we rehearse a lot. But it all depends on the actors. Sometimes they'll go through a scene and everything is right instantly; other times we have to maneuver.

DB: *As a rule, do you change a lot on the set or very little?*

JH: If the script is right, you change very little. And the nearer the script is to being truly right, the less you change.

DB: *Have you always been so confident in these things?*

JH: Yes. Provided you believe in your material. The only time you'll find a lack of confidence is when you doubt your own material. When you doubt a scene before even going into it, you stay up all night trying to re-write it and make it better than the original writing. Sometimes you do; sometimes you fail.

DB: *What about the actual shooting? Do you ever get up in the morning and say, "My God, what am I going to do today?"*

J H :   Have I ever awakened in the morning and said, "My God, what am I going to do today?" I've awakened in the middle of the night in a cold sweat saying, "My God, what am I going to do in the morning?"

D B :   *And what do you do then?*
J H :   You just have to keep your head and try to correct what is essentially wrong because you wouldn't feel that way in the first place if what you were working with wasn't wrong. If what you're working with is true and good, then there's no sense of that frustration you're talking about.

Making a film is like every other undertaking in life. Its success depends on whether or not you're equipped for it. And I'm not referring to learning. I don't know that I've learned a hell of a lot. I think I was probably as good a director at the beginning as I am now. Oh I've probably learned a few small technical things. But I'm not sure my understanding has deepened since I was nine years old.

I think one is born with a certain knowledge. And you can, to some extent, improve, embellish, and polish your equipment; but, essentially, I think that innate knowledge remains intact and you operate out of it.

D B :   *So, for example, when you search for material that is right it isn't with an idea of what is "right" but of what "feels" right.*
J H :   Of course. Something that itself develops; that makes itself known to me. I don't search for material; it comes.

D B :   *What happens when your instincts come in conflict with those, say, of the cinematographer? You say, "This is the way it must be done"; and he says, "No, it's got to be done that way"—and then gives you five good supporting reasons. Do you still reply with something like, "But that doesn't feel right"?*
J H :   The only experiences of that kind I've had have been with producers. Usually Johnny-Come-Latelies who don't know what the hell they're talking about. But they still talk with an authority you wouldn't have put up with in the old days when they really did know.

D B :   *Then you don't have many creative conflicts?*
J H :   Never. The cameraman is of course cast for the picture just the same as an actor would be. You decide what you want on the screen and then go to the right man for that. Over and over, in my experience, the right man has

been Ozzie Morris. I've done a number of pictures with him—*Moby Dick, Moulin Rouge, Beat the Devil, Heaven Knows, Mr. Allison,* most recently *The Man Who Would Be King,* and more.

And the reason Ozzie and I have worked together so often is that we speak in a kind of code. I rarely look through the camera except maybe to check the position of the actors or something like that. Usually I just stand in a certain position and look at Ozzie and he knows exactly what I mean so far as the set-up is concerned. Words are rarely necessary with us. And there's hardly room for any misunderstanding that way.

DB: *Disasters, gore, and mayhem seem to be the chief components of today's successful movie fare. Yet your most recent picture,* The Man Who Would Be King, *was an elegant, stylized adventure story.*

JH: It's just that I'm easily bored by clichés, and the more monumental they become the more my interest wanes accordingly. I will walk out of a disaster film if it's expressed in terms of clichés. And I have a low threshold for slow-motion bleeding: the first time I'm interested, the second time mildly interested, and the third time rather revolted by it.

DB: *But audiences tend to get bored if not enough is happening.*

JH: That is quite possible—if what is happening is a bore. The question is: are you *interested* in what is happening? I personally find it hard to distinguish between dialogue and action. What's going on in someone's head can be action, can have as much violence in it as slow-motion bleeding.

DB: *Do you think the audience of today is different? If you made, say,* Treasure of Sierra Madre *today do you think people would go see it?*

JH: They do. They watch it on television. When *African Queen* was shown on television, the ratings indicated they liked it as much as the old audience that saw it in the theater.

DB: *Do you feel a film like* Jaws *will have the same appeal over time?*

JH: I haven't seen *Jaws* so I can't comment on it. But good films—truly good films—will endure. Granted the camera used to turn at a different speed and the acting style was one of exaggerated delivery. Today we're closer to reality. Figures on the screen move at the same pace as we do in life. And the style has changed, of course. But a Chaplin film is as good today as it was then.

D B : *What is your opinion of the state of the art today?*

J H : One of the ill effects of the modern set up of the industry is that if a picture isn't immediately successful, they won't risk any more money publicizing it. I've seen a number of fine films that the public was barely able to see. Like *The Traveling Executioner* with Stacey Keach, or *Walkabout* from Australia. I think Altman's *McCabe and Mrs. Miller* was a kind of masterpiece. *Midnight Cowboy* was a wonderful film. Beautiful pictures—and our loss, as a result of the present economic set up.

On the other hand, *Earthquake, Towering Inferno,* etc. I haven't seen them and I'm not drawn to them because they seem to contain a formula. What I hear about them doesn't sufficiently attract me. I'd rather read a book.

D B : *What about the future of motion pictures?*

J H : I don't look at the history of motion pictures any more than I look at the history of art. I like a painter for the painting and for what the painter himself does. His position in the history of art is for historians.

I don't suppose every work is a masterpiece or even fulfills itself. And I don't necessarily see every work as a sign of progress. Very often it's a decline. But then, even in its decline something can be fascinating. The fact that we've got a new style doesn't mean the earlier works weren't fascinating. Or that pictures which weren't popular at the time they were made won't become so later on.

In sum, I guess it's probably as bad to be ahead of your time as to be behind your time. What we are looking for is instant, universal acceptance.

Interview with John Huston

URS EGGER/1977

THE FOLLOWING INTERVIEW, CONDUCTED by Urs Egger, took place in a soundstage at Metro-Goldwyn-Mayer Studios in Culver City, California. John Huston was acting in a film there, *Winter Kills,* an independent production directed by William Richert and also starring Jeff Bridges, Toshiro Mifune, and Elizabeth Taylor. With Huston on the set was Gladys Hill, his collaborator and screenwriter for many years. At one point she took part in the interview. It was Huston's last week of shooting, and a few days after the interview the two flew to Ireland and Italy to start pre-production on their next film, *Across the River and into the Trees,* which is scheduled to start filming in Italy later this year.

Do you enjoy acting?
Yes, within limits. I think of myself as a director.

Does the director Huston watch the actor Huston?
I try not to, but I probably do. I saw myself in the rushes today and I wasn't very good; but then I was looking at the screen as a director.

Many years ago you shot Asphalt Jungle *and* The Red Badge of Courage *in these soundstages at MGM. How much has filmmaking changed over these years?*
Well, it is still the same; techniques have improved, but that is of little importance. The studio system ended with the war, when the studios lost their

From *Cinema Papers,* October 1977, 139–41, 185. Reprinted by permission.

theatres, lost their monopoly. Being a liberal at that time I was very much for it—not so much now, though.

The studios had to fill their theatres then, and many films were made. When they lost them it became quite different and the agents came in.

You started as a writer at Warner Brothers, before directing your first film, The Maltese Falcon. *What made you make the transition from writer to director?*
Directing had always been in the back of my mind. It was a natural thing to go from writing to directing. I had written short stories, and I came to Hollywood exclusively to write for the screen. Then, after a while, I had it put into my contract that I was to direct my first film within a certain period.

Did you feel the scripts you wrote could have been rendered onto the screen in a better way?
Yes, I was not very happy with many of the films. Most of the directors at that time came out of the editorial department. There were a few cameramen, but they were mostly cutters. The only writer to become a director before me was Preston Sturges—unless you include Chaplin.

Was your father a big influence?
Well, I learned a good deal about direction from seeing him act—the way he would approach a scene.

Was he already in films when you started at Warners?
Yes, but I learnt more from seeing him work in the theatre than at Warners. I would attend rehearsals of plays he was doing and I'd see what he would do with a scene. It was mostly his creation of a role, to see how he went at it, that was a lead into direction. There weren't many great film directors whom he worked with at the time.

In your very first film you worked with him . . .
Oh, he just walked in. It was a good luck appearance, a token. He came into a room, took the furniture to pieces, broke a lamp, and died. The only true part that I ever directed him in was in *The Treasure of the Sierra Madre.*

What makes you decide to do a certain film?
My interest in the material—just how fascinating it is. I'm not trying to propagate an idea or anything of that sort.

So when you did Jean-Paul Sartre's No Exit *on the stage, it was because that particular piece interested you, rather than the existentialism itself?*
Yes, exactly.

How do you feel about existentialism now?
I think I am existential in my views of things. I know Sartre and I worked
with him. I think he made an enormous contribution. He's out of vogue now
though, isn't he?

How does existentialism relate to your film, The Bible.
Well, I look at the Bible as a collection of myths and legends, not from a
religious standpoint at all.

How did the producer, Dino de Laurentiis, feel about that?
He just wanted a very successful film. I don't think it was meant to be the
word of God.

*European critics, especially the French, have said that you are more interested in
the pursuit of your heroes towards a goal rather than in the goal itself. It is the
game, not the gain . . .*
It has been said to me so many times that I tend to believe it. But as I said
earlier, I don't look for certain themes. I don't even read with the intention
of finding material, I just read out of interest. One day something might
become a film. And unless there is a challenge in it, unless there is an element of experiment in it, I am not profoundly interested. But there are also
those films I do for money, and not for any other reason.

Miss Hill, you wrote many screenplays with Mr. Huston, including Reflections in
a Golden Eye, Fat City, The Man Who Would Be King. *How do the two of you
work together?*
HILL: If we are adapting a novel, I will first break the novel down, scene by
scene. I then memorize the book, so when John and I are discussing a scene,
action or sequence, I can say, "Remember, John, such and such happened."
He may say, "Where is it?" and then I find it in the book and read it to him.
    From there we talk about it and then I write it. I put in the description
and the dialogue. Then I take it to Mr. Huston to read. And if it has to be

redone, it's redone and we discuss it again. Then, Mr. Huston will, if he wishes, change the dialogue.

It's difficult to describe, because there is no formula. It's so dull to say, but writing is rewriting. And sometimes you are so close to it but you can't see what you're doing.

Then one of you will set it in perspective . . .
HILL: Huston always, he is the maestro. But often nothing gets changed. After all these years of working together we think quite similarly.

How specific is the script? As Mr. Huston is also the director, does it specify shots or angles?
HILL: Yes, but only generally. We might write "camera moves back," but we don't give any unnecessary camera directions. The screenplay we do is the shooting script, but when Mr. Huston sets up a shot, he does it the way he wishes.

A novel is something descriptive where many things happen within people's minds—memories and so on. How do you transfer these thoughts into a screenplay.
HILL: That's not an easy question to answer. Sometimes you let a person say what she or he has been thinking about; in another case you might have to select a thought and express it in words. I suppose in the old days people used flashbacks to show their characters' memories.

Each story has its own approach.

HUSTON: The dialogue and the scene itself should explain their thoughts. It's up to the writer to visualize the underlying thought of the scene. You try to explain through the behavior and the actions of people what their thoughts are.

I know a Bergman script was published, and he does go into the subconscious, and writes about the thoughts that are going through the minds of people. But I've never had an occasion to do that, except where the thought is at variance with the action.

In terms of style, you don't pan your camera a lot, you just cut. Is there a special reason for this?

HUSTON: A word that appears a lot in scripts is "masterscene," which means to shoot the whole scene in one shot with the camera in a fixed position. I never shoot a master scene and I think that word should be stricken from the vocabulary of films. I never do it, unless that's the way the scene is going to be in the film. After the first set-up I always know what the next shot is going to be: the size, how close, and so on.

I think the camera has many things in common with our physiology. You look from one point to another, now look back to me! *(I look over to the door of the wardrobe trailer we are sitting in, then back to him).* Do it again. Do it again. Well, as a rule, when you know what's over there, you know what the intervening space is. You blink. You exclude the space in between. And that's a cut! *(Laughs).*

It would be dull and boring to our minds to take everything in all the way over here. I would see out there *(Huston looks at the wall)* and so on, and I don't want to do that. I talk to Gladys *(He turns his head toward her)* and then I talk to you. *(He turns his head towards me).* And Gladys again. And you. So that I am cutting constantly. The size of a character on the screen is determined not by the technique, but by distance. For instance, we would not be having this conversation and talking as we are if I was standing over by the door. *(He points to a door on the wall of the set, about forty metres away).* I see Gladys, she is listening, and I am not talking to her, but if I would be talking to her in this way, I would probably get a little bit closer to her even than I am *(He frames her in a loose waist shot).*

On the other hand, I would never tell a girl that I was in love with her from the other side of the stage *(He points out to the far end of the sound stage),* unless I was calling to say goodbye or something of that kind.

There are certain kinds of conversation with a distance, and the size on the screen is very important to keep the right atmosphere. When you pan the camera you are making the space between important and that implies suspense of some kind, or that something is happening out there that is worth my glimpsing as I go to you. Every time the camera moves there should be a real purpose to it.

As for going closer, if Gladys says something very important and confidential, I find myself leaning forward *(He leans forward, and puts one hand to his ear like a person who has trouble hearing),* so the camera will lean forward, and so on. The camera is your mind and your emotion.

Now you shoot up at something, you aggrandize it—that's from being a child looking up at your parents or looking up at a heroic sculpture. By the same token, you wouldn't shoot something like a comedy scene, looking up at Charlie Chaplin or Buster Keaton. You would see them at eye-level, if not looking down on them a bit.

So it's psychology turned into behavior . . .
Exactly.

Do you have your shots figured out when you go onto the set?
I usually have an idea what the scene is going to be. I then bring the actors onto the set but I don't tell them anything, I just say: "Play the scene!" Usually they come around to doing exactly what I had hoped they would do, but sometimes they don't and do it better than what I had planned. But, as I said, the moment the first shot is made the rest is just following out the slack.

That would imply that the most important part, as far as the acting is concerned, is the casting . . .
Of course it is. if you have to direct actors a lot, in my instance at least, it means they aren't all that good, and you have to conceal their weaknesses. Very often I use people who have never been before a camera, and they can be wonderful. Just being professional doesn't make someone an actor, and being an actor doesn't necessarily mean that the artist is professional.

The African Queen *was enormously funny. Did that turn out through casting, or was it in the book?*
There was an element of humor in the book though I don't think it was as funny as the film. Of course they worked beautifully together; they complemented each other and became the film.

It was also quite different from what Humphrey Bogart had done before . . .
Yes, and he found the character. I remember him saying to me: "For God's sake, John, don't let me get out of it!" I was sure this was actually one part of Bogart, and it took him a little time getting into it—but he found it.

Another humorous film you made with Bogart was Beat the Devil . . .
It was a bit of a travesty—we were making fun of ourselves. Another actor in *Beat the Devil* was Peter Lorre. He was an extraordinary actor. He was always

so much better on the screen than you imagined he'd been when you saw him do it. He did very subtle things and I have a great respect for him as an artist.

You treat your heroes very sympathetically, but often in a very detached way . . .
The heroes themselves have that same detachment when they are confronted with their final destiny. They are alone there and they look at it objectively without undue sympathy for themselves or too great an emotion, but a kind of overall sense of the fitness of what's happening to them. They rise to the occasion and they become a little bit greater than themselves even. And that's what makes them heroes.

Can heroes not fail?
They always do, at least in my films.

Do you think films have an influence?
In a superficial sense, of course. Look at the enormous success of *Roots,* which I thought was very bad artistically. About eighty million people saw the last episode and that's the biggest audience that has ever seen anything. Certainly it has a moral, ethical, and political significance.

But isn't it perhaps just a manifestation of a change that has already happened?
Undoubtedly it's timely. *Roots* is not introducing a new idea, and how deep it goes is something else. If it effects any psychological change in the attitudes of the very people that watch it, well . . . but I'm sure it doesn't.

Do you think it could?
I doubt it.

So film is not really political . . .
I doubt that anything is. I wonder if any great work of art has had any profound political effect, including Beethoven, Scarlatti, Piero della Francesco, Michelangelo, and Rembrandt. I wonder if it has any universal impact. Sad and cynical observation.

You once said that everything in your films has a function. Could you talk on what one could call your "school" and compare it with what you see on the screen today?

I was raised on the classic concepts of filmmaking. Just like in the theatre there were requirements, and perhaps they were cast a little bit too tightly into a mould. There was the idea of organization, the internal combustion, where everything had to work. The drama was the tightness of the construction. A theme that you can render into a plot, lines that furnished the plot as well as the characters, so that the whole thing was like an internal combustion engine.

Today, or that yesterday more I think than today, points didn't need to be underscored, a film didn't have to have an ending, and this was in a sense certainly a liberating influence.

Are you now talking about Godard, for instance?
Yes, the *nouvelle vague.* However, I see now that the better films are reverting to the old form. A film like *Network* for instance, which is very complex. And even a film like *Rocky* which I fell for completely. *Rocky* was outspoken, and also you stand back in admiration of the way scenes were done.

Rocky has taken the best of both worlds, in a sense—the old and the new. A wonderful liberation occurred as far as censorship is concerned, to the great benefit of the better films.

Did you suffer under censorship at times?
Not really. Certainly I have seen films suffer under it, but I don't think ever my own. However, I worked with the conception of censorship. It was already in the grain of the film, and very often censorship led me to do things that were even better than I would have done had there not been that kind of censorship.

Nevertheless it's a fine thing for films that there is no longer that absurd requirement. For instance, when I came in, if Rocky and the girl had made love before they were married, they would both have had to die. It was immoral, absurd. I remember on some film I had nothing to do with, a boy came back from war and discovered that his wife had been unfaithful; so she had to die. Awful things were forced on us. They were harder with us than Moses.

You are going to direct another film soon . . .
Yes, it is the Hemingway story *Across the River and into the Trees.* Gladys and I

wrote the screenplay, and we are going to do it in Italy this year. The story takes place in Venice, and we are shooting it almost entirely on location. I have always preferred to shoot on location than use studios.

You don't plan to retire . . .
No, never.

John Huston

G. Y. DRYANSKY/1978

PUERTO VALLARTA, MEXICO—The Hollywood rumor you may
have heard, about the cows rampaging through John Huston's new house
and tearing it down, is not true. For one, there are no cows at Huston's compound at a cove edged by jungle although there is a pet macaw, a funny ant-
eating animal on a string locally known as a tejon, two pet boa constrictors,
and, most recently, a sort-of-tame ocelot. The houses, all six huts to be exact,
are still standing although some are not yet finished.

The other story going around, about Huston's being very sick, is equally
misleading. After major surgery and seven weeks of intensive care, the seventy-
one-year-old film director is now well, working hard—on an autobiography
and the script of his next film—drinking (moderately) and spinning yarns.

Huston's compound was a building last fall when he went to have his
emphyzema looked at in Cedars of Zion in Los Angeles. In examining him,
the doctors discovered an aneurism of the aorta.

"My father died of a ruptured aorta. They couldn't cure those things
twenty years ago," he explained. "Now I've got plastic tubing in me down as
far as both legs.

"You know, they tested my lungs to see if I could sustain eight hours of
surgery and the results were terrible—they couldn't sustain me for a half
hour. They said, 'It's quite extraordinary those lungs are sustaining you right
now.' So they worked on my lungs for ten days with a breathing machine

From *Women's Wear Daily*, "W" Section, March 31–April 7, 1978, 10–12. © 1978 by *Women's Wear Daily*. Reprinted by permission.

and they beat my lungs, and I came through the operation all right. But you know, it's a terrible thing, they put your intestines on a tray and there they lie smoking and writhing while your aorta is being worked on. I developed adhesions—when they're touched, something happens to your insides—so I had to be operated on for that for another four hours. Well, then the gall bladder started up, and the doctors said if we have to operate on that, that's it. Fortunately, I didn't need the operation."

Huston spoke about his battered body with the same counterpoint of awe and world-wisdom in his voice he has when he tells one or another of his famous long tales. He sat on the porch of the house, which consists of just his bedroom, in white peon pajamas, talking slowly, like Marlow in Conrad, to the sound of vodka swishing in a glass and the waves beating almost to the edge of the porch.

While a pretty young Mexican girl poured more drinks, he went on to a more savory story illustrating why he likes living in Mexico:

It was the tale of Candy Candelera, former chief of police and local desperado, who recently walked into the Puerto Vallarta office of the Federales and shot an old enemy, the captain, between the eyes.

"And then," as Huston puts it, "he turns to the two other officers with his gun smoking and he says, 'Have either of you any objections to what I've just done?'

" 'No, none at all . . . not at the present moment.' "

There's a pot-smuggling and a murder charge out on Candy, but he still comes into the town, which is speckled with tourists, has a quiet drink with his friends and moves on. "Oh, Candy is a very popular fellow."

Such is the "condiment" of Mexican life with which Huston has been in love since he explored the country's Pacific coast in a canoe at the age of nineteen. Several times, he's found the condiment a bit too hot, as when, only two years ago, a posse with "breach-loading rifles from the time of Maximilian" wanted to kill Huston and a friend to keep them from taking out samples from a silver mine the local mayor and doctor coveted. The gringos were saved in the nick of time by the Federales.

For Huston, the ocean is his Mexican retreat's answer to the horses he raised in County Galway, Ireland, until three years ago, when the cost of keeping his farm and twelve servants "meant you had to be away from the place working all the time."

Huston liked to ride and jump treacherous stone walls. Now he puts a mask on and paddles among the rocks offshore, where a teeming aquarium of huge needlefish, parrot fish, angel fish, and all manner of bright water life dart about, along with an occasional deadly sea-snake.

The baby boa he likes to hold between his legs and stroke while he meditates on his autobiography is far less dangerous.

Huston was prodded into doing the book by Swifty Lazar, who swept the lanky director through the offices of the New York publishing houses a year and a half ago, doing a sort of Mutt and Jeff routine with him for the highest bid.

"Swifty and I would go see a publisher or we'd go to lunch with one, and he would sort of intimate all the good stories I had, and I would sort of nod, and Swifty would rub his hands in the taxicab." Swifty rubbed his hands the hardest to the advance of Robert Gottlieb, of Knopf, at a figure neither Huston nor Knopf would disclose.

Huston is keeping most of his good stories to himself until publishing date, but the book, which will trace his career as a boxer, painter, writer, actor, and director of more than thirty-five films, is bound to say a little on the subject of women. Huston shrugs off the talk of his being rather hard on women although he has gone through five wives. (In any case, Evelyn Keyes, one of the five, later made clear in Los Angeles that "there was never anything kinky about John Huston.") Of all the women who spangled his life, Huston says he misses the late Pauline de Rothschild most of all, although there was just a whiff of romance between them, which led to thirty-five years of close friendship.

Pauline Potter, as she was then known, came out to stay with John Huston in his ranch near Los Angeles, smitten, as her friends described it, by the young director fresh from filming the Battle of San Pietro under fire in Italy, whom she'd met at the John Barry Ryans'. If Pauline was in love with him, Huston avows he wasn't aware of it, having been blindly in love himself, at the time, with Marietta Fitzgerald (later Marietta Tree), who was married.

Marietta's husband's solution to her affection for the wild director who stormed around New York looking like a lumberjack before that was stylish was to insist on her having analysis. And she did, pledging not to divorce Fitzgerald until the analysis proved her decision was a healthy one.

"Well, I was in a terrible position there," Huston says, with a pained expression on his prizefighter's face—or rather his poet's face toughened by a broken nose and cauliflower ears, souvenirs of his amateur boxing days. His solution was to up and marry Evelyn Keyes, whose current autobiography does in Pauline, Marietta, and what, for Keyes was their effete, fashionable set.

"Poor girl," says Huston, "poor, sweet girl, she was completely out of her element when she met them."

Huston never felt out of his element drawing up his chair, invited or uninvited, at the most sophisticated dinner tables in New York, but he shirks high-sounding talk and will not go on about women with a capital W any more than about film with a capital F.

"The French critics who read depth into every film say I'm interested in the game rather than the gain. The chase rather than the kill. I suppose that's right . . . , I like the statement a picture makes to be clear, whatever it is. There has to be a statement, not a doctrine."

Among Huston's three dozen films are such classics as *The African Queen*, *Reflections in a Golden Eye* and *The Treasure of the Sierra Madre*, but he admits no favorites—although he readily confesses having made about six turkeys.

"I get in trouble when my story isn't good. I don't particularly like writing my own script, but it's the best thing that can happen to a picture when I do.

"Pictures are made for diverse reasons. Usually, it's the head of the studio who's got a girl who read a bad book, and she considers it would make a good movie. You spend three years doing treatments and screenplays and they find they have an investment of $180,000 from a book bought at $10. You come in and try to keep it from disgrace but it's awful, and you're sorry you've ever done it. What can you do? Surgeons operate when they know the patient is going to die."

Huston lists *The Mackintosh Man* as his most recent bad picture, in contrast with *The Man Who Would Be King*, which he loved. "I love Kipling . . . I love the doggerel."

The list of the actors he worked with reads like a book of screen royalty—Burton, Taylor, Brando, Hepburn, Bogart, Mitchum, Newman. Huston says he gives very little direction to his actors. "I get them for the part. I don't try to adapt the role to the actor."

Huston's next film, if he is satisfied with the treatment he's started, will be based on the life of Ibn Saud, the great unifier of Saudi Arabia. Has he got the actor for the part?

"Not yet."

"What about Paul Newman?"

"Hardly."

John Huston, Grand Old Man of American Film

BARBARA THOMAS/1978

IN AN ABANDONED BUILDING near Grady Hospital, up four flights of crumbling, filthy stairs, one can find one of the great directors of American film.

John Huston, director, actor, ex-boxer, and once a painter in Paris, is in Atlanta for a role in *The Visitor,* an occult-sci-fi film from Swan-American Films.

"I play an old man from outer space," he says.

Twisting his expressive face into a smile, he adds, "I feel much like that already."

As a director, seventy-two-year-old Huston has been responsible for such film classics as *The Maltese Falcon, The Treasure of the Sierre Madre, Key Largo, African Queen, Moby Dick, The Misfits, Night of the Iguana,* and most recently *The Man Who Would Be King.*

As a young writer in Hollywood, he turned out scripts for films like *Sergeant York, Jezebel, High Sierra* and many others.

His 1948 film, *Treasure of the Sierra Madre,* brought him two Oscars for screenplay and best direction. Humphrey Bogart had the role of Fred C. Dobbs while Huston's father Walter took a best supporting actor Oscar for his role.

"I don't write with an actor in mind, but as I wrote it I realized Bogart would be good for it and my father would be good as the old man.

"On the set, a director is like a father, so in a sense, by directing my father, I became like my own grandfather, my father's father."

He chuckles at his twist of words.

Huston remembers Bogart as an "ideal collaborator and companion."

"*African Queen, Key Largo, Beat the Devil*—those are just some of the ones we made together. He's a joy to work with. Although I never wrote for him, his figure seemed to find its way into whatever I did.

"He's become a myth, a cult figure, hasn't he? Bogie seems to loom larger since he died than he ever did in his lifetime. He would be delighted and amused by it . . . and probably is."

Huston describes *Moby Dick* as the most perilous film he's ever made. "Whenever you make a film on the ocean you're instantly asking for it. We encountered the worst weather in maritime history for those waters. . . . We were dismasted twice; and how we missed anyone getting killed I'll never know, because we were so close to it the better part of the time. . . . Once there was no question that we were going to the bottom. Only a miracle of seamanship saved us."

Huston said he agreed to direct *The Misfits,* (with Marilyn Monroe and Clark Gable) unaware that Miss Monroe was "desperately ill."

"I had no idea she was in that condition. The picture had to be stopped once when she went to the hospital because of drugs . . . drugs she took to go to sleep, drugs to wake up. There were times when she was full of both and her own mind was blown. I agreed to do the picture because I was asked by her and her husband, Arthur Miller. He wrote it for her, you know."

Film directors, according to Huston, should be "well read, widely read, and even deeply read," with some knowledge of the associated arts.

"Film is a medium like any other. I don't, like Frank Capra, think it's the greatest of all the arts, but it's an art. You're constantly trying for perfection, depending on how high you pitch your sights. The other arts certainly do contribute to it. My own interests as a painter have played a large part in my life as a director. Paintings have a frame the same as those shadows you see on the screen."

Huston is amused by critics or film buffs who are awed by particularly flashy shots. "I move the camera a good deal, to a purpose I hope, and have never had a good shot pointed out by a critic. If it's good, you don't see it."

He alludes to a practice *Time* Magazine had of including a reference to "best shot" in their film reviews.

"They would note a reflection in a doornob or some other damn thing . . . they were all clichés of shots a good director wouldn't dream of having in a film. It would take a bad director to do it, but critics always like the cliché shots."

"There was a time there, after Orson Welles—and I think I'm partly to blame because of *The Maltese Falcon*—when everything was shot looking upward at the character.

"If a shot is well-conceived and moves as it should, it develops like a ballet with the camera. No one is allowed to become aware of it. Your mind is what is moving and looks at the idea, not the shot."

Huston has no favorites among his films, although there are a few he has sunk into his subconscious with "other murky incidents."

Quite by accident, he says, he turned on the television one night and saw *Key Largo* for the first time since it was released in 1949.

"Bogie was extraordinary in that. In fact," he laughs at what might be thought his immodesty, "I liked the whole picture. Whats-her-name, that girl in it, also got an award for it." (Claire Trevor took best supporting Oscar for the role.)

Huston is quite animated in his insistence that his role in the Atlanta movie is that of the good guy. "I have to convince the little girl not to destroy mankind."

When suggested that it's vital that he succeed in his efforts, that he help save the human race, he parries: "Are you absolutely sure of that?"

John Huston: At 74 No Formulas

BERNARD DREW/1979

IN 1941, WHEN JOHN Huston was thirty-five, he was best known as the son of actor Walter Huston. Then came *The Maltese Falcon,* his first directed film. It turned out to be a masterpiece, and its success, both critical and popular, made Huston a star director. In fact, later Huston was able to add to his father's fame when he directed him in *The Treasure of the Sierra Madre.* Both father and son won Academy Awards.

Today John Huston is seventy-four and has directed thirty-four movies since *The Maltese Falcon.* His most recent film, *Wise Blood,* which he shot on a limited budget in Macon, Georgia, is every bit as fine in its own way as his first picture. Somewhere in between, he made such enduring films as *The Asphalt Jungle, The Red Badge of Courage, The African Queen, Beat the Devil, Fat City, The Man Who Would Be King,* and one which is never revived and seems to be completely forgotten by everyone including Huston himself, but which I have always liked, *We Were Strangers.*

On a cold winter's day last December, on the shore of Lake Ontario in Toronto, Canada (where his father was born), Huston was shooting *Phobia,* his thirty-fifth film. *Phobia* deals with murders at a mental institution and stars Paul Michael Glaser as a psychiatrist treating convicted killers. Huston was busy directing on the grounds of an unused and weather-beaten asylum when I arrived, and I was told to please go into his camper and make myself comfortable.

From *American Film,* September 1980, 38–42. © 1980 by *American Film.* Reprinted by permission.

When I enter Huston's camper, I see Michael and Kathy Fitzgerald, the young couple who produced *Wise Blood*. We met during the movie's showing at the New York Film Festival, and Michael is still glowing over the reviews—the best Huston has gotten in years.

Huston comes in now, whitebearded, but somehow still not patriarchal, shivering through the many layers of clothing he is wearing because of bronchitis (he is as macho as ever, though he is also an elegant man with impeccable manners, almost courtly.

He offers us all sherry—he had to give up his beloved twenty cigars a day, but he can still take a drink—and he takes one, then settles down, looking fondly at the Fitzgeralds. "They are quite an extraordinary couple," he tells me, and they both blush as he goes on. "I didn't know a thing about them. A book by Flannery O'Connor was sent to me. Then someone called and said he was Michael Fitzgerald and he wanted me to direct the screen version of the book and that he already had the money. Then he'd call and say that the money just wasn't there. This went on for a couple of years, and I became rather fond of him, paternal. I'd feel sorry for him and say, 'Don't devote the rest of your life to this,' and he'd say, 'I'm going to do it, and it's going to be a good picture.' "

"Finally," Huston goes on, "he had the money, and we began the picture. There was nothing I wanted that he didn't go out and obtain, God knows from where. He spent money as if there were no limit. But no corners were ever cut, and the picture was brought in under budget. I must tell you that I'm intensely proud of it, as proud as of anything I've ever done."

The next morning there is no shooting, and I have been invited to the condominium Huston has leased on Lake Ontario. I meet Gladys Hill, his longtime amanuensis, who has written a number of his screenplays and who has just arrived to discuss something about the script of *Phobia*. After she leaves, he begins his story, skipping his sickly, book-filled childhood. "After I got out of school," he says, "I did a little boxing, then went to Mexico, where I was given an honorary commission in the army and trained horses for them. Then I got married, and I began writing because I didn't want to work. So I wrote some stories, and, of all things, they were published by H. L. Mencken in the *American Mercury*. I came to New York, got a job on the old *Graphic,* and turned out to be the world's worst reporter, absolutely no talent in that direction at all. I wrote a book, *Frankie and Johnnie*, illustrated by Miguel Covarrubias. It was then that Herman Shumlin brought me out to

Hollywood to work for Sam Goldwyn as a writer. But as soon as I came out there, Herman was fired, and that was the end of that job."

"This was in 1931," he recalls, "and Universal had a script they wanted dad to star in. I read it and saw that it would never be a good picture but it could be improved upon. So dad said, 'John, would you write out your suggestions,' which I did. The picture was called *A House Divided,* Paul Kohner was the producer—I was his first client when he became an agent, and I still am his client—and it was directed by Willie Wyler, who was then beginning his career."

"I worked for dad and Willie again in their next picture, *Law and Order,*" he goes on, "and worked on *Murders in the Rue Morgue* with Bela Lugosi and Sidney Fox for Bob Florey and then—." Huston stops and says vaguely, "I was going through a bad streak so I went to Europe to try to extricate myself. I was in Europe through most of the thirties, drifting somewhat, then came to New York and drifted some more. I went back to Hollywood, but this time I had immediate acceptance there. At that point I wanted to write films more than anything else; writing was my only thought.

"I wrote *Jezebel, The Amazing Dr. Clitterhouse, Juarez,* which I wrote with Aeneas MacKenzie and Wolfgang Reinhardt, *Dr. Ehrlich's Magic Bullet, High Sierra,* which I wrote with W. R. Burnett, and *Sergeant York,* which I wrote with three other people, and then several scripts which weren't made until years later—*The Killers, The Stranger,* and *Three Strangers.*"

"MacKenzie, Reinhardt, and I had spent about a year writing *Juarez,*" he recalls, "and we wrote, I must say, a fine script. Hal Wallis said it was the finest he'd ever read. Then Paul Muni came into it and complained that he didn't have as many lines as Maximilian and Carlotta did, so he just tore the script apart and ruined it. I knew that if I'd been the director instead of William Dieterle, this wouldn't have happened. So I knew I was going to have to be responsible for the things I wrote, that that was the only way I could survive."

"So I had it put into my contract," he continues, "that if they took up my option as a writer at Warners, they'd have to allow me to direct a picture. They were delighted when I picked a property they already owned and had made twice before without success. That was *The Maltese Falcon,* of course, and I had a great champion in Henry Blanke, who produced *Juarez.* I want to tell you that Blanke and Hal Wallis were the best producers I ever encountered. Those two men were entirely responsible for the great years at Warners. Wallis was a very solid man who had a real imagination, though he would never declare himself on the side of culture or aesthetics. But he had a real appreciation of quality, and under him Blanke was able to do *Pasteur, Zola,* and *Ehrlich,* which were a complete departure for that time."

Returning to *The Maltese Falcon,* Huston says, "I considered the Hammett novel practically a screenplay, and we had a wonderful time making the movie, no sense of making a classic, of course. Everybody just had a lot of fun doing what they were doing and liking themselves doing it. Imagine assembling that cast today—Bogey, Mary Astor, Greenstreet and Lorre, Gladys George, and the rest. That was something that only the old studio system could supply. And remember that outside of Greenstreet, who made his movie debut in this, everyone else had had their shots. Even Bogart's stock wasn't that high at that time. He'd already done *High Sierra,* but Warners wanted me to use George Raft. He walked around with bodyguards; I didn't want him, but I was prepared to deal with him. Then Raft happily decided that it wasn't for him, so, fortunately, I was spared."

"Perhaps there were some things that were wrong with the old studio system, but on the whole," Huston goes on, "I think its death has been a great loss. Its troubles began with the antimonopoly ruling and subsequent divorce of its theaters from the companies that owned them. Now, theoretically, I was all for that, but as it happened, it was responsible for the end of the studios."

"While we were under contract," he recalls, "our daily and future lives were assured, so we could afford to strive for quality. Nowadays, writers just want to finish their assignment and get on with the next one—it's all part of the package deal. But before, writers were under contract at so much a week, and with each success their aspirations rose and so did their economic status. Virtue was more than amply rewarded, which it isn't today. There is no way I could have made any of the movies I made through *The Asphalt Jungle* except under the studio system."

Following *The Maltese Falcon,* Huston made *In This Our Life* with Bette Davis and Olivia de Havilland. This was a steaming portrait of the Deep South with Davis doing most of the steaming. Walter Huston accepted a cameo in it, just as he had done in *The Maltese Falcon,* to bring John luck, but the picture was not one of his son's great successes. Huston next made *Across the Pacific,* again with Bogart, Astor, and Greenstreet. In the midst of filming, the Japanese bombed Pearl Harbor, and he was called into the army.

There is a story that may or may not be apocryphal that Huston received his orders just as he reached the climax of the movie, with Bogart being captured by the Japanese. Huston immediately wrote in a scene in which a dozen men faced Bogart with drawn guns while he was tied to a chair. Huston then walked onto the set, and while everybody waited for him to get Bogart out of this precarious situation, Huston merely smiled and waved and said, "Good-bye, everybody, I'm off to the wars."

It was just before the war began that Huston commenced his mild flirtation with the Broadway stage when he directed Walter Huston in *A Passenger to Bali*. "The truth is," Huston says, "that I was never really interested in the theater, but dad asked me to direct this play—I had never done a play before—and it flopped. But then Howard Koch and I wrote *In Time to Come*, which was about Woodrow Wilson and the League of Nations. Though it had a fairly respectable run and even won the drama critics award that year, would you believe it, I never even saw it."

"Then in 1946, when I came out of the army," he recalls, "I staged Sartre's *No Exit* on Broadway with Annabella, Claude Dauphin, and Ruth Ford. *No Exit* introduced existentialism to the United States, and the critics were confounded by it. I think they thought it was just another French triangle play. In any case, it closed in four weeks, and I went back to Hollywood to prepare *The Treasure of the Sierra Madre*."

This turned out to be Huston's second masterpiece, although at least one member of the cast had his doubts about the project—his father. I remember his father telling me before the picture started, "My son John wants me to do this B. Traven story, *The Treasure of the Sierra Madre*. It's a good story and a wonderful part, but he wants me to play it without my teeth, and I'll be darned if I work without them." Fortunately, he changed his mind and gave one of the most penetrating performances of his life—and won the Oscar for it.

Huston then turned his attention to *Key Largo,* based on Maxwell Anderson's play, which had failed on Broadway. He cast Bogart, Lauren Bacall, Edward G. Robinson, Claire Trevor, and Lionel Barrymore and made a film which was markedly different from the play. It was at this point that Huston, Bogart, Bacall, and many other important Hollywood figures began to busy themselves with politics. The McCarthy years were on their way in, and the Hollywood Ten stood accused of being Communists.

Huston still speaks of that period with passionate indignation. "The Mc-

Carthy years," he says, "weren't just a matter of censorship. Suddenly people were made into circus performers. If they didn't jump through hoops, they were disgraced, ruined, and destroyed. I had a great sense of shame at that time. Phil Dunne and I started the Committee for the First Amendment. Willie Wyler was in it, the Epstein brothers, and many others who flew to Washington to attend the hearings. None of us were Communists.

"The only one on that flight who was, as it later turned out, was Sterling Hayden. After that, we were all branded, though McCarthy hadn't reached his height yet. I went on to make *We Were Strangers, The Asphalt Jungle, The Red Badge of Courage,* and then I left the country because I could not abide what McCarthy was doing to America. That had a lot to do with my not coming back here. Except for three or four pictures I made in the United States over the last thirty years, I've remained abroad. I did not want to come back into an atmosphere that was permeated with the stench of that dreadful man. In some ways, I trace the Nixon years with its disgrace to the McCarthy period."

"I made *The African Queen* in Africa and England," he recounts, "*Moulin Rouge* in France, *Beat the Devil* in Italy, and *Moby Dick* in England. *The African Queen* was designed simply as a great entertainment. I think it was the one picture Bogey made in which he was not playing himself but doing a characterization. He would constantly say to me, 'John, keep me on it, don't let me get off.' He proved that when he stopped being himself he could still be an actor. He was superb as a little man who was way over his head, not knowing what to do about it. He was totally befuddled before Katie Hepburn and life."

"Katie didn't know me when she agreed to be in the picture," he says, "but she'd heard stories about Bogey and me drinking and roistering all the time. We put on a great show for her, pretending to be drunk even if we weren't and writing dirty words on her mirror. So she set about to reform us. There's something of the reformer in Kate anyway, and wasn't she wonderful in the movie?"

I ask Huston what ever made him cast Sterling Hayden in the lead of *The Asphalt Jungle,* when Hayden was then simply known as the hunk of man who had married Madeleine Carroll. Huston laughs and replies, "I always found Sterling a very interesting man. I used him way before he began to blossom. He was known then for his physique rather than his talent. But physically, he looked the part of what they call a gorilla, the strong man in a robbery. In recent years, Sterling's personality has become richer. There is a kind of kingliness or priestliness about him now. I can see him conducting a pagan rite, his beard blowing in all directions." I ask him what he had seen in Bogart when he picked him to play Sam Spade. "I saw in him what audiences today see in him," he says. "He was not a man of great stature physically, but the camera saw something in him that we, and even he, didn't."

"I'm always surprised that so many good actors are like the characters they portray on the screen," he continues. "Take Clark Gable. He was very much Gable offscreen. When I was directing him in *The Misfits,* I would see something he could do that would sharpen his performance, and I'd tell him. Now, he sought direction, really wanted it, but I saw that what he did by himself was much better than anything I could think of for him to do. He knew instinctively what was right and natural for him, though he didn't always trust it."

The next time I see Huston, it's the day before he is to be honored with a gala tribute by the Film Society of Lincoln Center. He is tanned and robust looking in his suite at the Pierre, happy and grateful for the honor he will be accorded. Paul Newman, Lauren Bacall, Richard Burton, and Eli Wallach will be among those giving him testimonials. I recall that Jack Nicholson, who has been living with Huston's daughter, Anjelica, for many years, once said that Huston was the only man in this business who has never had to make a comeback because he's always been up there. I think Nicholson is wrong. Huston has been down there more often than up. It's simply that when he's up, he's so spectacularly up that one forgets and forgives his previous downs. I still cannot believe that he made *The Barbarian and the Geisha, Sinful Davey,* or *The Mackintosh Man.*

"One of the biggest disappointments in my career was when the critics and public did not respond to *Moby Dick,*" he admits. "It eventually paid for itself, but it wasn't a big financial success, and that bothered me. I've developed a philosophy across the years about failure. If you're going to be a professional about it, once you complete a picture, it's on its own. I love to hear that a picture is a success, and I regret when it's not, but by the time it's out, I'm on to something else, so I can't kill myself."

Returning to *Moby Dick,* Huston says, "They took it out on Gregory Peck, which I think was unfair, because I liked him and I liked the film. Still do. I just saw it again the other day. As a matter of fact, I think that Greg is quite remarkable. He's not the ranting, raving psychotic of the book, nor the John Barrymore version of Ahab, which colored it forever for audiences."

Huston went on to make a series of forgettables, among them *The Roots of Heaven,* a film Huston calls "one of the most unfortunate pictures I ever made. I don't think it began to reach its potential, and I hold myself fully responsible for it. I hold others to account for several of my failures, but in the case of *Roots, A Walk with Love and Death,* and *The Kremlin Letter,* I was given every freedom. I chose those stories, helped write them, directed them, and virtually produced them, and they didn't turn out well. I feel responsible to the principals, in this case, Dick Zanuck and David Brown—and Darryl Zanuck, I owe a great deal to him. He was a decent man, full of moxie, and he wore his Boy Scout badge at the first dragon or sign of trouble. When I'd apologize to him for one of my failures, he'd say, 'Don't take all the credit. I gave you the go-ahead, didn't I?' A fine man."

I ask Huston now about his problems with Montgomery Clift. Both of Clift's biographers have painted Huston as a villain who tortured Clift all through the making of *Freud.* Huston replies immediately, eyes flashing, "I found him to be not a pleasant man," he says. "I shied away from him. He was, or had been, a wonderful actor, but I got the remnants of him, not the man himself. He was pretty shredded by the time he came to me. The troubles I had with him were not his fault. He was just not capable any more. The accident to his face had done great interior damage to him. He had been very good in *The Misfits,* but he had very few lines in it, mostly colloqualisms, and I was taken in by his performance and thought he could do *Freud,* but he couldn't."

Huston then turned to an eclectic set of films—including *The Night of the Iguana, Casino Royale,* and *Reflections in a Golden Eye*—but in 1972 he was back again in peak form with *Fat City.* "That was about an aspect of American life that I knew quite well at one time," he says. "Not the skid row aspect but the boxing world, and I think it turned out well." So did *The Man Who Would Be King,* which was his best sheer entertainment since *The African Queen.* "I wanted to make that thirty years ago with Bogart and Gable," he recalls, "but it didn't happen, and it went on not happening until all this time later."

I ask him how, as a director, he works with actors, and he replies, "I have no special system, but I direct as little as possible always. I don't want an actor to give my performance. I want to get as much as I can out of him. I'll go along with him. If he's a method actor, why then I'll be a method director. Some actors like to talk about their part at great length so that they can ease themselves into the role. Well, that's fine with me, I'll talk. I've never found the formula that would work in every case."

In the sixties, possibly to help finance his expensive life-style in Galway, Ireland, where he lived in feudal splendor, raising horses, writer-director Huston became an actor again—he had appeared in four films between 1928 and 1930—in Otto Preminger's *The Cardinal*. Since then he has appeared in some seventeen films, ranging from *Chinatown* all the way down to *De Sade* and *Candy*, and including Orson Welles's still unfinished *The Other Side of the Wind*.

Huston has little to say about his career as an actor, possibly because he considers it an easy, comfortable way to make money, just as he has accepted a number of directorial assignments that he didn't particularly relish. "Unlike the material I had to work with in *Wise Blood,* which was solid and true," he says, "I've made a number of pictures where I had to conceal all the bad things and try to display the little that was good. Many pictures I made, too many, presented that exact problem. I have a genius for getting into that kind of bind—mostly because I needed money. But now I've sold the house in Ireland, and I live in Puerto Vallarta—back to the jungle and facing the sea—where my life is irreducibly simple. The whales sail past, and the dolphins, and the manta rays leap out of the water, and I look on in fascination, just as a kid would." He does not always stand with mouth agape in Puerta Vallarta. It is where he wrote his autobiography, *An Open Book,* which will be published this month.

Of his present picture, Huston says, "*Phobia* is a thriller. I think it's quite well done, technically. It's a broad thriller, the premise is barely conceivable, so if it's brought off, it's a double triumph. I think it may be quite successful. I'm particularly enthusiastic about my next picture, *Escape to Victory*. It's about a soccer game in Germany during World War II between the Nazis and an assortment of Allied prisoners of war. Evan Jones, an Australian, wrote the script, and I'm leaving in three days for Hungary, where I'll film it with Michael Caine, Sylvester Stallone, and Max Von Sydow."

When I ask Huston what he thinks of the books and articles written about him and his style and the similarities between his films, he says, "I have great admiration for Fellini and Bergman, who create their own films. But I'm eclectic. I like doing one thing very different from another. I don't even recognize a style in my work. If there is a style, it's to adapt myself to the material consistently, and as it changes in each film, so does the style. I see each picture I make as being totally different from any other."

"And by the same token," he adds, "I see no line of continuity in my films, but that's beside the point. If others do, so much the better. I can see certain things that I've used more than once—the hunt being more important than the kill, the quest more important than the prize, the comradeship of men under fire—but I think you'll find those in a lot of stories in some of my films. I think I fly to the opposite after each picture I've ever made."

Then he smiles and says, "I'm a shallow soul, actually, who likes variety."

Saints and Stinkers: The *Rolling Stone* Interview

PETER S. GREENBERG / 1981

IN THE RAREFIED ATMOSPHERE of the entertainment industry, no one has lived longer—or better—than John Huston. It can be safely assumed that no other American film director—not even his friend Orson Welles—has been as worshiped or vilified. On first meeting him, the man seems to be a larger-than-life and less-than-perfect living legend. His face is a wrinkled road map, each line a historical marker of an incredible life, part Hemingway novel, part Bogart script.

Huston has been married—and divorced—five times; he's been a reporter and short-story writer, a lieutenant in the Mexican cavalry, an amateur lightweight boxing champ, a street artist, a millionaire, and barely solvent. He's been the subject of three biographies in addition to his autobiography, *An Open Book*.

Now seventy-four, Huston is still very much a "bankable" director. His movies have ranged from those of genius (*The Treasure of the Sierra Madre*) to the merely pedestrian (*Phobia*), but not one has failed to generate a certain excitement about the myth and the truth of the director labeled a "man's man." With each film, Huston seemed to take on the color of his surroundings. "In Africa I was a white hunter, in Reno I was a gambler," he says with a laugh. "At sea I was Ahab after the whale."

In Budapest last summer to make *Escape to Victory*, starring Sylvester Stallone and Michael Caine, Huston seemed at ease with the picture and with

From *Rolling Stone*, no. 337, February 19, 1981, 25–25 +. © 1981 by Straight Arrow Publishers, Inc. All rights reserved. Reprinted by permission.

himself. He also appeared to be going through the paces somewhat mechanically, as though the film had no meaning for him.

Still, the plot has all the ingredients of what some critics have come to call a John Huston film. There's an Allied POW soccer team playing a grudge match with their German captors. It is an opportunity for Huston to explore some of his traditional themes: the strengths in weak men (*Wise Blood*) as well as the weaknesses in strong men (*The Asphalt Jungle*).

Outside one of the POW barracks constructed for the film in the Hungarian countryside, Michael Caine was waiting to do a scene. "At first I didn't know what was going on with the man," says Caine, who last worked with Huston on *The Man Who Would Be King*. "We were on location in Morocco, and I'd do a scene with Sean [Connery], and we'd finish it, and John would say 'cut,' and then we'd do the next scene on the first take as well. I never thought the movie would work. And then I saw the movie. It was wonderful. Most directors today don't know what they want—so they shoot everything they can think of. They use the camera like a machine gun. John uses it like a sniper."

Behind Caine, the unforgettably deep, euphonious, and almost too well-paced voice of John Huston bellowed for action. The scene began and ended without a flaw. There were no retakes. "That's fine," Huston said to the crew calmly, his signal that the scene was a keeper and that the next shot should be set up. He was actually ahead of schedule.

I had been warned that John Huston might be a tough interview. "He's exceedingly polite and cordial," a close friend of Huston's had told me, "but he's been through these things hundreds of times before on dozens of movies. That's why he wrote his book. He didn't want to keep talking about the legends and the stories."

At first, the friend was right. Huston was cooperative but not terribly expansive. But at the end of the second session, Huston invited me to play poker with him that weekend. Anyone who has done any research on John Huston knows the man is a gambler, that he has a history of playing for high stakes, and that as the newest pigeon in this game, I stood the biggest chance of losing the house, the Master Charge and the matching set of luggage.

The game started promptly at one on Sunday afternoon. There were seven of us in Huston'a Budapest hotel suite, and the table was full with players and guests. Only one rule, a Huston tradition: women were invited to watch but not to play.

It was a table-stakes game, with more than a few thousand Hungarian forints on the wooden table. I think I developed a rash. There were no cute variations to the games; we played five-card draw or seven-card stud. No wild cards. Throughout, Huston maintained the ultimate poker face. It revealed neither garbage in his hand when he was bluffing nor a full house when he wasn't.

Eight and a half hours later, the marathon game ended. Before the cigarette smoke had lifted, two big winners had emerged. John Huston. And me. We each had won the equivalent of $500. We shook hands and smiled. I thanked him again for the invitation and suggested we continue our interview the next day. "Sorry," he snapped, with the same poker expression on his face. "I don't talk to winners."

But I had somehow passed the test. The next morning, our poker victories behind us, Huston was relaxed and talkative, and the interview proceeded in sessions lasting about one hour each for the next seven days.

In watching you work, I can't help but notice that you're not doing many retakes on scenes.
It's simply that when I shoot a scene, I know the way I'm going to cut it later. And that style is known as "cutting with the camera." If you make a mistake, why, you're in trouble. So you'd better *not* make mistakes.

Have you made some of those mistakes?
I have. But not often.

Certainly there are a couple of pictures that you probably wish you hadn't made.
There certainly are.

For example?
Well, some of the pictures that I most wish I hadn't made were pretty good pictures at one time. I mean, I wasn't responsible for their being bad. There was one called *Sinful Davey*. The executive producer, Walter Mirisch, wanted to try various things. I said they wouldn't work, and he gave me his promise that if he tried them and they didn't, he would restore the picture to the original cut. He gave me this promise and went back on it.

Another picture that was good for five minutes was *The Barbarian and the*

Geisha. And it was made into just a *ghastly* picture, an awful one. John Wayne was responsible for that one.

How did that happen?
Well, I had finished the picture and gone off to Europe and Africa to make *The Roots of Heaven.* Once I left, the decks were clear for John Wayne, who was the star and who had great influence and push and style in the studio. He didn't fancy himself in some scenes, so he got them to shoot those scenes over. When I saw the picture eventually, I can't tell you how bad it was. It was just terrible. They didn't even know how to cut a scene.

And The Roots of Heaven?
Roots of Heaven was my fault. Darryl Zanuck gave me only one requirement; that was Greco playing the woman; otherwise, I was to call the shots. And I did. The whole thing was done to my requirements. And the script was no good. By the time I got to Europe, all I had were excuses, but no excuse is good enough. The director *is* responsible. Darryl had established the company in Africa, and I hoped to make changes while we were going on. I just got myself in deeper and deeper and made what could have been a very fine picture into a not very good picture.

In the business, did that hurt you as a director?
No, I don't think so. When I assumed the blame for this, Darryl immediately published a reply saying, "What do you mean, John is to blame? I was as much to blame, if not more so." But that's not true.

You're hereby acknowledging all—
Absolutely.

When I was talking to producer John Foreman about The Mackintosh Man, *he told me a story that I would love you to confirm or deny here. He said that he once looked at you and asked, "Why did you do this movie?" And you said, "For the money."*
Oh, sure. Certainly. I've done a number of pictures for that reason, because I needed the money. Simply because you're doing it for money doesn't mean that you aren't making every effort to make it a better picture. And then there are the pictures that are done just for the love of the picture.

Like The Man Who Would Be King?

Yes, and it was extraordinary how little it was made for. Something like $6 million. Twice before, I'd been about to make it, and each time, something happened. Originally, it was for Humphrey Bogart, and then Bogie died. And the next time, it was Clark Gable. Then Gable died, so we put it away until one night in Ireland, I was in my library with John Foreman. He saw a portfolio of sketches that had been done for the movie. We cast Sean Connery and Michael Caine. I believe Connery and Caine gave better performances than either Bogart or Gable could have, because they are the real thing. They are those characters.

You and Gladys Hill were nominated for Best Screenplay Adapted from Other Material, and there were some other nominations as well for that movie. Were you upset more people didn't see it?

Yeah, yeah. The picture wasn't well presented. Allied Artists eventually went bankrupt to save their asses. And they were seamy. I never got my full salary.

Wasn't David Begelman involved, too?

Yes. Begelman had part of the European distribution.

You felt that he was a trustworthy individual?

Yeah. And certainly the best-educated, the most refined man in that whole bunch.

Were you surprised, then, when Begelman was caught forging Cliff Robertson's signature on a $10,000 check?

Rather. Surprised; not shocked. I'm not easily shocked. I'm too sympathetic toward the criminal mentality. Thomas Mann saw a very profound relationship between the criminal and the artist. So do I. I know what he meant. They're both outlaws.

The movie Wise Blood *didn't exactly make you rich either, did it?*

No, but it was one of the finest movies I think I've ever made. It all happened because a young man named Michael Fitzgerald came down to Puerto Vallarta and brought a copy of the book, and I read it. Fascinated by it. And he asked, "Would you like to make a picture?" And I said, "Yes, I would, indeed, but I'm going to have trouble getting the money." Financing for a picture like that isn't easy to come by because it's not box office. It never had a chance to be box office.

Why was that?
Because no major distribution company wanted to release it. It wasn't commercial. So eventually it had to be given to an art-theater group.

You made the movie for $1 million in a time when $1 million movies aren't being made anymore, in a time when everybody thinks that success has to cost thirty times that much. Do you ever wonder how they're spending the money?
Actually, I'm appalled some of the time. There's no justification for it. It's all very well to give people entertainment, but that, too, should be kept within limits, when Biafra is still a star. And going as far overboard as some of them do is, I think, objectionable, almost an obscenity. *Wise Blood* was originally supposed to cost $2 million. But it was finally brought in at $1.6 million. But much more important than that is the fact that it got undoubtedly the finest reviews of any picture of that year, universally. No question about it. And yet it could not get commercial distribution.

When you do a movie like that, and it gets great reviews, and you bring it in for $1.6 million, and it goes nowhere—
Of course you become cynical.

You mean to tell me that at your age, you've finally become cynical?
It's too late to become *anything*.

You don't really believe that, do you?
I am what I am.

There are many who have tried to analyze a sort of consistency in your work. I know you would argue that there is none, but a lot of critics look upon a John Huston film as a John Huston film.
I don't know what you're talking about or what they're talking about. It is a John Huston film if I wrote it and directed it—like Charlie Chaplan did his films. That's what constitutes a John Huston film.

What about a John Huston-style film? Some say that your films are men's films, like The Man Who Would Be King *or* The Treasure of the Sierra Madre. *Is that your style?*

You're calling the shots in this regard, I'm not.

No I'm not, I'm asking.
No, you're saying that those are John Huston types of films. I don't recognize them as being different from *The Asphalt Jungle* or *Reflections in a Golden Eye.* Is that a John Huston film? About an army captain who's a cocksucker? Not really, I don't think.

There have been critics in the past who have tried to say that a John Huston film involves men against unusual odds that show the weaknesses of men, strong men. And yet you take a look at African Queen, *and the strongest character there is—*
Oh, those are formulas they like to fall on. I don't believe in formulas.

You know what I'm saying. You find it curious.
I know what you're saying. I don't see it myself, particularly. Now and then there is a continuity, I suppose, but a hidden one. A deep analysis would probably reveal the real continuity, the deep current of intention.

What are those intentions?
I said a deep, profound analysis would reveal. I didn't say *I* know what they are.

You have always been considered a "bankable" director. And yet you've always had a money problem; you've seemed to cut yourself out of profitable pictures and cut yourself in on some bombs.
Well, I think my mistake, so far as money is concerned, is somewhat broader in nature. I've spent it before I've made it. Instead of acquiring money, I acquired debts. It was always on the come.

Except in poker.
You could say that. I think I'm a pretty good poker player. And I've won some money.

What was the toughest game you ever played?
It was with Mike Todd, the producer. He brought along a couple of profes-sional gamblers, and when one made a bet, the other would raise it to bring

the pot up. It's legal enough; I mean, it's not cheating, but it can be scary. And I saw what was happening.

What were the stakes?
High stakes. And five-card stud. Four up. And I won the biggest pot I ever had, on a pair of nines.

How much money, do you remember?
It was more than $20,000.

Is that the most money you've ever won?
Oh, in a poker game. I've won much more money on a horse.

You've been quoted as saying that you married a schoolgirl, a gentlewoman, a ballerina, an actress, and a crocodile. Is that correct?
That's exactly it.

In your book, you say that the liaisons that you have had were often more interesting than the marriages.
Than some of the marriages, I suppose. I think of them equally with marriages. I think marriage is passing out of its form anyway.

Your divorce rate isn't exactly helping it.
No, I've done a great deal for it.

Have you?
Well, certainly. I've done it five times.

Every time you did get married, though—did you ever think this would be the one?
Each time, always. Yup.

While we're on the subject, are there any women you wish you had married?
Yes.

Who, for instance?
Suzanne Flon, a French actress. She's still unmarried.

You mean to tell me you're still considering it?
No.

No more marriages. What about Ava Gardner?
She's a very dear friend, but no romance.

Not even a mild crush?
I did make a pass at Ava very early on, when I knew her. And she wanted no part of me. That was it.

With the exception of Ava Gardner, would you consider yourself generally successful with women in your life?
No complaints. Let's just say that women have been kind.

And have you been kind to women?
Generally. I've had very fortunate relationships.

How many women, children, and offspring of offspring are you supporting right now?
Quite a number. I wouldn't want to start counting. I could in two minutes. But I won't.

I get the feeling that there can be no middle ground in trying to describe John Huston. There are people who love you dearly and people who would do anything to rewrite history about you.
I don't give much thought to such matters. My ruminations and introspections haven't very much to do with my own character. Probably if it had, my character would have improved somewhat over the years.

In your own personal hall of fame, is there an actor you would want to work with again, more than any other?
Oh, several actors who I like working with enormously. Bob Mitchum, right on top. Richard Burton, on top.

Who would be at the bottom?
George C. Scott—no, that's not true. He's a very fine actor. A very fine actor.

Now that you mention it, what did *happen between you and Scott?*
It was during the making of *The Last Run*. In the beginning, I was doing it for
the money. Then my conscience got the better of me. And then I began to
work on it. And Scott's a fool. I wouldn't say he's a fool—he's a fine actor,
and that's *all*. That says it. He's not fine at anything else that I know of. He's
a shitheel, in fact. And I left the picture.

Okay, you're not a great admirer of him as an individual. But tell me why.
Well, he's a pain in the ass, that's all. He takes advantage of situations. He
pursued Ava in a terrible way, terrible. I think Ava liked him in the beginning,
you know. But he was just quite impossible.

Did you ever work with Ronald Reagan?
Never. But we almost did in *Treasure of the Sierra Madre*. He was a contract
player at Warner Brothers, and it certainly would have been to their advantage to have one of their own men play in the picture. But whatever his
reasons were, he didn't want to. And I was delighted. God, he's a bore. And
a bad actor. Besides, he has a low order of intelligence. With a certain cunning. And not animal cunning—human cunning. Animal cunning is too fine
an expression for him. He's inflated, he's egotistical. He's one of those people
who thinks he is right. And he's *not* right. He's not right about anything.

The Misfits *must have been an incredible experience—not just because of the movie
itself, but because so many of the people involved died soon after. Did you have any
premonition that it was going to be anyone's last movie?*
It was more than a premonition. I was absolutely certain that Marilyn was
doomed. There was evidence right before me every day. She was incapable of
rescuing herself or of being rescued by anyone else. And it affected her work.
We had to stop the picture while she went to a hospital for two weeks.

Did the fact that Arthur Miller was on the set help or hurt it?
They were having difficulties, and it certainly didn't help matters. On the
other hand, I don't think anything would have made things any worse. The
problems were all within her.

I remember Marilyn before she had any recognition at all. I was making a
film at Columbia with Johnny Garfield and Jennifer Jones, and she'd come
over and watch. A very pretty little girl, very young, very pretty. I discovered

they'd told her she was going to have a test. And I thought it was kind of a
come-on they were giving her, like so many producers did to struggling actresses. So I said, "Sure, I'll make a test with you. We'll do it in color. And
Johnny Garfield here will play opposite you. We'll make it a very fine test."
She never came on the set again, the studio whisked her away so fast.

The next time I saw her, Johnny Hyde brought her around to see me about
doing *The Asphalt Jungle*. He was her agent. I can't say now that back then I
had a notion that she would ever become the kind of star that she did. But
there was something about her, a kind of pristineness, and innocence, too.
And I remember a magazine article about her in which her masseur was
quoted. He said her flesh was different than anyone else's. But there was that
freshness about her, and that endured. And you'll see it . . . it's on the screen
in *The Misfits*. It's still there.

Despite all the problems she was going through?
Despite them, even though she was on her last legs.

Couldn't you get close enough to talk to her?
Oh, yes. And she was not easy to talk to. If she had a few drinks, she'd start
to talk. And I wouldn't like this to be said, but, you know, she'd talk out
against Arthur Miller, right in his presence, to me, and with others around.
And say things that embarrassed me, and certainly must have made him
cringe. He would pretend he wasn't listening. And all my sympathies were
with him. And I began to, I, I . . . I didn't like what she was doing to him.

Do you think she was aware of what she was doing to him?
She had to know. She was . . . there were sides to Marilyn that I didn't know
and didn't inquire into. I mean, there were things about her that . . . I've
heard people who knew her very well put her way down. When I discovered
that she'd become the sex goddess of America, I thought it was almost funny.
And I didn't take it all that seriously. In fact, I didn't take it seriously at all.
Then her figure loomed bigger and bigger. I remember Jean-Paul Sartre saying that he thought she was the hottest actress alive.

Did that change your impression of Sartre?
Oh, no. No, no. But it was a kind of eye-opener to realize that Europeans
held her in very high regard. Much higher than just a sex goddess. They

thought she was a very fine actress, too. And she was, oddly enough. Not an actress in the technical sense, but . . . she had that ability to go down within herself and pull up an emotion and give it.

How bad was her drinking problem?
Bad. She had to take pills to get up and pills to go to bed. Finally a doctor on the picture refused to give her any more medication. So Marilyn got it elsewhere. I talked at the time to Arthur Miller, before I knew how or what the relationship between them was, or rather, wasn't. It was, in fact, being just torn apart. He wrote the movie for her trying to save her, and, I think, the picture was made in an attempt to save their marriage. He was making every effort. But I remember saying to Arthur that whoever—and this was pointed toward Arthur, and I know I was way off base—but to allow her to have drugs, anybody who allowed her to have drugs, was just as irresponsible as she was.

Why do you think you were off base?
Because Arthur had lost all power to do anything about her, and I didn't know it. He was out, and I didn't know it. And I was talking to him as though he were there and responsible and would have some control. And I said, "You know she's going, and I see it coming. She'll be dead or in an institution within three years."

Oh, it was a tragic thing to witness, particularly since there was something ever so appealing about her. What interests me now—and this has been gone over ad nauseam—is the fact that interest in her endures. It just is . . . they're asking the same questions—you are—that they were fifteen years ago."

What does that mean to you?
Well, simply that she's still alive.

While Monroe's death didn't surprise you that much, I assume that Clark Gable's did.
Completely. Completely.

What about all the stories that surfaced later that you worked Gable too hard, that you insisted he do his own stunts?
Nonsense. He didn't do his own stunts in *The Misfits*.

Did he want to?
No. No. Look, as a rule, good actors don't want to do their stunts, for a very good reason. They're doing a stunt man out of a job. It's not a question of courage. Sometimes in scenes when Bogie was, my God, flipping a pancake over, he liked the stunt men so much that he wanted to see them get whatever loose change there was around.

But now and then you need the actor to do it himself. If he can, it simplifies things. The outstanding example of that in my career was Gregory Peck on the whale in *Moby Dick*. It was a dangerous scene, but he wanted to do it, and when we finished, and I said, "That's it," he said, "Let's do it again."

Well, you do add a touch of realism all the time. I mean, using real leeches on Bogart in African Queen *was a little much.*
He'd rather have had a stunt man do that [*much laughter*]. But when we brought the leeches around, we made sure they were chemically pure leeches. They really were.

Almost every movie you make is filmed on location. Any movies you would rather have done on a back lot?
Heavens, no. If I have a trademark at all, it's that I prefer to make my movies where they happen. I was on one of the first location pictures, *Treasure of the Sierra Madre*. And *African Queen* would have been very difficult to do on the back lot of some studio. The point is that in a sense, it's easier to just do it than to fabricate it.

Was Moby Dick *the most wretched location experience you've ever had?*
No, it was in Africa making *The Roots of Heaven*. That was the most physically difficult. Temperatures were quite unbelievable. One didn't eat, myself included. But *Moby Dick* was difficult. It was the worst winter in maritime history. Three of our lifeboats capsized. We just had one storm after another, wretched storms. Certainly once we were on our way to the bottom. And three times I *thought* we were. We had started out with three mechanical whales, and we lost two of them. And I knew that if we lost the third one, we were shit out of luck. This was our last hope. So I just got in the whale, and I stayed there. I knew they'd have to rescue it if I was in it. If that whale had gone, the picture would have died. Every day we would go out to sea. That didn't take long, but as soon as we got out, the storms would just sur-

round us—longboats would be separated, and everything would become disordered and chaotic.

I guess by today's standards, if you were that far behind, they might have stopped the picture.
By today's standards, it is nothing to be a few weeks behind. Think of *Apocalypse Now*. I thought there were wonderful things about it, some unbelievable things, but I thought it was a poor picture. It didn't know what to do with itself.

There is no plot to *Heart of Darkness*. It's an atmosphere, and it's a wonderful evocation, but it isn't a story with a beginning, a middle, and an end.

And there were absurdities in the film. I mean, why do they all go up the river in a boat, when they can take a helicopter and go up the river? And so on. The nonsense of that American placement of lights and so on and the bombing area. . . . And showing a bridge all lit up at night. It's absurd. Coppola took refuge. He escaped into the metaphysical at the finish. And, you know, shithouse writers have been doing that since time immemorial.

The problem is that the concept of story can very easily be misunderstood. I mean, a story is not necessarily something that's as wooden as a first, second, and third act, or that comes out with a moral and a message or something that's all underscored and in italics and capitalized. That's not what I mean. *Peer Gynt* has a dramatic structure. And even Tennessee Williams has a dramatic structure. When we were doing *African Queen*—and we were just about to film it—I discovered *myself* without a story. That's why I say I can put myself in Coppola's boots. Luckily I found the ending well before starting the cameras.

At what point did you decide that you were going to let Katharine Hepburn and Bogart sink that ship?
I wrote the finish in Africa. I didn't feel that it should have an unhappy ending. It wasn't that kind of a picture.

If people were obsessed with Monroe, they seem equally preoccupied today with the Bogart mystique. Is Bogart easier to explain?
Ah, yes. I understand it better. Bogie came in with a character who was highly moral to his own code. A code of individualism. And that came across.

I think the young people recognized this thing of laying down your own rules for yourself and abiding by them, rather than the orthodox.

Speaking of sticking by your principles, did you ever have a fight with Bogart?
I didn't.

Not even a serious argument?
Well, I took him to the nose one time.

What was that about?
He was a bore [*laughs*].

Like Ronald Reagan?
No, no. Oh, no, no. Heavens no, not that bad. No. At least *he* [Bogart] had something to say. He wanted to be in a race to Hawaii on his boat, *The Santana.* And he was *always* asking when we would finish. And, *oh* Jesus, it just got to be unbearable. And one night he was cross table and loud about it, and I took him to the nose [*chuckles*].

What kind of relationship did you have with Howard Hughes?
Oh, no relationship. We went bowling a couple of times and that was it. He cut quite a figure, too. In bowling, even, he had enormous energy. And there was something so vivid about Howard. Unthinkable, that was an unthinkable death.

You never talked to him after he withdrew?
The most interesting thing about Hughes happened when I helped to form something called the Committee for the First Amendment to fight the communist witch hunting of the House Un-American Activities Committee (HUAC). Hughes had been up before Congress on that plane—the *Spruce Goose*—that he didn't deliver. And he just knocked their brains out and showed them, if they really wanted to get rough, how to play. At the time our group was going to Washington, I was in a restaurant for lunch—not one of the well-known restaurants—and they came to the table with a telephone. It was Howard Hughes. He must have had his secretaries call every restaurant in town until they found me, and he offered me a TWA plane at cost to fly to Washington. And the funny thing is that Howard was very far to the right.

Why do you think he did it?
Oh, he didn't like what Congress was doing, generally, to him or me or anybody.

Was that the last time you talked to him?
That was one of the last times. I accepted his offer, and we had put together
quite a group to go to Washington to protest the constitutionality of the
hearings. There was John Garfield, Gene Kelly, Bogart, Danny Kaye, and Jane
Wyatt. And others. And off we went to Washington. It was a sorry spectacle
to watch those hearings, and our response as a group was miserable. We
didn't make an organized stand against HUAC. In fact, on the way home,
Bogie stopped in Chicago and made a statement to the press that he had
been "ill-advised" to go to Washington with us.

*But you just told me how principled a man Bogart was. Weren't you surprised by
what he did?*
I didn't say that this was personal. I said that it was his image—a part he
played in the pictures. But I was a little surprised by his behavior.

Almost everybody else did it, too. He was just the first in that group. Eventually, the whole fucking country got into line. It got pretty scary, I hope to
tell ya. The magazines that today take such a high moral tone were among
the worst offenders. I'm talking about *Time* and *Newsweek*. You know, they
were all scared. *Despicably* so.

*Well, your wartime experience as a documentary filmmaker was certainly affected
by politics.*
Yes, you could say that. I was in the American Army, in the Signal Corps. My
first picture was made in the Aleutian Islands, and although it was a very
small war out there, the people who were in it were certainly playing for
keeps. They were using a lot of fighters, and most of the time they had no
room for cameramen. Occasionally, I'd squeeze in above the pilot and ride
piggyback into battle in a one-seat plane. They didn't want us up there. Besides, every time I went with them, shit, something awful happened, and I
got to be known as a Jonah. Bombs wouldn't work; people would be shot out
from under me.

There was one crazy son of a bitch named Rey Scott—a cameraman who
loved being shot at. One afternoon, when I returned from a scouting expedi-

tion, there was a letter and his insurance policy and his watch and everything, laid out on a board. He didn't think he was going to come back. But
the bombing raid was a complete success. Afterward, I asked Rey, "What the
hell did you do this for? I told you not to." And he said, "Well, if I'd been a
journalist and this raid got the publicity that I'm sure it will get, I'd have
received a cable from my publisher asking, 'Were you on it?' And if I hadn't
been, I'd have been fired. And I figured I should do as much for my country
as I would have for a newspaper." Believe it or not, it was moving. He was
quite a bird, quite a bird.

Let me guess. He made it all the way through the war, too?
He made it all the way through the war.

And you?
I didn't take one successful photograph during the whole war. But I carried
the cameras as a sort of token. It was my excuse for being there, you know.
On one mission in a B-24, I was shooting over the shoulder of the waist-
gunner. I lower the camera and he's not there. He was dead at my feet. So
then the belly-gunner motioned for me to come back and take the belly-gun.
I dropped the camera and started firing.

I suppose it hit you then that it was no movie.
Sure. I think it's true of all photographers. The camera separates one from
the world. I used to take photos of sporting events for a while. Took shots of
bullfights. One day I realized I wasn't seeing the bullfights, so I put the fucking camera away and that was it. I haven't picked up a camera since. But that
B-24 incident was just the first thing that happened.

The first of many?
Yeah. I was soon sent to Italy and came back with a film about the American
Army taking a small town. It was called *The Battle of San Pietro*. When it was
shown, why, it wasn't very popular. The criticism from the Pentagon was
that it would demoralize the young draftees. And that it was pacifist. And
also because it was very real, very true. And I was really in some disgrace. The
film would never have been shown, except that a few days later, General
George C. Marshall saw it.

I assume he liked it.

Liked it? He said that every young man who was headed for combat must see this picture. At that point, I was suddenly elevated in rank from captain to major and given a medal.

And given a medal for surviving the first showing of your movie?

Yes. And then it was widely shown. And *Let There Be Light* was next. That was my most interesting experience with the government.

Whose idea was that? Was that yours?

No. It was done to reassure industry that men who were released from the army on a section eight were reliable, that they were not lunatics. I followed one group of patients for ten weeks, through its entire period in the hospital. And when they were released back to society from the army, why they were good men. And that's what the picture was about.

This particular group that we photographed happened to show greater progress than any of the other groups. And they became interested in the picture. They loved it, loved doing it. I believe our presence was actually therapeutic. It gave them something to do and centered their thinking and gave a point to their being there.

But when it came to the picture being shown generally, why the army refused. They said it was classified material, not to be seen.

They immediately classified it?

Classified it right away.* I said, "Why?" And they claimed we had violated the right to privacy of the men we'd filmed.

When you think of how movies were made in those days, just about every picture was censored. On almost every picture, they'd have things that they wanted corrected. It started off with not showing cleavage.

There was The Misfits: *that one scene where Marilyn Monroe's right breast was revealed.*

Well, that was censorship. It never made it into the picture, even though

---

Let There Be Light was finally cleared for public showing by the U.S. Army on December 15, 1980, and by the Department of Defense on December 29. The names of the soldiers will be removed from the authorized version to protect privacy.

Marilyn wanted it in the picture. She liked it. But at that time, showing the breast of an actress, God. You know, cleavage.

It was blasphemy.
It was unthinkable. You couldn't even use the word *damn*. It was absurd. I mean, it never really hurt me, but censorship in any film hurts pictures; it damages them. I think the only form of censorship that's at all significant is what the French do—burn the theater down. If the audience is offended, they should do it themselves. But certainly not allow officials to say what you can do and what you can't.

Let's get back to The Misfits. *Montgomery Clift also died shortly after the picture.*
Yeah. It's rumored that it was his last movie, when in fact it wasn't.

But did he show signs of deterioration while making The Misfits?
No. Only during *Freud.* I'm sure they were there during *The Misfits,* but I didn't see them. I wouldn't have had Clift in *Freud* if I had seen the signs.

How did they manifest themselves on the set?
Well, in the first place, he drank. In the beginning, I thought it was just nervousness. Not just on the set either . . . God, I remember he came over when I was working with a psychiatrist in my home in Ireland. John-Paul Sartre had withdrawn from the project, and I was writing the picture. Clift came over. He was a mess. I had a bar in the hall outside the study. He'd drink at this bar. Just take the bottles and turn them up. And then he'd want to be present at my meetings with this doctor. And he was just a nuisance at them. He'd interrupt all the time, not knowing what he was talking about. And finally I locked him out of the study where we were working. And he'd stand in the hall and cry. That's as bad as it had become.

There was something very sympathetic about Monty. He was the male counterpart of Marilyn—of that thing in her that touched people . . . a sense that she was headed for disaster. Well, Monty didn't bring a single tear to my eye, but I still liked him. Liked him and detested him. His behavior was just so offensive. Belching and farting and, you know, stinking. He was awful, awful. I couldn't bear him.

Yet there was something about him that particularly moved women. All of them. There was a little boy thing, I guess, about him. My stepmother was very fond of Monty. Even Rosalind Russell—Monty would take them, squire them around to first nights and concerts of that kind. No question of him having affairs or anything. None of that. But with me, he didn't know what he was saying. He couldn't remember his lines. Originally, I thought he wasn't making any effort to. Slowly it dawned on me—and it was unintelligent on my part not to recognize it earlier—that he had brain damage. There was. He wasn't responsible. He had a persecution complex. I was supposed to have been cruel to him, you know. Oh, once I came into the dressing room following right after him. And I slammed the door so hard a mirror fell and broke. I was trying to scare him, thinking fear would do something. And Monty said, "Are you going to kill me?" And as he said that, I had a hard time keeping a straight face. But, God, I could have killed him on occasion. He was just unbearable. Impossible. He was *also,* it turned out, going blind. And he was attributing that to something that happened during the picture. I mean, there was a scene where somebody knocked his hat off. And he thought it had brushed his eyes. So he went and had them examined. And he had cataracts in both eyes. Terrible cataracts. They had never been diagnosed before. And so, along with the drinking and paranoia and so on, was the fact that he couldn't see.

You directed Orson Welles in several movies, and then he directed you in at least one of his, which hasn't been released. There are those in the movie business who look on Orson Welles as one of the great wasted talents. Why is that?
Well, it's a combination of things: In the first place, he offended the establishment in two ways. He started off with *Citizen Kane*—which was conceived to be an insult to William Randolph Hearst. The industry was quite indebted to Hearst, and out of some extremely false sense of loyalty, mixed in with their own gains to be had materially, they went about detracting Orson, even while he was making it and immediately after it. And then Orson had the arrogance and downright insolence to have made the movie a great success. It was enormously popular. Right off the bat, in other words, he violated two cardinal rules. First, you're not supposed to go against the establishment. And if you *do* go against the establishment, you're supposed to suffer.

I remember the trade papers, after the opening of *Citizen Kane,* when Orson simply ran a recapitulation of the things that had been said against him, against the picture and so on. So he really made them eat dirt, as they damn well should have.

Then he made a very serious error as a poker player, which he is not. He was down in South America to do second-unit shots for a picture. And he got caught up in the gala, the festival in Rio, the carnival. And I forget how much film he shot, but it was a lot. And in the middle of it, they told him to come home. He didn't. He stayed down there and shot and shot until they wouldn't send him more negative. . . . This gave him a reputation for irresponsibility. When he did finally come back, he was again in deep disgrace.

What happened is quite understandable to me, because Orson's an artist. He was acting in the service of history. But the studio couldn't have been less interested in history—

Or art.
Or art. Either one. They wouldn't have sent a second unit out to see Washington cross the Delaware. Orson is not a man who can bow down to idiots. And Hollywood is full of them. Orson is a big ego. But I've always found him to be completely logical. And I think he's a joy. I also look on Orson as an amateur. I mean that in the very best sense of the word. He loves pictures and plays and all things theatrical. But there is something else that needs accounting for. So many of his things go unfinished. I don't know why. That is one I can't answer. Even one that we did together, *The Other Side of the Wind.* I haven't seen a foot of it myself, and I don't know why it hasn't been released. Now, there's always a reason. But it's happened too often with Orson for it to be entirely accidental.

Do you think he might have been afraid of failure after Citizen Kane?
No.

Or perhaps he's afraid of success again?
I don't know. I'm sure Orson doesn't. He'd be the last to know. If he knew, he'd try and do something about it.

Do you ever miss your days as a boxer? Could you have been a contender?
Well, I *would* have become one. I was pretty good. I had a lot of fun doing it. . . . But I grew out of that.

You mean you're no longer macho?
Shit, I never was macho.

There are just a few women who might disagree, though, right?
I'm sure there are.

When we played poker yesterday, I couldn't help noticing that women weren't allowed to play. Why was that?
Well, I don't like women to play because I always lose to them. I could never challenge them. When a woman's playing, I don't want to take advantage—I don't want to bear down on her. I don't want to call her and make her lose her money. I've only played with women three or four times in my life.

I've got to get something settled here about Errol Flynn. You took Bogie "to the nose" once. But with Flynn, you actually had a fight, right?
Yeah, it was a knockdown slug-out. It was over a remark he made about Olivia de Havilland.

Do you remember what it was?
Yes, but I wouldn't repeat it.

Were you very close with Olivia de Havilland?
I knew her very well.

But the remark was so bad—
It was bad enough.

So what happened?
Well, just a real knockdown drag-out. It was quite a night. We were both at a party at David Selznick's. We went out alone. We just went outside for a long time.

Who won?
I don't think either of us did. We both went to the hospital, although we went to different hospitals [*laughs*].

A nice, friendly fight?
Yes. It was, actually.

The latest revelation that has come out in a recent book about Flynn is that he was possibly a German spy.

I can't believe any of it. I can't believe any of it at all. But not on the grounds that he would have been incapable of it [*laughs*]. I think Errol was capable of practically anything. He liked living on the edge. Errol took chances. But in lots of instances, people take chances in order to be more aware of life. They aren't keen, their senses aren't quickened, when there isn't an element of danger. And they're only half-alive unless they're threatened. And they get addicted to this. And—

You?

I've certainly taken my share of chances.

Like your friend Ernest Hemingway?

Well, like all young men of that time, I was certainly influenced by his writing. It hit me right when I was trying to write. And I had one or two other rather huge literary experiences, the biggest being James Joyce. And then along came Hemingway, who was circuitously a product of Joyce's, too. I don't think Hemingway would have been exactly what he was if Joyce had never written, which doesn't take anything away from Hemingway, God knows. I was very influenced by his writing and by his thinking. I think he was perhaps a more important influence, just in his thinking. His values, his reassessment of the things that made life go, were probably more important than his writing. Although at times he wrote very well, magnificently.

His writing was difficult to translate into film, wasn't it?

Yes. Stories didn't come easily with him. Incidents did. And he had a wonderful way of being able to bring an incident to life. He was more of a short-story writer. He didn't conceive novels in the grand sense, but significant detail—not just factual, but details that reflect an attitude. I think some of his best writing was in *Death in the Afternoon*. Sometimes he's marvelously funny in it. The old lady, if you remember, and some of those little short stories were departures and vignettes. Do you remember the Italian surgeon who came with the wounded and wanted to give more feed to the soldiers? Well, Hemingway had to have witnessed some of that.

You spent time with him in Cuba. You ate with him. You went fishing with him. Was it a surprise to you when he put the gun to his head?

Ah, no, it wasn't. It was actually what I would have expected him to do under the circumstances. And I say this with profound admiration for both him and the act.

Really?
Oh, yes. He was on his way out mentally, and he knew it and didn't want that to happen. Who the hell would? He had tried once before. He was very canny about it. He had these flashes of sanity. Once they were taking him to Mayo in America on a chartered plane, and he tried to jump out of the plane. They subdued him. And then he talked his way out of Mayo and got home. And if you could see the pictures of him near the end, you could see it in his face. The smiling one of them—the flesh was gone—that was somebody else.

You say with profound admiration for the act itself under those circumstances. Do you think that that you would consider something like that?
I wouldn't dream of doing anything else. If I didn't, it would be out of cowardice and nothing else. I mean, Hemingway wouldn't have done it had it been cancer. But he was on his way to imbecility. That's a helluva thing to have around. I'm intrigued by the way suicide is approached by different cultures. Some places it's *the* thing to do. But the bourgeois of the United States legislates against it. In this society, death is a kind of shameful thing and is to be concealed even after the spirit has left.

Have you ever been at a point in your life where you've contemplated suicide?
Only theoretically.

Then you talked yourself out of it, too?
I don't mean that I came that close to it. No, I wonder if I would if—

If what?
Well, if I had a flash like Hemingway, for instance. Because I like to live. but in a situation like Hemingway's, I hope I would pull the trigger. I would be disappointed in myself if I didn't.

Hemingway was often described as a man's man. And often, so are you. What does that mean?
I always thought that was kind of an offensive description to make of any-

body—a man's man. It immediately calls for hair on the chest. I think Hemingway would have objected to being called a man's man, too. Speaking of Hemingway, he refereed a fight down in Cuba one time, and he was introduced in the ring as that "well-known playboy, Ernest Hemingway." That's funny as hell.

People call me a man's man, I suppose because of the life I've led, more or less. But I never want to be called a lady's man, either. I'll be happy to be called what I am and for who I am—nobody's man.

Dialogue on Film with John Huston

THE AMERICAN FILM
INSTITUTE/1984

JOHN HUSTON BEGAN HIS film career as an actor, established his reputation as a screenwriter, and made his mark as a director. He has cut a wide swath through Hollywood for more than fifty years—he's been called "King Rebel" as well as the quintessential Hollywood maverick. He is a commanding presence both on the screen and behind the camera, with a string of acknowledged classics to his credit, including *The Maltese Falcon* (his first directing job), *The Treasure of the Sierra Madre, The African Queen,* and *The Man Who Would Be King.*

Huston's greatest popular and critical successes have been lean, sardonic tales of men pushed to their limits, but his flamboyance and adventurousness have led him to tackle big subjects and weighty literature, too. He brought Moby Dick and the Bible to the screen, as well as the life of Sigmund Freud. He seems also to have a special affinity with the mavericks of contemporary literature, like Tennessee Williams and Flannery O'Connor, whose works (*The Night of the Iguana* and *Wise Blood*) he has filmed successfully. Shortly after this Dialogue took place, he embarked on a new project—one of the century's great unfilmable novels, Malcolm Lowry's *Under the Volcano.*

Nominated thirteen times for Academy Awards, Huston has won two, for writing and for directing *The Treasure of the Sierra Madre* in 1948. He also received AFI's 1983 Life Achievement Award. In the Dialogue he discusses his

From *American Film,* vol. 9, no. 4, January/February 1984, 19–22, 70–71. © 1984 by *American Film.* Reprinted by permission.

controversial experiments with color, his collaborations with Tennessee Williams and Truman Capote, and his relationship with actors.

QUESTION: *Why did you become a director? You had already established yourself as a screenwriter when you directed your first film,* The Maltese Falcon. *Was being a writer just a stepping-stone to directing?*

JOHN HUSTON: I discovered during my period as a screenwriter the desire to become a director. It wasn't to protect my writing, in the way I am told other writers have proceeded; it was simply the desire. Directing is just an extension of the writing. They're not different departments.

I can give you an example. There was a scene in *The Night of the Iguana* that Tennessee Williams and I were having difficulty with. We had written it quite well—we had written it two or three times. But it just didn't pan out. It was the scene where a young girl comes to Richard Burton's room to importune him again—she's trying to seduce him. He's had an unfortunate background, so far as the seduction of ladies is concerned, and he's trying to avoid this. He's doing his level best to avoid it. But she comes into the room and then this dialogue scene ensues, wherein he tries to explain to her why he cannot make—doesn't choose to make—love to her. The dialogue was good, but the scene wasn't satisfactory.

So I said to Tennessee, "Could you do something? Look at it, see if you have any ideas, Tennessee."

He came back the next morning with the scene. It opens with Burton standing before a chiffonier, with a bottle of whiskey on it. The girl opens the door and startles him. He's shaving. He cuts himself and the bottle of whiskey falls off the chiffonier. The dialogue then continues as he, barefoot, walks on broken glass. And presently the girl, in the spirit of martyrdom, joins him, and she, too, walks barefoot on broken glass; the scene proceeds in that vein. As these lines pass back and forth between them, they are walking on broken glass. That is one of the best scenes in the picture, an example of real *dramatic* genius in the writing of a scene.

QUESTION: *You made many pictures in black and white, each with a strong visual style—*The Maltese Falcon, The Treasure of the Sierra Madre, *and* The Red Badge of Courage *come to mind, as well as* The Night of the Iguana. *In* Moulin Rouge, Moby Dick, *and, later on* Reflections in a Golden Eye, *you tried to do something different from the conventional use of color in film. Why?*

HUSTON: Up until *Moulin Rouge* (with the exception of the first three-strip Technicolor feature, *Becky Sharp,* which was muted and very beautiful), there was no attempt to even choose a palatte in American films. The Japanese had done some fascinating experiments. When *Moulin Rouge* came along, I thought it wouldn't be right to just shoot it in straight color, when color could give another dimension to the picture; so we conceived a different approach. There was a wedding between color and black and white, reinforcing the color, as it were. Giving it a strength. Whereas color was apt to go limp—sentimental—we thought the black and white would give it the strength that the subject matter deserved.

And this was an innovation. (*Moby Dick* was the second picture I shot with the idea of using color as a medium of thought, to convey an idea.) The idea in *Moulin Rouge* was to flatten the color to give it a local, almost posterlike look reminiscent of the lithographs and posters of Toulouse-Lautrec. *Moulin Rouge* was bitterly fought by Technicolor. They didn't want to fool around. They especially didn't want us to do this effect within the camera. I showed them tests we had shot of what I wanted, and they said, "You can let us tape those up in the lab as an example." We said all right, but the samples they sent back were very poor matches indeed. We proceeded to shoot the picture, but before we even started, Technicolor wrote letters to all the people involved—the principals, Warner Bros., and so on—disclaiming any responsibility and advising against our proceeding this way. But our people backed us up, and the color was certainly the biggest triumph of the picture. Even as late as *Reflections in a Golden Eye,* I had to fight for color experimentation: I wanted to give a kind of amber, golden look to the whole picture.

I still think that black and white has a role in motion pictures and not everything should be in color. In fact, unless the color is perfect to the idea, it can come between the beholder and the idea of the picture. One's eye can be deflected by the color. And one's thoughts as well.

For instance, I cannot possibly see doing *Freud* in color—or other pictures of a deeply psychological nature. Unless the palette and the values coincide or are part of the idea, why, it's better for it *not* to be in color. In the case of *Reflections of a Golden Eye,* after valiant effort on the part of producer Ray Stark and myself, they agreed to let us open the picture in key cities in that special color, but the general release was in the old Technicolor. That special color, incidentally, was achieved in the laboratory, not in the camera, as in the case of the other two pictures.

QUESTION: *Your films have combined entertainment with substance, unusual in today's Hollywood. How does a young director avoid being captured by Hollywood slickness?*

HUSTON: The best answer to that is to not be a Hollywood slicker. Certainly you have to buck the purely commercial side of pictures today, more so probably than when I was starting out. I think there are exceptions that I make even as I utter these gems, but certainly as much if not more attention is paid to the commercial aspects of film today than occurred when the major studios were running the show. They could afford, I suppose, to be somewhat broader in their outlook. They had theaters to fill, but every picture didn't have to be a great box-office success. Every movie today is conceived to be, hoped to be, by someone (however foolish) a box-office triumph.

QUESTION: *In the long shelf of pictures that you've made, if you had to choose four or five to keep right by your bedside, which would they be?*

HUSTON: Otto Preminger was asked that question and he said, "You know, they're all one's children and one isn't to be loved any the less because it has a harelip or a clubfoot." Well, that's partly true. I've got my favorites, but it wouldn't be fair to the others to reveal them. However, I also have the ones that I can't bear, which brings me to another conjecture. Why we don't make over again the pictures that we did badly, instead of our successes. *The Maltese Falcon* had been done twice before I made it, and badly both times. But there was a good picture there, a great, wonderful picture there—the one that the book allowed me to make. That's true of so many other pictures that were failures either in the making or in the writing.

QUESTION: *In terms of the director-actor relationship, how did it feel directing your father in* The Treasure of the Sierra Madre? *How did it feel to be directed by, say, Roman Polanski in* Chinatown?

HUSTON: Well, on the set, the director is the father image. So I was my own father's father. And as I appeared in *The Treasure of the Sierra Madre*, I was *my* father also, so that made me my grandfather. It's like the play on Shakespeare in Joyce's *Ulysses*. When it comes to working for another director, particularly when he is as good as Polanski, who is very good indeed, why, I try to be just the most obedient of actors, so that I'll serve as an example to the actors who are in *my* pictures.

QUESTION: *Do you give the actors a little room to create on their own in different situations when you're filming?*
HUSTON: I give very little room to the actors. I don't look to them to make creative contributions when it comes to the dialogue. Very often I've deplored the script even as I went up to production with it, but, in general, the screenplay should be as nearly perfect before shooting as one can get it. I think it's deceiving yourself to believe that you can wing it on the set. It has happened, I know, and there are certain directors that have done it with a degree of success. Not me.

QUESTION: *How about* The Misfits? *You had a company of actors there—Clift, Gable, Monroe—who would need some room. The circumstances of their own lives must have had quite an effect on the film's story.*
HUSTON: That is true, but it wasn't an immediate affair. It wasn't something of the moment. Arthur Miller wrote the script for Marilyn, and he had been out to Nevada and had met the equivalent of the roving cowboy part, played by Clark Gable. It was made out of the materials at hand, sure, and then the things that happened in the course of the picture were almost a counterpoint to the story of the picture itself. Marilyn was on her way out. But, you know, in working with actors, most of my directing occurs before I ever reach the set, in selecting the actor. That can be a strong statement itself. And when I go to cast a film, I don't think in terms of the popularity of an actor—that comes later, if at all. But I think, Who in the past, in my own background, is like this part? Not an actor, but just a figure who was like the person in the script. One goes to an actor for a facility, but sometimes the individual himself is his own character—his own nature is more important than the facility that his acting can endow. I remember when Brando played Antony in Joseph Mankiewicz's *Julius Caesar.* To me it's one of the most extraordinary performances I've ever witnessed, but it was something that had nothing to do with technique. It outraged the British at first blush, and then they decided it was the best performance of Shakespeare they'd ever seen. The picture itself was rather a weak echo of Shakespeare, but Brando hit some vein, passion—suddenly, the furnace door opened and you were put into a

sweat and then withered from the very heat of it. It's that natural outpouring that you don't have to be an actor to have.

QUESTION: *When you chose three nonprofessionals to star in* The Red Badge of Courage, *did you try to encourage them to just be themselves when you were working with them?*

HUSTON: Oh, yes, I encourage a professional actor to be himself, too, always. Always try to get the most out of the actor in the way of his own spiritual—for want of a better word—or instinctive contribution. But to get as much of the man himself and to direct as little as possible. To get as little of myself into his performance as I can, and as much of himself.

QUESTION: *You said you had gone into some films deploring the script, but had to work with it anyway. I suppose that was because of contracts, money, and time?*

HUSTON: That's right. There was only one outstanding exception, and that was *Beat the Devil.* I went into that film reluctantly, because we had no script at all to speak of, or at least a very poor excuse for a script. Truman Capote and I rewrote it on the spot, but it wasn't done frivolously, as has been described. We worked very hard and tried to keep ahead of the picture. In fact, I remember that on one occasion I didn't want the company to know how bereft we were. So I staged the scene that was already in the script and made it as complicated as possible in its moves. Then I went upstairs with Truman and rewrote it while the crew laid out tracks and took down walls. I came back down and said, "I've changed it." We got away with it. And we got away with the picture. But it was just the most fortunate of accidents that permitted it. To this day, I think it's an amusing, good picture.

QUESTION: *What kind of relationship do you have with the editors of your films?*

HUSTON: The editor and I hardly even need to know each other. Of course, I'm just making a point. But I'm a particular case here. I edit my pictures in the camera. I don't protect myself; I don't take other shots of the ones that I need. One's almost forced to edit a film the way I shoot it. I don't believe that pictures are made in the cutting room. They're sometimes helped, but they're not made.

QUESTION: *Your work incorporates some of the most difficult location pictures ever made, from* The Treasure of the Sierra Madre *to* The African Queen. *What do you look for in a producer when you go into difficult circumstances like those?*
HUSTON: Help. To do the onerous things that permit you to give your entire attention to the quality of the picture rather than to the problems, physical or otherwise. A producer must have the ability to bring forth the people that will help you the most, to understand the requirements of the picture. Some producers have a false sense of the requirements, or they want to have a critical role. I don't mean to demean or reduce the producer. It's a very important role, and I'll probably be a producer myself—when I'm no longer able to navigate.

Cracking the Volcano

TODD McCARTHY/1984

SELDOM HAVE THE DREAMS of so many been realized by so few as in the making of John Huston's film adaptation of Malcolm Lowry's *Under the Volcano.*

In the thirty-seven years since the publication of the novel, some fifty screenwriters have tried to crack the nut of Lowry's tortured, memory and history-laden tale of the last day in the life of an alcoholic British former consul to Mexico. Numerous directors, including Luis Buñuel, Jules Dassin, Joseph Losey, Ken Russell, and Paul Luduc, worked to get the project off the ground. Countless others dreamed about it, and several actors, notably Richard Burton, Robert Shaw, and Peter O'Toole, have imagined the Consul as the role of a lifetime.

Others, of course, doubted that the book could be translated into a film at all, despite the occasional "cinematic" conventions employed in the text. Like *One Hundred Years of Solitude* (and Gabriel García Márquez is said to have made a stab at adapting Lowry's novel), *Under the Volcano* is so vast, so complex, so overflowing with literary flights of fancy that it seemed advisable, in the opinion of many, to leave well enough alone.

Nevertheless, Huston's film received a highly respectful response when it premiered at the Cannes Film Festival in May, and the critical reaction in general has been one of some surprise as to how successful the filmmakers

From *Film Comment,* July/August, 1984, 59–60. © 1984 by *Film Comment.* Reprinted by permission.

have been in putting such intransigent material on the screen in coherent, compelling fashion.

As Huston acknowledges, many people associated him with the Lowry work over the years, even if in the end this was perhaps a dream project thrust upon him rather than one he had doggedly pursued. Huston's concentrated, character-oriented approach to the adaptation was clearly of the utmost importance to the shape the finished film has assumed, but in retrospect, he may have had a relatively easy job compared to those taken on by coproducer Wieland Schulz-Keil and screenwriter Guy Gallo.

HUSTON: I first read the book when it was first published. I didn't think of it as a film at the time. Then people kept sending me scripts. Different producers would come to me and propose making the book. I wasn't trying to do it. For some reason, the Lowry fans coupled me with the material, and I'd get these scripts. I must have received more than twenty. The last producer to come to me was Schulz-Keil. He didn't have a proper script, but I said, yes, I was very interested. That was well before Guy's script.

Were you of a mind that it was impossible to make into a film before you saw Guy Gallo's script?
No, there was another script that was quite good. But, as you know, the book's excellence is literary. There's an awful lot to wade through. It's not an easy book. Guy's script came to me through Michael Fitzgerald. Michael didn't know Guy, but he sent it on to me as a favor to this man he didn't know. It was the first script which seemed to me to be headed in the right direction. It did away with the character of Laruelle, if I remember, or it combined Laruelle and the brother. And it held to the essence of the story. From then on we worked just at purifying the material. I think now, probably more than any picture I ever made, it's seen as an experience, instead of a narrative thing. It's all immediate, it's right there, you're present, it's happening.

You've adapted weighty literary works to the screen before. Would this rank as perhaps the most difficult to transfer?
Of course, I had the benefit of all those other scripts that had gone before,

seeing the mistakes that had been made. But this and *Moby Dick,* certainly, were the most difficult.

The book has a certain resemblance to another novel you wanted to film, Hemingway's Across the River and into the Trees, *which is also about a man at the end of his life.*
The last twenty-four hours, yes. But I never got a proper script. I worked on it myself, but I never got it.

That project would also seem to call for flashbacks laced throughout the narrative. Do you think the flashback technique could work in that case, but not in this?
There's no need for it in this picture, the whole thing is so immediate. But in *Across the River and into the Trees* I did use flashbacks, but the script didn't come off.

What is the essence of the book for you?
The whole thing is bound up with the Consul. Someone asked me the other day, "Why was the Consul a drunk?" Of course, this question had come up during the writing of the picture, and it refused to be answered in an expository way. I mean, had he turned to drink because he'd killed those men on the ship, and the memory of that haunted him and so on? Well, obviously not. It was something bigger than that. And in answer to this question, I said, "God Almighty, looking at what's going on here, or having looked at what's been going on here for the last generation or so, must surely have turned to the bottle, and he's obviously away on an extended bat in another constellation." It's a Divine attribute. The Consul is a hero, and his reaction to life is to get drunk, and he gets drunk in an heroic way.

Why is it heroic?
Well, his talk, his very talk is heroic. The words in his mouth are the words of heroes.

He does make life difficult for those around him.
Sure. So do heroes. So does God. I'm now contradicting myself. I prefer to think of God as away on a bat. Not dead, just drunk.

Two Encounters with John Huston

MICHEL CIMENT/1984

ENCOUNTERS RATHER THAN INTERVIEWS.... John Huston
does not like interviews, strictly speaking, and would rather have a conversation. After two evenings spent with him when *Fat City* was shown at the
Cannes Festival of 1972 (see *Positif* 142), we met him again at the same festival,
this time in 1979 following the screening of *Wise Blood.* He kindly agreed to
talk to us before the camera of *Ciné-regards,* a TV show of Pierre André Bou-
tang. This is the complete text, without any editing, that is printed here. The
second meeting occurred this year, when *Under the Volcano* was being presented in competition; the meeting was at the Grand Hotel du Cap where
Huston likes to stay. This time Jan Aghed, our colleague and Swedish friend
with *Sydsvenska Dagbladet,* was participating in the conversation.

First Encounter (Cap d'Antibes, May 1979)

M . C . :   *Your private life has always been as important to you as your movies, if
not more so. What made you decide to live in Mexico?*
HUSTON :   I live on the west coast of Mexico, facing the Pacific Ocean and
with the jungle behind me; and I have a creek that is entirely mine. I am
totally isolated. The only way to get there is by boat and one can only leave
by going through the jungle. No roads. I look out at the sunlight shining
brilliantly on the water and the whales gliding in it. It is a nice place, the
ultimate place where I would want to live.

From *Positif,* no. 283, September 1984, 26–35. © 1984 by *Positif.* Reprinted by permission.
English translation by Gamo Tounkara and Robert Emmet Long.

M . C .   *How did you choose it?*

H U S T O N :   I was familiar with it for a long time before I decided to live there. Actually, I came back there to shoot *The Night of the Iguana*. It is close to the city of Puerto Vallarta. When I came there for the first time, before *The Night of the Iguana*, there were two thousand and five hundred people living in Puerto Vallarta. Now there are seventy thousand.

M . C . :   *A lot has been said about the incidents that happened during the shooting of* The Night of the Iguana. *You have been warmly received there in spite of those incidents?*

H U S T O N :   Oh! The truth is that nothing happened during the shooting of the movie. All the media gathered in Puerto Vallarta hoping that something terrible would happen, but nothing happened. Everything went along fine. However, I think that the changes this country went through have not always been for the best.

M . C . :   *You've been having a long love affair with Mexico that started a long time ago.*

H U S T O N :   When I was a young man. . . . I went there for the first time when I was nineteen. I lived there for a while and I kept going back after I left.

M . C . :   *What were you doing in Mexico when you were nineteen?*

H U S T O N :   Horseback riding. . . . I was a rider. Just like my mother was before me. I took lessons from a man who broke in horses, one of the best in the world. Equestrianism is a tradition in Mexico. Then I was called into the army. I was given the rank of lieutenant and was part of the Mexican cavalry.

M . C . :   *For how long?*

H U S T O N :   Many months. I left and came back. I must have spent a year and a half there in all.

M . C . :   *Before Mexico, you were living in Ireland, a totally different country. Why did you settle there and why did you choose to live there?*

H U S T O N :   Well, it was, once again, about horses. I think they were one of the major attractions of that country, and I lived there for more than twenty years. It is a sweet country to live in. I took out Irish citizenship and, of course, I still have it. I go back there regularly. The house I used to own, in the south side of the country, in Saint Clarence, was becoming too expensive for me to keep up. At the beginning it was possible. But it needed a lot of staff, twelve or fifteen people. Twenty years ago it was feasible, but I realized that I had to work constantly to pay for all that and I would end up not enjoying my house at all. I was always going away to work to pay the bills. I was never in the house.

M.C.: *What were you doing, hunting?*
HUSTON: Yes, fox hunting. I was hunting with the Galway Blazers. I was "Joint Master of the Blazers" for ten years and that was a wonderful period of my life.

M.C.: *You are, as you confessed, a person who is fundamentally not religious; it is funny that you chose to live in countries as deeply religious as Ireland and Mexico. It is true that they are also rich in mythologies.*
HUSTON: Yes, of course. Maybe I am not a religious person but that does not mean that I don't like religious people. I am not, in any way, an orthodox believer.

M.C.: *But do you believe in God?*
HUSTON: I do not want to get into that. It would not be wise to give an opinion. I am an onlooker at the spectacle of life, all amazed.

M.C.: Wise Blood *looks a lot like what you did before, but when seeing the movie one also feels, at the same time, the pleasure of an adventure and the discovery of a country.*
HUSTON: Plus, for me, the discovery of a new region. I shot this movie in Georgia. I am not only talking about a new geographical area but of a side of American life that I did not know.

M.C.: *What did you like about Flannery O'Connor? The style?*
HUSTON: Yes, that is a wonderful and fascinating book. As fascinating as she is herself. We can say that of late she has been ranked among the great American authors. She died fifteen years ago and it is just now that her talent is being recognized.

M . C . : *She was a Catholic and she used to mock Protestant sects. This is clearly a point of view different from yours. What do you think about the main characters of the story?*

HUSTON: I look at those people just the way they are. It seems to me the drama of a young man who is trying to rebel. It is as if someone were recovering from an illness, fighting against something that had afflicted him when he was a child. Let's try to say it more clearly: he was captivated by the idea of Christ when he was a child, which made him suffer. He tried to cure himself by denying the existence of God. It is a courageous rebellion but he fails, the flag in his hand.

M . C . : *There are many styles in the movie: realistic, fantastic, etc. . . .*

HUSTON: Yes, but all that comes from Flannery O'Connor. Many writers that we know are sometimes funny, sometimes awful, sometimes strange, but she could be all three at the same time.

M . C . : *Your taste for traveling and the diverse occupations you have had come from your childhood, from the influence of your father and mother, which was very important.*

HUSTON: Yes, I traveled a lot for a great part of my life, but always within the United States. From city to city, in different states. My parents were separated. My mother was a journalist and my father was in the theater, and I was passed back and forth from one to the other.

M . C . : *Being a producer, a writer, and an actor, you brought together all of your parents' jobs.*

HUSTON: In a way, yes. But it is something I never thought about.

M . C . : *Can you tell me about your childhood?*

HUSTON: I was born in Nevada, Missouri, where the gas and electric company was won by my grandfather in a card game. My parents met during the World's Fair in Saint Louis. "Meet Me in Saint Louis. . . ." They were on tour with a theater company and were in a play called *Convict Stripes,* but the company went bankrupt. I think that the director skipped town with the money, leaving my parents stranded and without resources. They wrote to my grandfather who told them to join him, and he made my father chief engineer for gas and electricity in Nevada, Missouri. He knew nothing about engineering, however, one day there was a fire and one whole side of the city was damaged; my father, who was of no help in this crisis, decided that it was time for him, and my mother and me, to move to Weathersport, Texas. That was the beginning of long trips by train, Pullman most of the time, through the Middle West, but sometimes up to New York. My mother married again, this time to an employee of the Northern Pacific railroad company. I lived in Saint Paul for some time, but when I became ill they sent me to the warmer climates of California and Arizona. I was eleven or twelve years old then and remained bedridden for some time. I was in a sanitarium and from its windows could see others swimming in an irrigation canal. So one day I got out through the window and dove into the canal. I had a lot of fun and nobody saw me. I even crossed the cascades formed by the water gates. Finally when I was allowed to leave my bed and go swimming, I did not tell anybody about my past experiences that had lasted for weeks.

M.C.: *You told me one day that you never wanted to become an actor like your father. You acted in twenty movies, however, seven of which were your own.*
HUSTON: I played the role of a minor character, that of an American tourist in Tampico, Mexico, in one of my own movies, *The Treasure of the Sierra Madre.* But I never thought about acting for other producers. It was Otto Preminger who had me become an actor. He called me one day unexpectedly and said: "Would you like to have a part in one of my movies?" It was *The Cardinal.* And everything went very well. Then other people wanted me to play in their movies. It became an adventure. I had a lot of fun, there wasn't any responsibility involved. It is easy to be an actor.

M.C.: *The waiting between the shootings is not too boring?*
HUSTON: Not if you have a good book! I had a wonderful time with Otto. Everything is very strict with him. He imposes discipline. He takes care of everything. I personally give others a lot of responsibilities. But Otto likes to supervise everything—the time when you get into your car, the name of the hotel where you sleep at night.

M.C.: *The roles you played in your movies must not have been accidental, they must have meant something to you.*
HUSTON: In *The List of Adrian Messenger,* I was a fox hunter because I knew how to ride a horse and I was a huntsman. For *The Bible* and the character of

Noah it was different. I had asked two actors who weren't available, and I resigned myself to being the poor third one. I tried Charlie Chaplin first and he liked the idea. He was living in Switzerland and we were good friends, so I called him and asked him to read the scenario. He was not interested in reading it, but the idea of playing Noah excited him. He asked me to give him some days to think about it, then he told me that he had never been in someone else's film and that he wasn't going to do it now. So I told him that he could rewrite the scenario and direct himself. He laughed and laughed. . . . I still remember his laughter on the phone. Then I asked Alec Guinness but he was busy. So I did it myself. One thing that made me decide to do it was that I have always liked animals; in making the film I taught them many things.

M . C . : *What are the animals you like best after horses?*
HUSTON: In *The Bible* there was a whole range of animals, starting with the hippopotamuses. One of them became my favorite. He would open his big mouth and let you caress his tongue. A female elephant loved being caressed behind the ears. She would lower her head down so far that you would wonder what was going on. And whenever I wanted to leave her, she would grab me with her trunk to make me stay so that I would keep on caressing her ear.

M . C . : *To you, being an actor seems to be more like a game than a job.*
HUSTON: It is true. I have never taken myself seriously as an actor.

M . C . : *But you take the other actors seriously?*
HUSTON: Yes, yes, very seriously.

M . C . : *So why not yourself? You are not different from them, are you?*
HUSTON: You are right. I respect the profession, but I don't feel burdened by responsibility when I am playing a role. It is almost a sensual pleasure for me. And it is wonderful to be paid to have fun.

M . C . : *In* Wise Blood *you were playing the role of the grandfather preacher.*
HUSTON: Yes. As I think about it, I played Noah as well as being the voice of God in *The Bible,* and in the Preminger film played a Catholic cardinal. So I often found myself in religious roles.

M.C.: *You worked six times with Humphrey Bogart. I assume you were friends.*

HUSTON: We were friends but it was the image Bogart projected on screen that made him right for my movies. I never wrote a scenario with Bogey in mind. After the screenplay was written, however, I would say, "Only Bogey can play this role." I have always been surprised to see how much actors resemble the characters they play. Bogart in real life was what he was in the movies. But we cannot say that he was always exactly the same. I believe there was a little bit of himself in the character he played in *The African Queen*. We were good friends, we would drink together, we liked to tell nonsensical jokes and laugh together. I had a good time with Bogey in Paris, in London, in Africa. He was a wonderful companion. He did not know what being serious meant. And if he noticed that other people were being pretentious, he would attack them in the most direct way.

M.C.: *Brando is an actor of another sort; he comes from the Actors Studio, which is a different type of school. You directed him in Reflections in a Golden Eye.*

HUSTON: He is a great actor, someone that I respect a great deal. We are not close friends but I like him very much. You know, the better the actor is the easier it is to work with him. I have definite preferences in casting actors for roles. I prefer using an actor who himself resembles that character he plays. Of course if you have an actor who is not only very talented but also has a personality like that of the character he plays, it is best of all, and that was true for Bogart. He was a great personality and a great actor at the same time. Brando is the most powerful and the deepest actor I have ever known. I remember seeing him in *Julius Caesar,* when he was playing the character of Marc Antony. Well, the experienced English actors who were with him were not as inspired in their interpretations as he was, and they paled beside him. He gives a brilliant coloring to everything he touches. I am overwhelmed with admiration for Brando and his art.

M.C.: *You were in a fight with Errol Flynn.*

HUSTON: We were at a reception and he said something offensive about one of my friends, and I could not let that go. I spoke out. He asked me what I intended to do. I told him he was going to see. We went to the garden and had a fist fight. A long time after that incident we became good friends and he played in *Roots of Heaven.*

M . C . : *Many books have been written about the making of your movies, and they read almost like novels.*

H U S T O N : Yes, it is a little bit like that. There were three books. I do not think of making movies as a job. Movies are part of my life. Only the making of one of the movies was unfortunate . . . that was *Freud*. Monty Clift was at the end of his tether and was a victim of many things. He was mixing alcohol and drugs. He also had physical and emotional problems. He suffered a head injury in an automobile accident. It was very hard.

M . C . : *What attracted you to Freud's writing?*

H U S T O N : It came about when I made a movie in the army, *Let There Be Light*. It has never been shown to the public. It was about soldiers coming home from the war who were suffering from nervous breakdowns and other psychological disorders. In following the treatment of the patients at the hospital I discovered the role Freud was playing in modern psychiatry. Of course in the thirties, I had already read two or three of Freud's books. But it was the filming of *Let There Be Light* that made me feel that I would like to devote a whole movie to Freud.

M . C . : *The making of* The African Queen *must have been particularly memorable.*

H U S T O N : It was a wonderful experience. One of the happiest I have ever had. For me it was an opportunity to discover Africa: we shot the movie in three different locations. Between those shootings, I would go hunting big game. I would not do it today; at that time the species were not endangered. The shooting of the film, which allowed for a certain amount of improvisation, was very exciting. I had a lot of fun. Everybody was very dedicated, and they were all dear to me—Bogart, Betty Bacall, Katharine Hepburn and the others.

M . C . : *What kind of experience was the shooting of* The Misfits, *which featured three of Hollywood's legendary stars?*

H U S T O N : There was a feeling of misfortune throughout that experience, but it was not like the making of *Freud*. There were some difficulties but they were not too important. We had to stop the shooting for a while because Marilyn was sick. It was about drug abuse again. Not heavy drugs, just sleeping pills to help her sleep. She would wake up in the middle of the night and be afraid that she would not fall back to sleep. And since she wanted to be in good form the following morning, she would overdose herself. In the morning she would take stimulants to prevent her from sleeping during the day. A vicious cycle.

M . C . : *Did Gable and Clift like horses as much as you do?*
HUSTON: Not at all. Gable was experienced with horses, and Clift had some experience and acquired more during the shooting. But neither of them was passionate about horses.

M . C . : *Would you be miserable if you could not make movies any more?*
HUSTON: Certainly. I love making films. If I were prevented from doing it I would be very unhappy.

M . C . : *You take a lot of your inspiration from literature. Is transforming literature into a visual medium what cinema means for you?*
HUSTON: I believe so. You just put it very well. I want to express my pleasure in having read something. For example, *The Man Who Would Be King* was one of my oldest projects. I began reading Kipling at the age of twelve. If you tell me the first verse of one of his poems, I will tell you the second. I believe I read every line of his prose writing when I was a child. I thought that *The Man Who Would Be King* could be a great and beautiful story. I like the strong narrative line of his fiction, the sense of breadth and depth of feeling he gives.

M . C . : *Were you impressed by Kipling's idea of a man who wants to be powerful?*
HUSTON: Yes, but that is the final stage, the stage that people reach when they attain great power. The air becomes rare over there and one becomes the victim of that terrible illness, illusions of grandeur. He starts to believe that he is very important and the last stage is reached when he believes that he has supernatural powers and is seated among the gods.

Second Encounter (Cap d'Antibes, May 1984)

M . C . : *Bergman recently declared that he did not have enough energy to keep on making movies. You are fifteen years older and it doesn't seem as if you want to retire. Where do you get all that strength from? Under the Volcano is certainly not your last movie!*

H U S T O N :   We never know what will be the last movie. But, of course, Berg-man has another alternative, theater, and he can concentrate all his energy there. In fact that is what he prefers and is his first love after all. I do not share his love for the stage. It is certainly an easier life and in a way I envy him. Obviously, it becomes harder and harder for me to make movies, just as everything else is harder for me now—going up the stairs for example.

M . C . :   *When you think about your first movies such as* The Maltese Falcon *or* The Treasure of the Sierra Madre, *does it seem to you that there are some aspects of filmmaking that interested you once but no longer do, and certain other aspects of filmmaking that now interest you more?*
H U S T O N :   Not really. I believe my attitude did not change; I must say that I never thought about that.

M . C . :   *You are perhaps the last of the great Hollywood storytellers. Your famous contemporaries have more or less disappeared.*
H U S T O N :   That is what happens with age! People describe me as an old lion. Nobody caresses my tail of late, that is where the problem is.

M . C . :   *What is striking in your adaptation of* Under the Volcano *is that you do not try to be faithful to Lowry's style. You remained faithful to yourself, made the film in the naturalistic style of your other movies, a style that is closer to Ham-mett or Hemingway.*
H U S T O N :   I believe that being faithful to yourself gives extra strength to any style of drama. But I would like to come back to the old lion. When I was shooting a sequence of *The Bible* in Egypt, I wanted a lion to attack the pagan king, but this turned out to be impossible to do. We went to the zoo to see the old lion. He would not hurt a fly, and would certainly escape to the desert where we would have to hunt him down; I could not bring myself to do that. And that old lion was so sweet and so nice in his cage! He was at the end of his life, and the following day it was an act of kindness to put him out of his pain. I hope that my life will not end like that.

M . C . :   *How did you work with the screenwriter Guy Gallo on* Under the Vol-cano, *and how did you reach the decision of cutting out the fourth main character, Laruelle?*

HUSTON: In a letter Lowry says that should he adapt his novel for the cinema, the character he would cut out would be Laruelle. I did not know Lowry personally but I discovered when reading his biography that many of my friends had met him. I have a lot of admiration for the novel; I think that it is a fascinating book but not a great book. There are times when the author is really inspired and produces unforgettable passages of writing. But I would not compare it to the great novels of my generation. Lowry tends to use symbols, images, and allusions in an almost suffocating way. All that is literary. Sometimes we feel that Lowry made use of everything that was within his reach, and he put into this book all that happened to him in his life. We feel that if he saw a cat cross a street or read a sign in a park, the cat and sign would be in the book. That is certainly the reason why he is, in a way, a man of only one book. He put all of his experience into one book. It is this that prevents it from being a great book. All those digressions, all the banter allowed him to hide himself rather than to reveal himself nakedly. He expressed himself through allusion, in an indirect way, without the directness of his contemporaries.

M.C.: *Do you think it was the most difficult film adaptation you had to do?*
HUSTON: Without any doubt. There were some difficulties with *Moby Dick* also, but they were not of the same kind. All that Melville put into his novel was directly related to the theme.

M.C.: *You dealt with great writers: Hammett, Stephen Crane, Carson McCullers, Tennessee Williams, Melville, Kipling, Flannery O'Connor. Sometimes you also found your subject in books that are less well-known. Did that make any difference with your adaptations?*
HUSTON: I consider each case separately. Each movie presents a different problem. And if I have a similar point of view towards some movies I am not aware of it. Of course, adapting Flannery O'Connor was easier than adapting Lowry. We just changed some sentences, cut out some parts. It was the same for *The Maltese Falcon*. The book was ready to be put into images. On the other hand there were many original contributions in *The Red Badge of Courage* and *Moby Dick*, but I think and hope that the authors would have approved those additions.

M.C.: *Toward the end of the movie, in Finney's long monologue, you use the florid, baroque style of Lowry. Did you consider using more of that style for the remainder of the movie?*

HUSTON: It would have been easier to use more of that kind of monologue, but we decided to make very sparing use of it because we didn't want
it to become a literary movie. We wanted people to confront a human experience, not to have them listen to the text of a book reproduced on the screen.

M.C.: *Many Hustonian heroes face up to a challenge, and even if they are defeated at the end we remember their struggle before anything else. The Consul is
not one of your typical heroes. He seems condemned from the beginning.*
HUSTON: I think that the Consul is striving even though his fate is actually fixed from the beginning. But in that way he is not different from Captain Ahab in *Moby Dick*. That is the definition of tragedy: the unavoidability
of death. Tragedy doesn't lie in the fact that the hero dies or that we pity
him, because that also happens in comedy. Comedy is governed by the accidents that can change the unfolding of the story. In a tragedy, on the con-
trary, we have only one possible conclusion. The Consul's weapon against
fate is alcohol. Many people feel that his drinking is a form of self-destruc-
tion. I don't agree. He does everything to win: he wants to love that woman,
he wants to love the brother, but he cannot accept betrayal. From that moment, he feels as if life itself has betrayed him. When at the end he faces his
enemies, he calls them by their names and tells them what they are. The
movie is therefore about a struggle, not about a man who is waving a flag of
truce.

M.C.: Under the Volcano *and* Paris, Texas *both deal with the presence of the
past without any use of flashbacks. Did you try to use them?*
HUSTON: If you take a close look at the scenario, you will see that there is
not much exposition, and what exposition there is has an immediate appli-
cation to what is happening in the present. We are not told about what happened in the past. In a certain way, the past is dramatized in the present.
When the Colonel speaks of the German officer who was thrown in an oven,
it is not something that is being recalled but has a bearing on the present
moment.

M.C.: *How did your great knowledge of Mexico help you to make that movie?*
HUSTON: Strangely, it was rather by accident. We wanted to shoot in the
same locations that inspired Lowry. Any change would have been a mistake
and I had no intention of doing it.

M . C . : *Some countries live on stereotypes, and these stereotypes are rooted in a deep truth. It is the case with Mexico with the Celebration of the Dead and the tortillas, or with Spain with corrida and flamenco. Many critics have reproached Rosi, in* Carmen, *for making use of Spanish dance and the running of the bulls, considering them a recourse to clichés.*

HUSTON: They criticize him for that? [laughter] But what else is *Carmen?* The music of *Carmen* also has something of the cliché. I was not afraid of using those stereotypes in *Under the Volcano* because they are true. If they were not, if they were a distortion of the truth or were falsified, I would have discarded them.

M . C . : *Did you always have Albert Finney is mind for the role of the Consul?*

HUSTON: We thought about Richard Burton, then we even considered Peter O'Toole. Even though he is a remarkable actor, he was too old for the role and did not have the necessary strength, because he is described as possessing the power of a horse. Richard Burton would have been perfect but he had other obligations. So we contacted Albert Finney and I must say that I don't regret it. For the first time I was showing an alcoholic on the screen, and I needed someone who could be the embodiment of that character. To me, he was ideal, he is the Consul. He is an actor that I put at the top of his profession.

M . C . : *You must also have been attracted by the political ideas that are expressed in Lowry's novel, which are close to your own at the time of the Spanish Civil War and during the period of McCarthyism. In the adaptation, we see the character of the German Consul that does not exist in the book. The emphasis is put more on the Nazi threat than on the civil war in Spain.*

HUSTON: The Spanish Civil War is a way of showing the idealism but also the sentimentality of the idealism that inhabit the Consul's soul. Idealism is a very complicated thing: it is both genuine and full of falsities.

M . C . : *It is what we find in many of your movies, a mixture of engagement and detachment, of romanticism and irony.*

HUSTON: Yes, my characters know how to laugh at themselves.

M . C . : *What do you think about American cinema now?*

HUSTON: I find it miraculous that so many good movies are produced now, given what the studios became. I do not know how under such bad auspices people manage to make interesting pictures. With a few exceptions, I have a poor opinion of the system on the whole. Yet talent flourishes there. Somebody was asked if nowadays there are actors who can compare with those of the "golden age" of Hollywood, such as Gary Cooper or Clark Gable; and he answered, justly, that it was not so. Those former actors cannot compare with the ones that are here now, such as Robert De Niro and Dustin Hoffman. They are wonderful actors.

M . C . :   *Is there any great writer that you think about adapting, after having adapted the work of so many others?*

HUSTON: Yes, I would like to film *The Autumn of the Patriach* of Gabriel García Márquez. To me he is a great novelist. It is a very complicated novel and I hope that Márquez will help us with the adaptation.

M . C . :   *Do the comments of the critics matter to you? When they say, for example, that you make great movies, but also* Phobia. . . .

HUSTON: If I did a bad job, I don't have any problem with its being described in that way. But if I did something that I like and it is not well understood by critics who attack it, I am hurt by it. For example, I do not think that the harsh criticism of *Moby Dick* and of Gregory Peck's portrayal of Ahab were deserved. I am all the more sure of that now after seeing the movie again on television.

M . C . :   *Do you know that they just published Sartre's scenario of your* Freud *in France? How do you feel about your experience with him on the film?*

HUSTON: The problem is that he was inexhaustible whether he was talking or writing. He did not have any discipline. He would not even listen to what people would tell him and would keep on writing and talking without getting tired. He did not know a word in English and the interpreters could not follow the rapid flow of his speech. I have a lot of respect and admiration for him. But as a scenarist he had a problem. And not only as a scenarist. When asked to give an introduction to Genet's work, he provided a text that was longer than any of Genet's books. It is very strange. He would simply not stop talking or writing. . . .

M . C . :   *It has been more than thirty years since you have lived in the United States. Why?*

HUSTON: If I were living there I would be as far from the mainstream as I am when I live in Ireland or Mexico. I love the countryside and I would probably settle in a place like Idaho. I have never liked Hollywood a lot, the life the people live there. In Hollywood I could indulge myself with poker games, but in general it does not attract me. I have a wonderful life in Mexico. I rent a creek there from some Indians, who will have it back when I die. No problem! I do not go horseback riding as I used to when I was in Ireland, but I swim in the sea, which has so much salt in it that you could be transformed into a statue before being drowned in it. And the old idiot I am likes to row in his canoe.

Playboy Interview: John Huston

LAWRENCE GROBEL/1985

THERE'S TROUBLE IN PARADISE as John Huston looks up at the sky again and sees no sign of rain. He has been living in Las Caletas, Mexico, which is south of Puerto Vallarta and reachable only by boat, for ten years, and when the rains don't come, the wells dry up and there's no running water. His hacking, recurring cough expresses his displeasure.

The short-wave connection to his secretary in Puerto Vallarta is not coming through, and when it finally does, he's told that Maricela, the young woman who is both companion and caretaker, missed her flight and won't be back until tomorrow. So even here, where pelicans float on the sea and iguanas rest on boulders, it's beyond snafu (situation normal, all fucked up), at tarfu (things are really fucked up) and closing in on fubar (fucked up beyond any recognition)—favorite expressions of Huston's—but that's OK with him.

He would probably scoff at being called a national treasure, but if John Huston doesn't fit the cliché, no one in America does. As writer, director, and actor, he has been a force in our culture for more than four decades, from his first hyphenated credit as writer-director of the 1941 remake of The Maltese Falcon *to his recently released and highly charged Mafia black comedy,* Prizzi's Honor, *starring Jack Nicholson, Kathleen Turner, and his daughter Anjelica.*

Over his long life, Huston has lived in New York, Arizona, California, France, England, Africa, Ireland, and now Mexico, which has always fascinated him. In 1948, he wrote and directed The Treasure of the Sierra Madre *there and received*

separate Oscars as director and screenwriter. Nearly two decades after that, he de-
cided to film Tennessee Williams's The Night of the Iguana *in Puerto Vallarta*
and helped turn a sleepy village of 2500 into a bustling tourist attraction of 80,000.

Huston is one of the last of a breed of rugged individualists who had enough
talent and courage to carve out a life that reads a lot like an overblown Kipling
story. Born in Nevada, Missouri, in 1906, Huston has been a semipro boxer, painter,
writer of fiction and screenplays, big-game hunter, actor, director, horseman, great
drinker, womanizer, husband (five times), father (of five children, one adopted),
animal lover, architect, storyteller, narrator, and, at appropriate times, the voices
of Noah and God.

He was dared to adapt such great works of literature as Melville's Moby Dick,
Kipling's The Man Who Would be King, *Stephen Crane's* The Red Badge of
Courage *and Flannery O'Connor's* Wise Blood *and turned B. Traven's* The Treasure of the Sierra Madre, *C. S. Forester's* The African Queen, *Dashiell Ham-*
mett's The Maltese Falcon, *W. R. Burnett's* The Asphalt Jungle, *Arthur Miller's*
The Misfits *and Carson McCullers's* Reflections in a Golden Eye *into some of*
the most memorable stories ever put onto film.

It was his father, actor Walter Huston, who not only encouraged him to direct
but showed him the fundamentals of drama when he took his son to the 1923
Dempsey-Firpo heavy-weight-championship fight at the Polo Grounds. Dempsey
was, to the seventeen-year-old Huston, a god. "Nobody in my lifetime has ever had
such glory about him. He walked in a nimbus." When the fight started, he dropped
the much larger Firpo in the first fifteen seconds. Firpo got up, went down, got up,
went down again—and the crowd went crazy. Then, incredibly, Firpo threw a
mighty punch that sent Dempsey through the ropes. Huston thought it was over,
but Dempsey got back in and knocked Firpo down at the bell. In the second round,
Dempsey won the fight and young John learned a lessen in courage and drama he
would always remember.

As a fighter himself, Huston won his 140-pound division at Lincoln Heights
High School in Los Angeles and then boxed in clubs for five dollars a fight, winning
twenty-three of twenty-five bouts, until he discovered painting and enrolled in the
Smith School of Art. Painting has remained a passion, but it was the theater that
enthralled him. His mother, a journalist, and his father had divorced, but Walter
Huston kept in touch with his son—and passed along a love for the theater.

In 1924, John acted for the first time with the Provincetown Players in Greenwich
Village. He married his first sweetheart, Dorothy Harvey, and they lived in Malibu,
broke but happy; Huston returned to the ring to pick up some cash. His career lasted

one bout, in which he was pummeled so hard that he decided to return to the haven of the arts.

His mother had smuggled a copy of James Joyce's Ulysses into the country, and it affected Huston in much the same way as Dempsey's flattening Firpo. He tried his hand at writing stories. One, called "Fool," was accepted by American Mercury.

He became a journalist, working for the New York Daily Graphic, then wrote a play for marionettes and acted in a short film called Two Americans in 1929. When his friend Herman Shulin (who had directed Grand Hotel) suggested he go to Hollywood as a contract writer for Sam Goldwyn, Huston gave up journalism and crossed the country once again.

Although he wrote a few scripts (A House Divided, Law and Order, Mruders in the Rue Morge), his first experience in Hollywood was disappointing. His marriage dissolved when his wife discovered he was having an affair. He had a car accident in which he ran over and killed a girl crossing the street. Shaken, he took an offer to write scripts in London and moved to England.

The job proved to be a bust, and Huston soon found himself sleeping in London parks and singing cowboy songs in the streets. Twenty-eight and penniless, he returned to the States, where he fell in love with an Irish girl named Lesley Black. They married and went to Hollywood, where Huston was asked by his friend William Wyler to doctor a script he had been writing called Jezebel.

Next, Huston wrote The Amazing Dr. Clitterhouse for Edward G. Robinson and Humphrey Bogart, collaborated on Juarez for Paul Muni and moved to the San Fernando Valley, where he designed his first house. He wrote Dr. Ehrlich's Magic Bullet in 1940, and his screenplay was nominated for an Oscar. He then wrote Sergeant York for Warner Bros., followed by High Sierra and then by his directorial debut, The Maltese Falcon.

Before Bogart's death in 1957, Huston directed him in five other films: Across the Pacific, The Treasure of the Sierra Madre, Key Largo, The African Queen and Beat the Devil.

The outbreak of the Second World War coincided with the breakup of Huston's second marriage, coming soon after he and his wife had lost their daughter, born prematurely. He accepted a commission as a lieutenant in the U.S. Army Signal Corps, and between 1943 and 1946, he made three of the most powerful and controversial war documentaries: Report from the Aleutians, The Battle of San Pietro and Let There Be Light. The effect of the San Pietro documentary was so vivid, its depiction of war so bitter, that it was classified as secret by the War Department;

it took a direct order by General George C. Marshall to override the classification. And it wasn't until January 1981 that Walter Mondale, as vice president, got Let There Be Light released.

By the war's end, Huston had fallen in love with a married woman, Marietta Fitzgerald. While waiting for her to leave her husband, he met actress Evelyn Keyes, who proposed to him at a restaurant. Ever the gentleman, Huston accepted and they flew to Vegas to marry that night.

During the McCarthy era, Huston helped form a group called the Committee for the First Amendment, which was falsely described as a Communist-front organization. Disgusted with the politics of the time, Huston left the country to make The African Queen, Moulin Rouge and Beat the Devil. He eventually found a haven in Ireland; he bought an estate in Galway and became a fox-hunting gentleman farmer. By then, he was married to his fourth wife, Enrica "Ricki" Soma. In 1964, he became an Irish citizen. Eleven years after that, ever restless, he moved to Mexico.

To find out more about this legendary man, Playboy sent Contributing Editor Lawrence Grobel (who has conducted "Playboy Interviews" with two actors who have worked for Huston, Marlon Brando and George C. Scott) to Las Caletas for a week of intensive conversations. Grobel's report:

"It shouldn't be easy getting to see John Huston and, by God, it isn't. After the flight to Puerto Vallarta, it's a twenty-kilometer drive along a narrow road between the mountains and the sea to an unpaved, rocky turnoff at a place called Boca de Tomatlán. José, Huston's boatman, was waiting by his ponga. A washing machine was already in the boat, being transported to Huston's coastal hideaway, and José suggested that I sit behind it as we made our way through choppy seas.

"When I realized that it wasn't secured, the trip became a ride of terror; the machine slid from side to side as we plowed through the waves, and I feared being crushed to death by an errant washing machine.

"The sun was bright, the weather warm, the sky blue and unpolluted. The huge boulders that made up the shore line of the Mexican Pacific are scarred as if sliced by the ax of some angry Mexican god, and the jungle glowers behind the shore.

"The house Huston lives in is a simple one: An arched trellis provides shade over the path to the house, which consists of living room, bedroom, and bathroom. A satellite dish and a short-wave radio provide him with all the contact with the outside world he needs. In his bedroom, books and scripts cover his large bed; vials of pills line the top of the bookcase.

"Although racked by emphysema and worn down by heart surgery, he is still a *vigorous, unvanguished man whose life force is strong. He takes a daily morning swim in the sea, works a full day and reads long into the night. He was a gracious host, conscientious, thoughtful, insightful, I liked him enormously."*

PLAYBOY: *Coming to Puerto Vallarta to interview you is an adventure in itself.*
HUSTON: Well, this is the most primitive home I have ever had, with the jungle at my back and the ocean a few steps from my house. No running water, either. It hasn't rained in more than three months, so the spring has run dry. You get used to it. It's a hell of a lot better than living in Bel Air, which is the kind of life I can least imagine myself living—where if your neighbor has a Colonial mansion, you have a Swiss chalet and, depending on how rich you are, you live north or south of Sunset Boulevard. [*Laughs*]

PLAYBOY: *At least in Bel Air, you could get help in an emergency. You're seventy-nine years old and an hour's boat ride away from a hospital. Doesn't that concern you?*
HUSTON: Not an hour; it's a day from anywhere, because the hospital in Puerto Vallarta is not what I would call space-age outfitted. But what the hell. If you think like that, you can have a heart attack in the Beverly Hills Hotel and be dead before you get to the ambulance—which is how my father died.

PLAYBOY: *What kind of shape are you in?*
HUSTON: I'm in terrible shape. I've got emphysema as bad as you can have it. A flight of steps is a short climb up Mount Everest for me. I went to Mexico City, where the smog is ten times as bad in Los Angeles, and, Christ, I didn't think I could make it to the curb.

PLAYBOY: *Do you miss Ireland?*
HUSTON: Yes. It was wonderful; I loved it.

PLAYBOY: *Why did you leave?*
HUSTON: Two reasons. When I went to Ireland, it was one of the cheaper places in Europe to live. But prices kept going up, salaries kept rising, until today it's one of the most expensive countries. The other big consideration was the hunting, which was a strenuous sport. I was joint master of the Galway Blazers for ten years. But when I couldn't hunt any longer, those two things just decided it for me. But it was one of the best periods of my life.

PLAYBOY: *Are you still an Irish citizen?*
HUSTON: Yes.

PLAYBOY: *Are there any other locations for which you feel nostalgia?*
HUSTON: I liked Africa, but a lot of the places that I've been to are quite impossible today. When I was in Africa to shoot *The African Queen,* for instance, there was no conflict, the people were friendly and hospitable, and you felt perfectly safe in places that now no one dares mention, such as the backwaters of Uganda, where you can get killed. it's hard to imagine those gentle, delightful people, who were very well governed, by the way. . . . I was, and theoretically still am, against colonialism, but, my God, they were a lot better off under the English.

PLAYBOY: *Wasn't that when your expatriate life began—with* The African Queen?
HUSTON: Well, I didn't exactly pack my bags and leave America. It's just that I had one son, my wife was going to have another baby, and since I had to cut that movie in England, I took them all over. Then came the idea of doing *Moulin Rouge,* so I went to France, and after that came *Beat the Devil.* During that time, I would go over to Ireland for hunting weekends. It was something I had never experienced before, the best hunting in the world. That led me to rent a house in Ireland.

PLAYBOY: *There's lots of talk about—writing, directing, acting, your rich personal life—but since you mentioned it,* The African Queen *seems as good a place as any to begin. What memories do you have of that location—of Katharine Hepburn and your friend Humphrey Bogart?*
HUSTON: We had some funny encounters in Africa. To start out with, we had talked with a local king who said that his people would be villagers for us, but when the time came, no one showed up. So we drove a considerable distance to this king's native village. I said, "Why aren't the people coming?" He said, "They are afraid you are going to eat them." I said, "Oh, no, we wouldn't dream of doing anything like that." By that time, there was quite an audience of villagers around us, and he asked for volunteers. Two of the bravest men I have encountered held up their hands. Just two. So we took them back with us, wined and dined them and drove them back to their village. The next morning, they all came. They called it the Third World, but,

my God, Africa was the ninety-seventh world! It was so far removed from our awareness, there was no basis for comparison.

PLAYBOY: *The stories about that film are that Hepburn was very much put off by you and Bogart and the project in general. Just how skeptical was she at first?*
HUSTON: Extremely. Katie was born suspicious, and she had great reservations regarding me that she was in no pains to conceal. She knew that both Bogart and I were wastrels, but Katie has a weakness for wastrels. Spencer Tracy was also one. But we put it on for her. We pretended to be even bigger wastrels than we were.

PLAYBOY: *How?*
HUSTON: By writing dirty things on her mirror in soap—childish things that shocked her. She always rose to the bait. She was suspicious of my advice as a director and wasn't sure how she was going to play her character in the film. I advised her to play her as a lady rather than a shrew. She said, "What lady?" I said, "Eleanor Roosevelt." That made sense to her, and her performance thereafter was everything I had ever hoped for.

PLAYBOY: *Did you become close?*
HUSTON: I don't think I was ever closer to anybody than I was to Katie out there. Not in a romantic way; there was only one man in her life, and there was no room for anybody but Spence.

PLAYBOY: *Wasn't there a story about the two of you getting caught in the middle of a herd of elephants?*
HUSTON: Well, that was a bad moment. I used to go out shooting in the morning to get game for the pot. It was always in my mind to get a really impressive trophy, a big tusk. There was a book written about my quest for a big elephant, but I never shot one. I wouldn't commit the sin—not the crime but the sin—of shooting an elephant unless the reward were sufficiently handsome. I wanted nothing less than 100 kilos in the way of a trophy. Anyway, Katie took a very dim view of my shooting. She said, "John, this just doesn't go with the rest of your character. You're not a murderer, and yet you shoot these beautiful animals." I said, "Katie, you can't really understand unless you come with me and experience it." So she did, and from that day on, Katie was a veritable Diana of the hunt. We shot antelope, water-

buck. You couldn't restrain her. She would come into my cabin and wake me before dawn to get in an hour of shooting before we started work on the picture. One of those mornings, there were elephant signs. It was a very heavy forest in Uganda, and we worked very carefully down wind. All of a sudden, there was a very loud growl, which was the elephant's insides digesting, about five feet away. We froze, of course, and the elephant didn't know we were there. But then the breeze changed and our scent drifted and hell broke loose. There were elephants going by like train engines. You must not run under those circumstances, because that only confuses the elephants, which are trying to get away from you. But if they're confused, they're likely to pick you up and throw you away for good. I turned and looked at Katie, who had my light rifle up to her shoulder. She was going to go down like the heroine she is. Fortunately, those locomotives all went by us, and I breathed very deeply and wiped the sweat off my brow. Katie wasn't shaken by the experience. I was profoundly shaken. It was a hell of a note, my taking my star out, submitting her to that sort of thing.

PLAYBOY: *You once nearly did away with the picture's other star, too, didn't you?*

HUSTON: Yes, in Italy, just before we began shooting *Beat the Devil*. There was an element of absurdity about that whole experience. I found myself in Rome with the company, the crew—everything but a script. It was no spot to be in. I said to Bogey, "Let's forget the whole thing." He surprised me very much, saying, "John, it's only money." Then he and I got a chauffeur-driven car to go to Naples, and at a fork in the road, the driver couldn't make up his mind and went straight ahead through a stone wall. I was sitting in the front seat and braced myself, but Bogey was asleep in the back seat. His teeth had been knocked out; he had bitten through his tongue. We got him to a hospital and had to wait ten days for his bridge to be duplicated and sent over.

PLAYBOY: *You say you were stuck without a script. How did you come up with one?*

HUSTON: I met a young man named Truman Capote on the street in Rome and asked him if he could help us out. He said sure. He was an extraordinary little man who had the courage and the determination of a lion. We worked on the script together. We had been writing feverishly for a few days when his face got swollen to half again its size. He had an impacted wisdom tooth. So I called an ambulance and we took him to the hospital; and that night, pages came back to me from the hospital. That was typical of Truman.

PLAYBOY: *When you have your writer's hat on, how do you work with a collaborator?*
HUSTON: As a rule, I write a scene and the other person writes a scene; then he takes mine and I take his and we rewrite.

PLAYBOY: *How good a screenwriter do you think you are?*
HUSTON: I think I am one of the best.

PLAYBOY: *Are there many others?*
HUSTON: There aren't many. Ingmar Bergman. Robert Bolt writes beautifully for the screen. Screenwriting is such a very special branch of literature. In some ways, it's closer to the poetic form than it is to the dramatic. A lot of book writers think that they write down to an audience if they do a motion-picture script.

PLAYBOY: *Speaking of writing up or down to your audience, it seems as if some of your latest films, such as* Under the Volcano *and* Wise Blood, *have been smaller, more personal than the adventure films for which you're famous—*The Maltese Falcon, The African Queen, The Treasure of the Sierra Madre, The Man Who Would Be King. *Why have you gone in this direction?*
HUSTON: Nothing conscious about it. I don't think of those films as art films, nor do I think of adventure as something that simply implies action or exploit. The consul in *Volcano,* played by Albert Finney, is an adventurer. *Volcano* is an adventure of the mind, of the soul.

PLAYBOY: *Nevertheless, these films are different in appeal. Is that what interests you more now?*
HUSTON: No, there's no design in any of this. My new movie, *Prizzi's Honor,* is not a small film. But, yes, I am less concerned with having to make a buck.

PLAYBOY: *In writing about* Under the Volcano, The New York Times *called you a "bold visionary." Are you?*

H U S T O N :   I'm a bold visionary with other people's work. I haven't origi-
nated my films in any true sense. As for the acting, that is largely the work
of the artists themselves. Just as I had done with many other actors, I often
said to Albert Finney and the others, "Work something out; I'll leave you
alone." I'd leave them for an hour or two and they'd come up with something.

P L A Y B O Y :   *Isn't that a favorite expression of yours—"Work something out"?*
H U S T O N :   Yes. And if they are the right people playing the part, what they
choose to do is right, as a rule, and that's a great help. It's a practice of mine
to get as much out of the actor as I can, rather than to impose myself upon
his performance.

P L A Y B O Y :   *But what happens when you ask your actors to come up with something and they can't—or when a scene isn't working, no matter what you do?*
H U S T O N :   You go back to the sources, to the writing. You may even discover that the scene isn't needed and can be dropped; that's happened a time
or two. I'll give you a very good example: I had such a scene in *The Night of
the Iguana.* The dialog and the situation were good, but for some reason, the
scene wasn't coming off. It was between Richard Burton and the young girl,
Sue Lyon. He's in his room at that hotel in Puerto Barrio, and she comes to
see him surreptitiously. She wants him to make love to her and he resists.
He's shaving, there is a whiskey bottle on a shelf, and they have this dialog
that doesn't work.

Well, Tennessee Williams was down there on the set, and I said to him,
"I'm having trouble with this; see if you can do anything about it." He had
it for me the next morning. What he had done with it made it perhaps the
best scene in the picture: When she comes in, instead of dialog, her very
appearance startles him and he bumps against the shelf and the whiskey
bottle falls off and breaks on the floor. He's barefoot. He begins to tell her
why they must not make love and, in talking, he walks up and down, the
broken glass cutting his feet. She watches him become a kind of martyr with
fascination; then she takes off her shoes and joins him in his martyrdom,
cutting her own feet as their dialog is played over that. I think that's a striking example of the answer to your question.

P L A Y B O Y :   *Yet Williams wasn't happy with the way you ended* Iguana, *was
he?*

HUSTON: We talked a lot about the finish of the picture and disagreed on it. The most amusing character in the play was the one played by Ava Gardner, who had the most penetrating remarks. Yet, in the end, he wanted her to be a female spider. But he himself had written her sympathetically, and it seemed to me he was pulling back his sympathy at the end. He resisted the finish as we had written it for the screen but couldn't come up with anything as good. He just wanted to make the Ava Gardner character consuming and destructive. Finally, I said, "Tennessee, I think you've got it in for women; you don't want to see a man and a woman in a love relationship, and that's at the bottom of it." He didn't contest that; he just thought about it and stopped arguing. Yet years later, in London at a luncheon party, the last thing he ever said to me, just before he left, was, "John, I still don't agree with you about the finish. I think that finish was a mistake."

PLAYBOY: *Was Williams a genius?*
HUSTON: Yes.

PLAYBOY: *What is a genius?*
HUSTON: Someone who sees things in a way that illuminates them and enables you to see things in a different way.

PLAYBOY: *How many have you known?*
HUSTON: Well, one knows men of genius only through their work. I'd say Williams; Eugene O'Neill; Manzù, the sculptor; Henry Moore, the sculptor; Mark Rothko, the painter; Henri Cartier-Bresson; in a funny way, Robert Capa, the photographer; Ernest Hemingway; William Faulkner; Dashiell Hammett; Marlon Brando. I've seen flashes of it in others: Bergman; Vittorio De Sica; Akiro Kurosawa.

PLAYBOY: *Brando is the only actor you include. What about some of his peers from the old days, such as Montgomery Clift and James Dean?*
HUSTON: Clift and Dean were in the same league, but Brando was something else entirely. Brando had an explosive thing; you felt something smoldering, dangerous, about to ignite at times. Did you see *Julius Caesar?* Christ! I will never forget that; it was like a furnace door opening—the heat came off the screen. I don't know another actor who could do that.

PLAYBOY: *You directed him in* Reflections in a Golden Eye. *What comes to mind?*

HUSTON: An extraordinary, amazing actor. If you remember the scene where he talks about the Army, standing at the mantelpiece, it's a long speech and he fiddles with a candle. Well, he did it, and after the first time, I could have said, "That's it," as I often do; but knowing Marlon and the way he works, I said, "Let's do it again." We did it three times, and each time was different; any of them could have been used!

In another scene, he gives a lecture on leadership to a class as his wife is in the background, on horseback, with the man she was having an affair with. He did that completely differently two or three times. I've never seen any other actor do that.

PLAYBOY: *Do you think Brando's disdain for his profession is real?*

HUSTON: Yes, I think it's real, though he takes his acting very seriously. He is not a dilettante in that sense. I'm not sure that he felt about acting the way Laurence Olivier does, or John Gielgud, or those who are dedicated to the art of acting. His doing a season at Stratford is beyond one's imagination. But, God knows, he is a fine actor and a very intelligent man. I don't know whether Brando has done some of the things he has simply because of the money, but I can't imagine him being bad in anything, though I think the worst thing I ever saw Brando do was *Apocalypse Now,* which was just dreadful—the finish of that picture. The model for it, *Heart of Darkness,* has no finish, either, and the moviemakers just didn't find one. It's very good for a picture to have an ending before you start shooting. [*Laughs*]

PLAYBOY: *Of your several careers, when did you start thinking of yourself as a writer?*

HUSTON: H. L. Mencken, the legendary editor of *American Mercury,* accepted a short story I'd written called "Fool" in 1929. It was the first time anybody had ever published anything of mine. I can't begin to describe the importance Mencken had in my young manhood. He was the most prestigious figure in this country, as far as I was concerned; the arbiter of taste and judgment as the editor of the finest magazine. When his letter came saying he wished to publish my story, why, that was a high moment in my life.

PLAYBOY: *Soon after that, you became a reporter for the New York* Daily Graphic. *Did you like being a journalist?*

HUSTON: No, I was the world's worst reporter. There was a night city editor who hated my guts. He would fire me and the day city editor would hire me back. I was hired and fired three or four times. All my sympathies, by the way, are with the night city editor. He was quite correct. The thing that finally brought about my separation from the paper forever happened when I was sent to cover a murder in a tobacco factory in New Jersey. One of the workers had killed another one, and I got my notes mixed up and had the owner of the factory down as the murderer. That ended my career as a newspaperman.

PLAYBOY: *And when did your career as a director begin?*
HUSTON: Let's see: I was a boxer while I was in high school, and I was also going to the Art Students League in California; I had a half notion that I'd be a painter and a half notion I might have the makings of a welterweight champion. Then I went to New York on a visit to my father, whom I wasn't living with. I had only seen him in vaudeville, not in the New York theater. He was in *Desire Under the Elms*. That's when I met O'Neill. I was about seventeen, and it influenced me enormously, seeing one of the great American plays come together.

   Anyway, some years later, when I had had some success as a writer in Hollywood, my father asked me to direct him in a play, *A Passenger to Bali*. I'd never directed, of course. I'm trying to remember whether I had ever expressed the desire to direct. . . . No, it was his idea, as I recall. The play had a modest success, but it confirmed my desire to become a director.

PLAYBOY: *So the credit goes to your father?*
HUSTON: Yes, yes.

PLAYBOY: *But how did you get your chance to direct—getting as your first movie a small property called* The Maltese Falcon?
HUSTON: It came from my being a writer first. My standing as a writer was quite high at Warner's; and after I had adapted *High Sierra*, my agent had it written into my contract that if they took up my option, they'd let me direct a picture. When it came time, Henry Blanke, who was a producer at Warner Bros. and a man of great taste and discrimination, became something of a champion of mine, and he backed me up. When I said I wanted to direct *The Maltese Falcon*, the studio heads were astonished and delighted, because they

owned it. It had been a bad picture twice before, but it makes sense to remake a bad picture.

PLAYBOY: *George Raft was Warner's first choice to star, not Bogart. Had he made it, would it have been——*
HUSTON: Not nearly as good. I couldn't have been more pleased when Raft turned it down.

PLAYBOY: *Did you have any idea that you were making a film classic?*
HUSTON: I knew it was a marvelous book. Hammett is one of the great American writers, a great stylist.

PLAYBOY: *Did you cast the picture yourself?*
HUSTON: Yes. Just think of a completely inexperienced director's bringing Sydney Greenstreet out from New York. They gave me the actors I wanted. Being in charge of my own casting has allowed me not to have to do as much directing through the years. If the actors aren't right, then you have to direct and conceal that fact.

PLAYBOY: *Casting your father in another picture,* The Treasure of the Sierra Madre, *was apparently a right decision.*
HUSTON: Yes. [*Laughs*] He got the Academy Award for it; I regard that film with great sentiment. And since I learned a lot about direction from seeing my father work, it was very gratifying.

PLAYBOY: *Were you close to your father?*
HUSTON: I didn't see a great deal of him until I was about fifteen years old. I had merely been told by my mother that he was an actor, which meant he was away. Then I remember my mother's saying they were getting a divorce. I stayed with my mother and my grandmother. But every month, he would write a letter and send money. Every year or two, they would send me to see him; and because I saw him so infrequently, he would put himself out, so it was always a very pleasant relationship. And since he had never played a father, he never assumed that role with me. We were more like brothers or good friends. He was a great companion; he loved great humor. I've never laughed with anyone else as much as I did with him.

PLAYBOY: *What was your mother like?*

HUSTON: Nervous . . . very active . . . smoked. When I say nervous, I mean tending toward the neurotic. She was better with animals than with people. She liked excitement. Still, I was closer to her than to my father, closer to the women in my family.

PLAYBOY: *That reminds us of a story we read about your mother's leaving you with your nursemaid when you were a boy. . . .*

HUSTON: Oh, yes, I know what you're talking about. I was very young, maybe five or six, and my mother was working and left me alone with this nursemaid. I lay on the bed with her, and somehow her dresses got up and her behind was bare, and I fiddled with her behind and thought it was marvelous. I thoroughly approved of it. I remember my mother coming to the front door, but I didn't tell her what had happened. There was some sense that I should keep this very strictly to myself, looking forward to further exploration.

PLAYBOY: *And?*

HUSTON: Unfortunately, the nursemaid disappeared from our lives almost immediately. [*Laughs*] But from that time on, I was trying to get little girls to show me their genitals.

PLAYBOY: *So you were advanced sexually?*

HUSTON: I don't know about that. I was comparatively late in having any coitus. I was about fifteen or sixteen, it was with a girl I met in the park. My mother was away, and I took her to my bedroom and pulled the shade down. My mother later noticed that the shade was down and asked me if I had been home during the afternoon. I confessed ignorance of that mystery.

PLAYBOY: *You must have made up for your ignorance by the time you got through school. There's another story we seem to remember involving you, a lady, and a commission in the Mexican army—all before you were twenty.*

HUSTON: Oh . . . that was when I first came down to Mexico. I loved horses and there was a well-known teacher of dressage in Mexico, and I thought if I could get down there, maybe I could get lessons from him. I had jumped horses, but I had never done dressage. I found the man, who was a colonel in the Mexican army, and he gave me lessons at a stable in Mexico

City. We became friends. I didn't have much money, and one day, the colonel said, "Look, you don't have to pay me for the dressage lessons anymore; why don't I just give you an honorary commission so you can ride horses and go to the officers' mess and not have to pay the expenses?" Well, that sounded good, and that's what I did.

The whole scene in Mexico and the army around that time was pretty abandoned. I became a kind of a Mexican-army pet, a mascot. It was a crazy country, much more so than now. I had never seen an outdoor swimming pool owned by an individual, and one night, a powerful bureaucrat named José Avelleneda, who later became secretary of the treasury, invited a group of us to his house in the country, and he had an outdoor swimming pool— and he had it full of whores, without any clothes on. He had brought them out for our visit. We dived right in. Life was a constant revel.

PLAYBOY: *And what happened with the woman—and a supposed duel?*
HUSTON: That was just an absurd thing. There was a count from South Africa whose main claim to glory was that he had lured Mata Hari, the German spy, over the Spanish border into France to be shot. That was his demonstration of patriotism. He was in hot pursuit of the wife of an American I got to know. She was afraid to tell her husband about the count, but she wanted him warned off. So I undertook to do it. There was a quarrel, we scuffled, were separated and he said, "I will meet you in an hour, where I will kill you."

I hurried downtown, where guns could be bought without a license. I wasn't an expert with handguns at all, so I bought the one with the longest barrel and took up my position, behind a tree, well before the stroke of the hour. I was going to shoot him as he turned the corner, aim the gun like a rifle and just shoot him [*laughs*]—so there would be no question of the outcome. Well, the count didn't turn the corner; my mother did! She had come down a few weeks earlier, had heard about the duel and had come to disarm me. And that was the end of that.

PLAYBOY: *That's not the only time you've been involved with guns and a lady-friend. We're thinking of the filming of* Moulin Rouge *in Paris, in 1952, and the actress Suzanne Flon.*
HUSTON: That happened on Bastille Day. I had been with Aly Khan, Zsa Zsa Gabor, José Ferrer, and Suzanne Flon. Afterward, I took Suzanne home in

a taxi, and when the taxi door opened, somebody came in and belted me—
hit me two or three times before I knew what was happening. I got out of
the cab and the man disappeared through an archway. I followed and he
came down some steps with a pistol, which he pointed at me. I went toward
him and he pulled the trigger, and I heard the pistol click and decided it
wasn't loaded. The taxi driver and a bystander got between us, and Suzanne
kept begging me to leave, so I did. But he had bruised me around the eyes
and I had to put on some dark glasses. He was in love with her; he was jealous
and he had been waiting to see who was taking her home.

Well, I found out where he lived, and I had a kind of goon in the company
who I asked to come with me, since I knew he had a gun. I knocked on his
door and he opened it, and I hit the door hard enough to knock him back,
then proceeded to kick the shit out of him. He couldn't fight; he tried to kick
me in the balls, so I gave him a little extra punishment for that. [*Laughs*] I
was still angry at this son of a bitch. Then he began to beg, saying he had
loved her for so many years and so on, and there was a knock at the door—
the gendarmes. We answered, said it was just a friendly scuffle—he was
bleeding from his nose and mouth. [*Laughs*] I said, "Let me see your gun,"
and he brought it; it was only a .22, but you can kill somebody with a .22. I
took the clip out of the gun and, son of a bitch, the round had misfired.

PLAYBOY: *Was Suzanne worth getting killed over?*
HUSTON: She was the most extraordinary woman I have ever known.

PLAYBOY: *Another, more publicized altercation was an hourlong fistfight you
had with Errol Flynn. How serious was that?*
HUSTON: He went to one hospital and I went to another. [*Laughs*] To reduce the publicity.

PLAYBOY: *You didn't say in your memoirs why you had that fight, but other
sources say it was over a remark Flynn had made about Olivia de Havilland.*
HUSTON: I've never said that.

PLAYBOY: *Still, it seems as if you feel a man needs to test his courage with an
occasional fight. True?*
HUSTON: It depends on how severe the test. I think it's of primary importance in the make-up of a man, the part that courage plays in his character.

It's happened to me frequently. Let's say that I've been able to conceal from others the anxiety that I felt at the time. *[Laughs]*

PLAYBOY: *That's straight out of Hemingway—whom you sparred with, correct?*
HUSTON: I had been told by someone that Hemingway had his doubts about me as a boxer. I'd been on the boat with Papa in Cuba—I think I began calling him Papa at that time—and instead of swimming directly to shore, he took a long walk instead. That evening, we had some cocktails and we were at his house and I said, "Have you got some gloves here, Papa?" And he said yes, and I said, "Let's put them on; I just want to see what your style is." He said, "You have longer arms and you're supposed to be a good boxer; you wouldn't stay out there and jab my face, jab my nose, would you?" And I said, "No, no, I wouldn't do anything like that." I meant it.

Well, Papa went into the other room with [writer] Peter Viertel, saying, "I'm gonna cool the son of a bitch." But Mary, his wife, said to me, "John, don't box with him, please; he has been having trouble with his heart; that's why he walked in today and didn't swim. No one is supposed to know that, but, please, don't box him." When he came out, I said, "Let's forget it," and that was the end of that.

PLAYBOY: *Did you ever consider working with him in any way?*
HUSTON: I was going to do a picture of Hemingway's at one time and the idea was for him to do a voice-over, a foreward to it, but it was impossible. His voice had a funny lack of expression in it.

PLAYBOY: *Does anyone today remind you of Hemingway?*
HUSTON: I'll tell you the actor who looks more like him than anybody else but doesn't resemble him in any other way: Burt Reynolds. He could be his brother.

PLAYBOY: *What do you think of Hemingway's choice of death?*
HUSTON: I approve completely. He knew he was on the way out; his mind was gone. Papa had been having persecution complexes, phobias, and life was dreadful for him. He had a moment or two of sanity and killed himself in one of those moments.

PLAYBOY: *You've been married five times. You're obviously a good judge of actors and actresses; how good a judge of women are you in your personal life?*

HUSTON: Quite good. I've delighted in the women I have known, been married to, and been in love with. It's really gone to make a very good life. I regret that I wasn't constituted, as some men are, to stay with one woman, though I believed implicitly each time that I would.

PLAYBOY: *Do you really regret this? After all, you seem to be in the mold of Hemingway, Norman Mailer, adventurous men who apparently outgrow their women.*
HUSTON: No, I think they grew just as fast as I did . . . and for the most part, they were extraordinary women, except the last, who was a crocodile. *[Laughs]* And even she was extraordinary, in a sense. Let me put it this way: I regret that lack within myself that enables a man to pour all his affection into one individual.

PLAYBOY: *Why do you call your last wife a crocodile?*
HUSTON: It's just the best description I have of her. *[Laughs]* I've been friends with all of my wives except the last. We were never good friends, from the word go.

PLAYBOY: *Were you surprised at your lack of perception about her?*
HUSTON: I was, indeed. I was shocked by it.

PLAYBOY: *Have you ever known a woman who you felt was your equal?*
HUSTON: Oh, many. A few, even superior. *[Laughs]* For sheer strength of character, I wouldn't have dared to cross swords with [Maria] Callas. I would rather have gone six rounds with Jack Dempsey! I had an aunt Margaret who was a very strong and intelligent woman. I didn't like her or have great regard for her, though. A woman we've talked about, for whom I have enormous respect and regard for her intelligence and humanity, is Suzanne Flon. Another is Iris Tree.

PLAYBOY: *You have five children, including an adopted son. Do you feel differently about each of them?*
HUSTON: Yes, I have different emotions toward each.

PLAYBOY: *Is it tough for them, being the children of John Huston?*
HUSTON: One of my sons has a little difficulty being a son of mine and the other one none at all, and neither of my daughters has any problem. Anjelica has a role in my new movie and is wonderful in it.

PLAYBOY: *Anjelica has been living with Jack Nicholson for some time; that makes him a kind of son-in-law. Is he a good one?*
HUSTON: As far as I'm concerned, he is.

PLAYBOY: *Do the rumors linking Nicholson to alleged cocaine use bother you?*
HUSTON: I don't think there is any truth to the stories. I have seen a good deal of Jack and never once have I seen him under the influence of drugs.

PLAYBOY: *You acted with Nicholson in* Chinatown; *now you've directed him in* Prizzi's Honor. *How do you assess him from both sides of the camera?*
HUSTON: Oh, he's a wonderful actor, one of the best. He just illuminates the book. He impressed me in one scene after another; the new movie is composed largely of first takes with him.

PLAYBOY: *Let's talk about some of the themes of your movies. There seems to be an element of despair in some of the recent ones. Does that reflect your own philosophy?*
HUSTON: I certainly don't know what the point of life is . . . but I don't indulge in depression. I think I see the world very clearly, though.

PLAYBOY: *Has life always seemed futile?*
HUSTON: Not always. In World War Two, I think I had as high hopes as anybody. It looked to me as if we were on our way to some kind of understanding of life.

PLAYBOY: *What changed that vision?*
HUSTON: The McCarthy era, the whole Red-baiting thing. The idea of America, the America of our founding fathers, was lost. It stopped being that America and became something else. And then one wondered whether it ever had been America except for the founding fathers and a few rare souls. Was it all an illusion? I know that what Roosevelt was doing with the New Deal seemed to hold the promise of a return to those original values. He was the only President in my time I thoroughly approved of. Red baiting did nothing to me and my career, because my nose was completely clean; I had no Communist inclination; but I had a few friends who were Communists, though they never told me they were. The thing is, I saw nothing reprehensi-

ble; if they chose to become Communists, that was their business. In America, there is supposed to be political and religious freedom!

PLAYBOY: *Your Committee of the First Amendment was described as a Communist front.*
HUSTON: Only afterward, you see.

PLAYBOY: *Why weren't you subpoened by the House Un-American Activities Committee?*
HUSTON: Because the members all knew I wasn't a Communist.

PLAYBOY: *Still, many Hollywood writers and directors were brought before HUAC.*
HUSTON: I think many of them were Communists. I know of one who was not, but he was never called to the stand. That was Howard Koch; he was subpoened but not called. HUAC had a pretty good idea of who was a Communist and who wasn't. The people who did get caught up in it were, for the most part, well-intentioned boobs from a poor background. A number of them had come from the Lower East Side of Manhattan, and out in Hollywood, they sort of felt guilty for living the good life. Their social conscience was more acute than the next fellow's.

PLAYBOY: *Didn't the head of MGM, Louis B. Mayer, want you to do a documentary tribute to Joe McCarthy?*
HUSTON: Yes. I just laughed. L. B. was a great patriot.

PLAYBOY: *Did he actually crawl on his knees and kiss your hand, as reported, begging you to make* Quo Vadis *for him?*
HUSTON: Yes, he was the kind of man who would do such a thing. *[Laughs]* He wanted that picture to be warm and emotional, and he described to me the way he had once hired Jeanette MacDonald against everyone's advice. Everyone said MacDonald pissed ice water—I'm quoting L. B.—but he knew that she had heart, and he said he sang her a Jewish song and was able to bring tears to her eyes. She went on and did *Ah, Sweet Mystery of Life* in that picture, and it was an experience that no one ever forgot. Now he wanted me to make *Quo Vadis* that kind of picture, and if I were able to, he

would get down on his knees and kiss my hand, and then he proceeded to do exactly that. Needless to say, I didn't make the film.

PLAYBOY: *Another example of your outlook was* Fat City, *a bleak look at one of your favorite pastimes—boxing—which contrasts, for example, with the upbeat tone of such movies as* Rocky.

HUSTON: Yes, one asks the questions, Why is a prize-fighting film such as *Rocky* a great success and a picture such as *Fat City* not successful at all? *Rocky* isn't the true world of boxing. *Rocky* is a world of boxing that's in people's minds. But the first *Rocky* was very good; there were some extraordinary moments in it—his seduction of the girl, getting her to take off her hat, standing there mute . . . it was memorable.

PLAYBOY: *Coming from an old boxer, that's at least some praise. You have a fondness for tough guys, don't you? Robert Mitchum, for instance.*

HUSTON: Yes, I like Mitchum enormously.

PLAYBOY: *Why?*

HUSTON: It's just his viewpoint, his attitude toward life. He doesn't dramatize anything; he's—I don't even like the word, but he's cool, he underplays everything and he has a wonderful humor. He's extremely intelligent, has marvelous powers of observation, can re-create a scene with all the funny aspects that it originally had. Mitchum is, essentially, a gent. I like his easy attitude. God, I've seen some funny things happen with Mitchum.

One night in Tobago, I went into the hotel where we were staying and Mitchum had a sailor over a balcony, holding him by the throat, slapping him around. Dorothy, his wife, was crying and begging him to let go, which Mitchum did. Then he laughed and strolled back to the bar. I said, "What in hell happened?" Turned out these two sailors had bothered him and he put up with them as long as he could and finally they jumped him; he knocked them both down. Mitchum could fight. It ended with them, so one sailor said, trying to be friends, "Give me a free one." Bob said all right, and the sailor hit him once for all he was worth. Bob said, "OK, you've had your free one," and turned away. Then the son of a bitch hit him again! Bob turned loose. That's when I came in, as Bob was throttling the guy, about to throw him over the balcony eighty feet down. *[Laughs]* But there is no element of the bully in Bob, no strutting his stuff. He's quite the opposite.

PLAYBOY: *A tough guy for whom you don't have much affection is George C. Scott. You once called him a shitheel in* Rolling Stone. *When you filmed* The Bible, *who was more difficult, the animals or Scott?*
HUSTON: Scott was more difficult, because he got drunk.

PLAYBOY: *How much abuse did he give Ava Gardner on that film?*
HUSTON: Considerable.

PLAYBOY: *Did you ever see him slap her?*
HUSTON: No. I saw him try to, but I was on his back and stopped him—with six others.

PLAYBOY: *Has your opinion of him changed?*
HUSTON: No, not in the slightest.

PLAYBOY: *Would you ever consider him for another role?*
HUSTON: No.

PLAYBOY: *Any other actors with whom you wouldn't have done a second film?*
HUSTON: Paul Muni. He was certainly an amazingly good actor, but he had a huge ego. He ruined a picture that I depended a great deal on—*Juarez.* He really ruined it. I can say this without bragging, because two other men worked with me on the script for almost a year; it was a very fine script and was written so Juarez would just come into the story at vital, special moments and when he spoke, every word counted. This was in contrast to the grace and eloquence of Maximilian. Well, the first thing Muni wanted was more dialog. A humorless man, vastly impressed with himself.

PLAYBOY: *Montgomery Clift was supposedly a difficult actor to work with, yet you starred him in two of your pictures—*The Misfits *and* Freud.
HUSTON: Emotionally, Clift was very fragile. He was a mess; he was gone. I remember that on *The Misfits,* Clark Gable had a bad back, a slipped disk; Monty would slap him on purpose. Gable didn't have much use for him, I must say. But it wasn't Clift who made filming *The Misfits* an ordeal; it was Marilyn Monroe. She was always trying to wake up or go to sleep.
    Marilyn and her husband, Arthur Miller, were at odds. I hadn't realized that until we were well into the picture. I was impertinent enough to say to

Arthur that to allow her to take drugs of any kind was criminal and utterly irresponsible on the part of anyone who had any feeling for her. It was only shortly after that I realized that she wouldn't listen to Arthur at all; he had no say over her actions.

PLAYBOY: *Do you believe her death was a suicide?*

HUSTON: No, no, I think it was an accident. You know, when I cast her in her first big picture [*The Asphalt Jungle*], I didn't have any idea that she was going to become America's sex queen. There was something very touching about her; one felt protective about Marilyn—and this is not simply after the fact, either. You felt that she was vulnerable and might get hurt, and she damn well did. The phrase sex queen may be a misapplication; that was no more than half of her attraction. She moved women as well as she did men.

PLAYBOY: *Getting back to Clift, is it true that he would cry when you excluded him from discussions during Freud?*

HUSTON: Tears came very easily to Monty. I was amazed how good the end result was, because it was really an ordeal.

PLAYBOY: *Was your reputation for being cruel to him unjust?*

HUSTON: Completely so. I was never kinder to anybody than I was to Clift. Sometimes I spoke harshly to him, but it was an attempt to awaken something in him. The combination of drugs, drink, and being homosexual was a soup that was just too much.

PLAYBOY: *There was talk of brain damage. Do you think that was true?*

HUSTON: Undoubtedly. He was never the same after his automobile accident. He lost the ability to memorize. In *The Misfits*, his lines were easy to learn, short, colloquial. *Freud* called for something entirely different, another language, as it were, the easy deployment of scientific terms—and he couldn't memorize anything.

PLAYBOY: Freud *didn't get the kind of reception you had hoped it would, did it?*

HUSTON: Well, I didn't like the beginning, but I did like the rest of the picture. I was surprised it didn't have an audience—and it certainly didn't. I'd thought that there would be more people curious about Freud's work. At one point, the studio changed the title to get a wider audience—*The Hidden Passion* or some goddamn thing—but that didn't fool anybody.

PLAYBOY: *Jean-Paul Sartre wrote the first draft of* Freud, *didn't he?*
HUSTON: Yes. I had promised him that we wouldn't be censored, and he understood that to mean we could have an eight-hour picture, so he wrote a script of that length. I then took his material and tried to organize it, and it was a hell of an undertaking. I have never had a worse time writing.

PLAYBOY: *What was your impression of Sartre?*
HUSTON: I don't think I knew Sartre at his best. He was on drugs—not hard drugs, drugs to stimulate him; he couldn't stop talking. He stayed with me in Ireland for three weeks, during which he talked. He had no English; my French isn't good; there were a couple of interpreters, who just added to the babble. He wore a cheap, ill-fitting three-piece suit with the same necktie, and although his shirts looked laundered, it was always as though he had the same clothes on. He was without egotism and was probably the ugliest man I have ever laid eyes on—one eye going in one direction, and the eye itself wasn't very beautiful, like an omelet. And this pitted face.

PLAYBOY: *Before* Freud, *you tackled another huge subject. What made you decide to film* Moby Dick?
HUSTON: I had read *Moby Dick* twenty years before I made it. I hadn't read it as a child. Most people say they read it when they were children—well, they're liars. Nobody in his early teens ever read *Moby Dick*. They've read abridged versions. Ray Bradbury and I wrote the script; we simplified it into picture terms. The fact that multitudes didn't clamor to see *Moby Dick* was a great disappointment. The greatest criticism leveled against the picture was the casting—Gregory Peck as Ahab. Well, I'm a pretty good judge of actors. I saw *Moby Dick* recently on TV, and Peck is good. But the image the audience of that time had of him was different; they wouldn't accept him.

PLAYBOY: *That was the only film on which you ever went over budget, wasn't it?*
HUSTON: Yes, because we encountered the worst seas in maritime history for that part of the Atlantic. We lost two quite expensive whales, and the picture had to stop while they built a new one. The cable holding it broke

three times, and it was a question of rescuing either the men in the boats or
the whales. Each time, we allowed sentiment to overcome our better judgment—we saved the men. [*Laughs*] When we were down to our last whale, I
knew that if I got inside it, they weren't going to let it go, so I grabbed a
bottle of Scotch and got inside the whale.

PLAYBOY: *How do you rank* Moby Dick *among your films?*
HUSTON: I like particular things about it. I like things about *The Red Badge
of Courage* and about *Freud,* too.

PLAYBOY: *You're naming three of your least appreciated films. How do you feel
about your body of work?*
HUSTON: I am delightfully surprised every now and then at something
that I see is good. I am not unduly impressed with my *oeuvre,* as some call it,
but every now and then I see something of which I approve.

PLAYBOY: *Which of your films made you the most money?*
HUSTON: For me, *Moulin Rouge.* The producers were unscrupulously hon-
est; instead of trying to conceal profits, they took pleasure in giving me my
dues.

PLAYBOY: *What about* The African Queen*?*
HUSTON: Just a salary. I wanted to get out of my partnership with Sam
Spiegel, and giving up my profits got me out of it.

PLAYBOY: *What about* The Man Who Would Be King*? Didn't Michael Caine
and Sean Connery have to sue to get their money?*
HUSTON: Caine and Connery eventually got their money. I never got my
full salary.

PLAYBOY: *Which of your pictures would you like to either forget or remake?*
HUSTON: I'd like to forget *The Barbarian and the Geisha* [with John
Wayne], which was a good picture at one point. I went away to Africa for
several months, and during that time, they changed it and released it, and it
was really a fucked-up proposition, terrible, awful. I would have had my
name taken off the picture, but the producer, the head of the studio, was a
friend of mine; he was dying of a brain tumor and I didn't want to have a

further complication. I would remake *Moulin Rouge* more realistically. At that time, censorship didn't permit the telling of the real Toulouse-Lautrec story.

PLAYBOY: *Given your interest in art, do you think there are other painters' lives that might make good pictures?*
HUSTON: Yes. I don't think justice was done to either Van Gogh or Michelangelo in *Lust for Life* and *The Agony and the Ecstasy*. Pictures could still be made about them, more serious, deeper pictures. But I've been influenced by painting in my own pictures. One of the things I look for in a color film is the palette: What palette do I use? Just as a painter, when he approaches a subject, decides what colors and tonalities. *Moulin Rouge* was in part an attempt to re-create something of the effect of the Lautrec posters.

PLAYBOY: *Which films by other people do you most admire?*
HUSTON: I find it easier to talk about the work of the director than about individual films. I like, of course, William Wyler enormously, the whole body of his work. John Ford, George Stevens—not unexpected names. Pictures from my youth—*Covered Wagon;* I was enormously moved by the profundity of *Four Horsemen*. [*Laughs*] Among the French, *Hiroshima, Mon Amour,* Henri-Georges Clouzot's *Wages of Fear*. De Sica's *Bicycle Thief*. The original *Mutiny on the Bounty*.

PLAYBOY: *How do you feel about remakes?*
HUSTON: Awful. They ought to remake the ones they did badly, but to remake a great picture is the ultimate in absurdity. Even if the remake is good, it can never be as good as the original. By Christ, you would think they would begin to realize that!

PLAYBOY: *What contemporary films have impressed you?*
HUSTON: The last picture I saw that I liked without reservation was *Gallipoli*. It was a marvelous picture, unrecognized for how good it was, simply a great picture from every standpoint. Another that impressed me not as a great picture but as interesting was the one about the three old men who robbed a bank, *Going in Style*. *Ordinary People* was well written, not inspired but excellent. That other Australian film, *Breaker Morant*. *Godfather II* was a hell of a picture, beautifully acted. Who played in *Taxi Driver*?

PLAYBOY: *Robert De Niro.*

HUSTON: Jesus, that was good. I didn't know it was De Niro when I began watching. I just knew it was marvelous. Christ, what a performance! I've seen a few pictures on TV that I would have missed otherwise. One was kind of awful but more interesting than people realized—De Niro in *The King of Comedy.* I found it distasteful and boring at first; then, about the third time I saw it on TV, I was fascinated. It was realism taken to the point of excruciating, sickening truth. It's a rather important document, I think, but mine is the first voice I've heard in praise of it.

PLAYBOY: *What about the blockbusters—the* Star Wars *and* Raiders *pictures,* E.T.?

HUSTON: Yes, fine . . . they've been done now. It's fascinating that such a large segment of mankind fell in love with the E.T. creature. It shows a good impulse.

PLAYBOY: *And what do you think of Steven Spielberg as a director?*

HUSTON: My God, I think he is as inventive as hell; I take my hat off to him. He's an ordinary man with an extraordinary expression.

PLAYBOY: *And George Lucas?*

HUSTON: I would lump them together.

PLAYBOY: *What do you think of actors, such as Warren Beatty and Barbra Streisand, who turn to directing?*

HUSTON: Beatty did an extraordinary job with *Reds.* What I most admired was his taking that subject. He is someone to contend with; his choices of material indicate quite a well-furnished apartment upstairs. I think, by the way, *Bonnie and Clyde* was one of the important pictures of our time.

PLAYBOY: *And Streisand?*

HUSTON: I'm impressed with her choosing *Yentl*; it was extraordinary. But for some reason, Hollywood turned against her.

PLAYBOY: *Why?*

HUSTON: I don't know; perhaps because she had some romantic hookup with this guy who was her hairdresser and she was calling the shots and they were out of their depth . . . there was a lack of sympathy toward her, I felt. I always felt Streisand was capable of far more than playing the Pussycat or the little Brooklyn Jewish girl. Christ, she could have played Cleopatra better than Liz Taylor, with her enormous power and the subtlety of her singing. I said to my friend Ray Stark [the producer of *Funny Girl*], "You are not doing the best thing you could with this girl."

PLAYBOY: *Would you like to direct her?*
HUSTON: I certainly would, because she is one of the great actresses and she hasn't been well used.

PLAYBOY: *What do you think of Meryl Streep, Faye Dunaway, Jane Fonda?*
HUSTON: Meryl Streep and Faye Dunaway are quite extraordinary. I like Jane Fonda for what she does, but it hasn't that scope to it. I think Jessica Lange has something that's very fine.

PLAYBOY: *How about Kathleen Turner, who's in your new film?*
HUSTON: Superb. I don't think there's any question she's a major actress. She's got it all. It's the kind of acting that you're born with; it's not learned. It's channeled and, my God, it flows.

PLAYBOY: *Does she remind you of anyone?*
HUSTON: No, and that's why she's wonderful: The good ones don't remind you of anybody else.

PLAYBOY: *How do you feel about your own acting?*
HUSTON: I don't put any great store in my acting; I don't take it seriously. I liked myself in *Chinatown*. And when I saw the picture about the Kennedys, *Winter Kills*, I thought that was amusing. But not much else. I just spoke my lines. But do you know who the best reader of lines is—at least on cue cards? The master?

PLAYBOY: *Who?*
HUSTON: Ronald Reagan. I saw him give a speech when he was in South Korea, and it was a damn good one. He spoke to the audience and he didn't look at the camera, you didn't see him reading his lines. It was the only thing about Ronald Reagan that ever impressed me.

PLAYBOY: *You and Reagan go back a long way, don't you?*

HUSTON: Yes, I have known him for a long time, since he was working with Warner Bros. I knew his wife, Nancy, who is the daughter of great friends of my father's, Dr. Loyal and Edith Davis. When Nancy went out to Hollywood, she was sort of under my wing for a while, and then she married Ronnie. I'd see them occasionally.

PLAYBOY: *Did your opinion of Nancy lower any when she married Reagan?*

HUSTON: Oh, no. I love Nancy—and I don't dislike Ronnie, I just disagree with his politics. But I submit one thing: The idea that Nancy is archconservative and reactionary and that she is the influence on Ronnie that has guided his political thinking is absurd, absolute nonsense.

PLAYBOY: *Do you miss the old Hollywood?*

HUSTON: Yes, I miss the order that the old Hollywood had. It was much easier then to get a picture made than it is today. It's become a cliché that the studio people were picture makers then, but there is a large element of truth in it. They were people who wanted to make pictures, and they knew how to make them. They weren't accountants and bookkeepers, tax consultants and efficiency experts who don't know how to make pictures, or wheeler-dealers; that element just seems to have taken over today—promoters who just want to get a part of the action rather than people who want to make good pictures. They'll get a picture, get an actor, wheel and deal and get a package together and present it to a studio and the studio will then pass on it. It's amazing that pictures ever get made—and a bad picture, a picture with no qualifications whatever, can get made as readily as something like *Terms of Endearment,* which was turned down by every studio in town. As to the Hollywood social scene, I've managed to avoid that for a lifetime, except in very small doses. I like country life—not farming but the sports that attend to country life: huntin', shootin', and fishin', as it were. I like making a picture if I feel I'm on the way to getting something good. I despair of making a picture if I feel it's going badly, which occasionally happens. Only occasionally, thank God—otherwise, I wouldn't go on making films.

PLAYBOY: *After all these years, are you still affected by reviews?*

HUSTON: Yes, the bad ones hit me. I read something recently that disturbed me no end. There's a female reviewer for *The New Yorker* who was writing about *The Night of the Iguana,* saying it was a badly made picture. Well, it's not a badly made picture. I know damn well it's not. She is a cunt. I'm prepared to forgive her for a lot of things but not for that. [*Laugh*].

PLAYBOY: *With cassettes and cable and satellite dishes, do you think seeing movies in a theater will become a thing of the past?*
HUSTON: I should think so. I find it very difficult to go to a theater if I have to line up round the block to see a picture. I'd go to see a fight or a horse race that way, but I would be goddamned if I would go to see a picture under those terms.

PLAYBOY: *Did you once tell Bogart that you were forever and eternally bored?*
HUSTON: No. Perhaps I was saying I was afraid of being bored, which is true. If I'm threatened with boredom, why, I'll run like a hare.

PLAYBOY: *Is there a secret to maintaining your creativity through a long life?*
HUSTON: Have I told you the story of a *jai alai* game I attended once? No? Well, there was a point that went on and on, an unbelievable rally that lasted five or more minutes, until one of the players lost. I heard the man behind me say, "He didn't lose it; his grandfather lost it." Well, it's not me; it's my grandparents.

PLAYBOY: *It's in the genes?*
HUSTON: Yeah, though you have to keep exercising the brain—it's a muscle like any other. I say this as the gates of senility open before me like a Beverly Hills estate.

PLAYBOY: *Are you afraid of death? Would you like to be in control of your own death, as Hemingway was?*
HUSTON: No, I don't care about that. What I wouldn't want to do is to hang around half out of my mind. I hope death approaches me very quietly, gently, touches me with a sleeve, says, "Lie down," puts its fingers over my eyes.

PLAYBOY: *But until then—*
HUSTON: There is usually something to do to keep from being bored— read a book, see a painting, ride a horse, skydive. . . .

PLAYBOY: *You've left out something.*
HUSTON: Oh, yes, make another picture.

INDEX